MILITARY ROLES IN MODERNIZATION
*Civil-Military Relations
in Thailand and Burma*

SAGE SERIES ON ARMED FORCES AND SOCIETY

INTER-UNIVERSITY SEMINAR ON ARMED FORCES AND SOCIETY

Morris Janowitz, *University of Chicago*
  Chairman and Series Editor

Charles C. Moskos, Jr., *Northwestern University*
  Associate Chairman and Series Editor

Also in this series:

Vol. I	HANDBOOK OF MILITARY INSTITUTIONS	
	Edited by Roger W. Little	
Vol. II	MILITARY PROFESSIONALIZATION AND POLITICAL POWER	
	by Bengt Abrahamsson	
Vol. III	MILITARY INSTITUTIONS AND THE SOCIOLOGY OF WAR:	
	A Review of the Literature with Annotated Bibliography	
	by Kurt Lang	
Vol. IV	THE UNITED STATES ARMY IN TRANSITION	
	by Zeb B. Bradford, Jr. and Frederic J. Brown	
Vol. V	SOLDIERS AND KINSMEN IN UGANDA:	
	The Making of a Military Ethnocracy	
	by Ali A. Mazrui	
Vol. VI	SOCIOLOGY AND THE MILITARY ESTABLISHMENT	
	Third Edition	
	by Morris Janowitz	
	in collaboration with	
	Roger W. Little	
Vol. VII	THE SOLDIER AND SOCIAL CHANGE:	
	Comparative Studies in the History and Sociology of the Military	
	by Jacques van Doorn	
Vol. VIII	MILITARY ROLES IN MODERNIZATION	
	Civil-Military Relations in Thailand and Burma	
	by Moshe Lissak	
Vol. IX	FAMILIES IN THE MILITARY SYSTEM	
	Edited by Hamilton I. McCubbin, Barbara B. Dahl, and Edna J. Hunter	

MILITARY ROLES IN MODERNIZATION

Civil-Military Relations in Thailand and Burma

Moshe Lissak

The Hebrew University, Jerusalem

SAGE PUBLICATIONS   Beverly Hills / London

Copyright © 1976 by the Inter-University Seminar on the
Armed Forces and Society

All rights reserved. No part of this book may be reproduced or utilized in any form or by any means, electronic or mechanical, including photocopying, recording, or by any information storage and retrieval system, without permission in writing from the publisher.

For information address:

SAGE PUBLICATIONS, INC.  SAGE PUBLICATIONS LTD
275 South Beverly Drive   St George's House / 44 Hatton Garden
Beverly Hills, California 90212   London EC1N 8ER

Printed in the United States of America

Library of Congress Cataloging in Publication Data

Lissak, Moshe, 1928-
    Military roles in modernization

    (Sage series on armed forces and society ; v. 8)
    1. Thailand—Armed Forces—Political activity. 2. Thailand—Politics and government. 3. Burma—Armed Forces—Political activity. 4. Burma—Politics and government—1948- 5. Sociology, Military. I. Title.
UA853.T5L57   322'.5   75-5015
ISBN 0-8039-0436-3

FIRST PRINTING

CONTENTS

Preface		7
Acknowledgement		11
Chapter 1.	The Role Expansion of the Military: Stimulus and Propensity	13
Chapter 2.	The Multidimensionality of Modernization and the Issue of Unevenness	47
Chapter 3.	Thailand: The Permeable Boundaries of a Military Establishment	73
Chapter 4.	Patronage and Sociopolitical Hierarchy in Thailand's Social Structure	117
Chapter 5.	Burma: Political Breakdown and Military Experimentation with Role Expansion	143
Chapter 6.	Burma: The Vulnerable Points in the Stratification Order	185
Chapter 7.	Some Notes on Economic Development and Value Predisposition in Burma and Thailand	207
Chapter 8.	A Comparative Analysis and Some General Conclusions	227
Index		251

PREFACE

Since the end of World War II and the beginning of the era of decolonization, there has been an almost immediate association between the political and economic crises in developing countries and the military revolts and coups. Ten years of independence were generally sufficient to bring about an almost total erosion within the civilian elite and the discrediting of many of the charismatic leaders of various societies in Asia and Africa. This phenomenon aroused the curiosity of many political sociologists and political scientists. As a consequence, the academic world has produced a large amount of research, part of which is descriptive and part, theoretically oriented. The latter suggested various comprehensive theories which were intended to explain and predict fundamental trends of military coups and their positive or negative effects on processes of change and modernization in the respective countries. As may be expected, any attempt to suggest a comprehensive theoretical framework was followed by counterattempts to discredit the theory and even to question the possibility of generalizing about such a complex and unpredictable issue as coups and revolutions.[1] On the other hand the empirically oriented researchers have been criticized for not making any serious attempt to suggest general hypotheses and to reach more analytical conclusions. It should be said, however, that in many cases the unavoidable gap between the empirical evidence and the theoretical framework exposed the scholars to unfair criticism from their colleagues.

Being aware of this disturbing situation, we have made a modest attempt to bridge the gap between the empirical data on the one hand and the theoretical and analytical conclusions on the other. One could call the modus operandi the "sandwich approach." As will be seen, the first two and the concluding chapters are what may be called analytical; the intermediate ones are basically descriptive. We prefer this way of presentation instead of other legitimate methods employed by other scholars—i.e., in which the evidence serves only as illustrations to the analytical discussion. With all the advantages of this latter approach, it seems that its main disadvantage is that in many cases it leaves little room for the reader to judge the reliability of the author's interpretation of the empirical data. The "sandwich approach" has of course its own disadvantages. However, its main advantage is that it tries to present the empirical evidence in an uninterrupted fashion, thus enabling the reader to evaluate the reliability of the author's interpretation. It should however be emphasized that this research is not intended to be a historical account. The presentation of a chronology of historical events serves only as a background to the analysis and not as an end in itself. Moreover no attempt was made here to be entirely up-to-date as far as recent events in the two countries are concerned. This is why the historical survey terminates in the late 1960s. This is also the reason why the "students coup of October 1973," probably a landmark in the political history of Thailand, is treated only with the utmost brevity.

The desire to combine an analytical approach with a sort of monograph research compelled us to limit the number of case studies. Although it was planned to include four case studies which seemed to us to be important prototypes of military-civilian relationships in developing countries, the vast amount of data available convinced us to confine ourselves to two case studies—Burma and Thailand. These two societies were selected because, as is explained in detail below, they have very different characteristics in spite of a basic similarity between their cultures.

This research is therefore basically a comparative analysis: although it is in general sociologically oriented, it has some historical elements. The combining of these two disciplines raises the question of the feasibility of a synthesis between the two methodologies, which to many seems a contradiction in terms. Even those who think otherwise cannot ignore the obligation of the historian to look at each phenomenon as unique in itself.[2] In order to resolve this contradiction, one should perhaps follow the advice of Shils:

> We are not historicists. We aim at generalized categories and analytical propositions, both because we regard them as among the highest intellectual achievements and because we think they are indispensable for the better understanding of concrete and particular events. It is obviously necessary to ascertain the unique features of societies and polities. These are already so apparent that their detection as such will not cause us any great difficulty. Indeed, the likelihood that their particularity will overwhelm us, is rather the greater danger. Our task in this regard is to find the categories within which the unique may be described, and in which its differences with respect to other situations may be presented in a way that raises scientifically significant problems.[3]

Even with the more limited issue of civil-military relationships in developing countries, we are not deluding ourselves into believing that we are successful in raising the most "significant scientific problems." Nevertheless, as the reader will observe, we try to focus the analysis around some significant problems concerning the processes of modernization and the role the military plays with regard to them. It should also be noted that we have tried to incorporate into the discussion the dimension of social stratification. Thus, we did not confine ourselves to the more conventional type of analysis, which is limited only to the

Preface [9]

political or cultural structure and which does not systematically deal with the social stratification of the society concerned. In this way, we hope to contribute to the understanding of processes of modernization from the stratification point of view, which has been more or less neglected. Moreover, it seems that a more systematic reference to social stratification adds to the understanding of the officer corps as a status group which has claims for partnership or monopoly of the economic, political, and social resources of the society.

The compilation of the data is based on primary sources (government documents, newspapers, interviews and short visits to the area). However, the analysis is essentially based on a re-interpretation of secondary data—i.e., books and papers which deal with the various aspects of Burma and Thailand. In this respect, the empirical data and the theoretical framework will interest not only military sociologists but the area experts as well.

The book is composed of eight chapters. Some of them were published in various journals and they have been rewritten and revised, although the chronology of the historical background (of the fifties and sixties) of course remains the same. The first version of some of the chapters appeared in the following places: Chapter 1, "Center and Periphery in Developing Countries and Prototypes of Military Elites," *Studies in Comparative International Development,* V, 1969-70, no. 7, 139-150; Chapter 2, "Some Theoretical Implications of the Multidimensional Concept of Modernization," *International Journal of Comparative Sociology,* XI, no. 3 (September 1970), 196-207; Chapter 4, *A Socio-Political Hierarchy in Loose Structure: The Structure of Stratification in Thailand,* Jerusalem Studies on Asia. Modernization Series No. 1, Institute of Asian and African Studies, The Hebrew University, Jerusalem, 1973; Chapter 5, "The Military in Burma: Innovations and Frustrations," *Asian and African Studies,* V, 1969, 133-163; Chapter 6, "The Class Structure of Burma; Continuity and Change," *Journal of Southeast Asian Studies,* 1, no. 1 (March 1970), 60-73.

NOTES

1. See, for example, R. E. Dowse, "The Military and Political Development," in *Politics and Change in Developing Countries,* ed. C. Leys (Cambridge: Cambridge University Press), 1969.
2. S. M. Lipset, "History and Sociology: Some Methodological Considerations," in *Sociology and History: Methods,* eds. S. M. Lipset and R. Hofstader (New York: Basic Books), 1968, pp. 20-58.
3. E. Shils, "On the Comparative Study of the New States," in *Old Societies and New States,* ed. C. Geertz (London: The Free Press of Glencoe), 1963, p. 15.

ACKNOWLEDGEMENT

The publication of this book became available thanks to many friends and colleagues. Professor Morris Janowitz enabled me to spend a year with the Committee for Comparative Study of New Nations at the University of Chicago in 1961-1962 and was the first to introduce me to the fascinating subject of civil-military relations in developing countries. Professor Janowitz's comments on the manuscript certainly improved greatly the final product.

While spending a sabbatical year at the Center for International Affairs at Harvard University, I benefited greatly from the discussions with Professor Samuel P. Huntington and the insight and wisdom of other members of the center. I am very grateful to Professor S. N. Eisenstadt who made valuable comments on the manuscript and helped to clarify some basic concepts concerning the theoretical framework. Thanks are due also to Professor Amos Perlmutter. Needless to say, none of the above-mentioned persons is in any way responsible for the remaining errors and deficiencies. The work was supported in part by the fact that I had the privilege of spending a sabbatical year at the University of Chicago and at Harvard University.

Financial aid has been also given by the Harry S. Truman Institute, and the Faculty of Social Sciences at the Hebrew University. I am profoundly grateful to all those institutions and individuals for their support, advice and assistance. I am grateful to all journals' editors for permission to use the articles which appeared in their journals.

Chapter 1

THE ROLE EXPANSION OF THE MILITARY:

STIMULUS AND PROPENSITY

A. THE BASIC ISSUES

It is customary to link military coups in developing countries with allegedly insurmountable obstacles and hindrances to the process of modernization. Many policy makers, political scientists, and sociologists unfortunately have toyed with the idea that young Turks will be able to overcome such obstacles and change drastically the social, political, and economic scenery of the developing societies. They watch with utmost interest and enjoyment as the different militaries in the developing countries of Asia and Africa emerge from their limited role of security maintenance into new roles. And, indeed, the relationships between the military and the civilian authorities in Asia, Africa, and certainly Latin America are undergoing a profound change, especially in terms of the expansion of the military's roles. This is not confined to the political sphere—a traditional phenomenon—but is reflected also in the military's inclination to assume, directly or indirectly, roles in economic development, manpower training, and ideological indoctrination.

In this chapter, we shall outline part of the panorama of issues and current opinions dealing with military takeovers or, to use a more generalized term, with the role expansion of the military establishments in developing countries. By "role expansion," we mean the penetration by the officer corps, either collectively or as individuals, into various institutional fields, such as economic enterprises, education and training of civilian manpower, fulfilling civilian administrative functions, and engaging in different forms of power politics.[1] Although some may characterize this phenomenon as deviant and even abnormal, the claim is not relevant to our discussion. After all, the definition of an "abnormal situation" is contingent on, among other things, social norms. Thus the phenomenon of role expansion may indeed be exceptional and "abnormal" in one situation and normal and acceptable in another.

Let us make some preliminary suggestions to relate this general issue to problems of modernization and social change and the role of the militaries in this context. We are not searching here for a clearly defined and indisputable relationship between specific stages and forms of modernization and particular types of military role expansion. The complexity of such a relationship necessitates a full-scale study.[2] However, we shall attempt a partial exposition.

The issue of role expansion of the military establishment in developing countries may be broken into more specific and concrete issues. First, military takeovers actually occur in dissimilar societies and under very different regimes. As well as differing in their structure and organization, these societies have achieved different levels of economic, political, and social development. Since this is indeed the case, as ample statistical evidence substantiates, any logical relationship between processes of modernization and frequency of military intervention in domestic politics is itself suspect and must be further probed.

Second, if such a relationship is found, yet another question arises. Can any uniformity in the role expansion of the military be shown? If not, are there any unpredictable variations or are all the variations explicable?

Third, what conditions are conducive to the emergence and rate of proliferation of various types of role expansion (if and where role expansion exists)? Why is the military inclined to role expansion in certain circumstances, reluctant but active in others, and enthusiastic in yet others?

Fourth, not all attempts by the military to take over civilian control and initiate change and reforms are successful. To what extent is the military capable of becoming an agent of modernization, or does the military function in fact as a pseudo-modernizer?

Fifth, under what conditions and in what circumstances does the military relinquish its power to an acknowledged and indisputable civilian elite?

The rationale for presenting these five questions is based on the prevalent —unfulfilled—expectations that the armed forces would become one of the major agents of modernization in the second half of the twentieth century. Reconsideration indicates that these expectations were unrealistic to begin with. In other words, it seems that one was compelled to hypothesize that the armed forces were capable at most of rule—even though not in the most efficient way. Although this hindsight is dubious, we would like to dwell on this issue.

In searching for those factors which incite the military to exceed its traditional role of defending the country from external and internal dangers, scholars have concluded that a distinction must be made between two sets of factors:

a. Structural and functional characteristics inherent in the military social system per se that, under certain conditions, may intensify previous latent inclinations or create new ones, and thus shift the focus of activities from the specifically military domain to a more diffuse political and social sphere.

b. Potential points of breakdown within either the social or the political framework that could serve—directly or indirectly—as focal points of "inflammation." It could then be alleged that they could be "healed" only by drastic measures which, depending on the particular circumstances, the military alone could undertake.

This distinction—between the impact on role expansion of the structural and functional characteristics of the military subsystem and the functional determinants of the society as a whole—is a significant one. However, this is not always so easy to establish as would initially appear. Moreover, while this distinction is accepted by all, scholars are divided about the respective weight to be attributed to each of these general factors.[3] It is even difficult to find a common thread in the views of those who place relatively greater emphasis on the intrinsic characters of the military establishment—let alone among those who stress the characteristics of the society as a whole. This lack of consensus stems from the fact that one confronts a complex array of variables and dimensions.

B. THE DIMENSIONS OF THE MILITARY AS A SOCIAL SYSTEM

When referring to the military establishment, we must make an analytic distinction among four basic dimensions: the instrumental, the managerial, the internal cohesive, and the self-identity dimensions.

By *instrumental dimension* we mean the quantity and quality of material and other resources necessary for the implementation of military rule. To assess the structural features and the material resources of the military, one needs information not only about the absolute size of the military personnel—on active duty as well as on reserve—but also about internal divisions between army, navy, and air force. Data on military participation ratio (military personnel as a percentage of the total population) are also valuable. Military expenditure must be evaluated as a percentage of the national income. Indexes of military size and finance may yield the "economic-demographic mobilization index."[4] The *managerial and logistic dimension* refers to the extent of mechanization, the number of units, and the degree of coordination between the different services (the army, the navy, the air force).

Most scholars consider that the degree of *internal cohesiveness* of the military (defined as "the feeling of the group's solidarity and the capacity for collective action")[5] plays a very significant role in the military's propensity to intervene in the society's political life or expand its influence to other spheres. Janowitz, for example, states that "armies with high internal cohesion will have greater capacity to intervene in domestic politics. Moreover, once they embarked on political intervention, cohesive military elites are more able to limit their involvement, if such is their interest, or they are better equipped to follow consistent policies."[6]

Another factor to be considered with regard to internal cohesiveness involves the types of military in terms of their system of recruitment. Here one may distinguish between a mass army based on universal conscription and an army where recruitment is voluntary or even dependent on mercenary corps. When these and additional factors and variables are taken into account, it is at once noticeable that the problem of cohesiveness in this respect is much less relevant to a consideration of the military framework as *a whole* but very significant to a study of more specific and select groups within it, for example, the army, navy, and air force.[7]

A further structural feature that has the potential of influencing the internal cohesion of the military is the possibility—both real and theoretical—of personal and professional advancement. If it is indeed true that one of the major motives for choosing the military profession stems from a desire to be upwardly socially mobile, then such a possibility should contribute to the development of common status symbols, and, as a result, internal cohesion, and also help to determine the course of relations of the officers with the political elite.[8]

The concept of *self-identity* or self-image is certainly one of the most central components of the internal structure of the military system. Mutual influence and interdependence exist between it and the particular character of the cohesiveness, the technological culture, and the managerial level of the military qua system. Apparently, however, the military personnel's "spiritual world" is no less under the influence of processes and social patterns outside the limited confines of the military system.

The most generally acknowledged determinant of the self-image is socioeconomic origin. Some observers—for example, Janowitz—note that there are many intervening steps between the impact of social origin and the political perspectives of a professional group. Nevertheless, they are inclined to believe that "in shaping the political perspectives of the military, however, social origin seems to be of the greater consequence in the new nations than in contemporary Western industrialized countries. Differences in background, such as rural versus urban, are sharper in their social meaning."[9] A total defense of the argument that class origin has a crucial impact on the political and social orientations of the officers can be found in Nordlinger's paper. With statistical evidence, he tries to prove that, in certain circumstances, social origin leads to radical stands and, in other circumstances, to conservative and antidevelopmental attitudes.[10] Despite its great appeal and the corroborating evidence, it is advisable to investigate this assumption further rather than accept it unquestioningly.[11]

Concepts such as "social-economic status" or "rural background" are highly diffuse, imprecise, and ill defined. Sometimes they must even be discarded in comparative research, since one cannot confidently accept that the concept of "lower-middle class," or even of "rural origin," has the same sociological meaning as an independent variable determining political behavior. Is it permissible to compare, without further specification, the rural society of the Yemen to that of Thailand or Ghana? Recent research into the relationship between social status and various attitudes has shown that the definition of the concept of "status" requires finer sophistication and that the circumstances in which the status of origin may have a greater or lesser influence need more elaboration. When status is examined by considering only one of its dimensions —occupation, income, or whatever—one arrives at an impasse. Status is, after all, a multidimensional complex. In the institutional sphere, it involves problems of internal harmony which affect the stability of the system. This reciprocity holds true when the reference groups are either individuals or small groups.[12]

A plausible counterargument may be based on the tenet that the new nations exhibit simpler stratification patterns and that consequently potential complications (arising from incongruent status configurations) are less likely to occur there. This contention, however, is undocumented by substantive evidence. In such societies, as in modern industrial society, problems of status anxiety and frustrations caused by inability to achieve a more congruent status (by comparable achievements in all status components) are very acute and potentially disruptive. Even though there is still room to toy with the variable of social origin, the approach must therefore be more systematic and sophisticated.

An additional contention is directed toward the pseudo-Marxist determinism implicit in the social origin thesis. Offered in its simplest form, it ignores the results of later effects of socialization frameworks, particularly of high schools and military academies. To evaluate the political behavior of the officers more accurately, we must consider education and other variables indicative of social participation in conjunction with social origin.[13] Finally, the class argumentation must by all means be extended in the direction suggested by Finer, i.e., by making a distinction between "corporate interests" and "class interests."[14] By "corporate interests," he means inter alia the demand for large budgets and other material privileges. By "class interests," he means more diffuse interests related to the balance of power within the society. Finer assumes, it seems correctly, that the corporate interest is the more important and even the overriding factor in determining the military's political attitudes and its desire to intervene at any time.[15]

C. THE CONCEPT OF MILITARY PROFESSIONALISM

The concept of "professionalism" is a key one in our discussion. Its quality and the attention paid to its meaning determine the character of many other potential components of the self-identity and the *Weltanschauung* of the military. Professionalism has been defined a number of ways. Huntington, for example, sees it as composed of three elements:

First, expertise: "the direction, operation and control of human organization whose primary function is the application of violence in the peculiar skill of an officer."[16]

Second, social responsibility: weapons may not be used or force exerted except for socially approved aims. A similar restriction is actually placed on all the professions but, in the case of the military, society's endorsement of measures involving the use of force and weapons is all the more vital, since the existence of the society as a sovereign entity is at stake. In many respects, the society is the client of the military, since the society expects to receive from the military a professional service; nonetheless, this professional-client relationship is different from all others. Where the military is involved, the client sees himself as privileged and qualified to define unequivocally the terms of the treatment he expects.[17]

Third, corporate loyalty to fellow practitioners: feelings of solidarity arise because of the uniqueness of the professional skill involved and particularly as a result of the military's responsibility to society at large.[18]

One can, of course, argue that a soldier may claim to be a professional only when *all* these three (or more) elements have been internalized and are properly balanced. Huntington maintains that when the emphasis is only, for example, on the expertise and corporate loyalty components, the military is to be defined as *partly* professionalized. The same applies where the expertise component is omitted and only social responsibility and corporate loyalty are stressed. One can also contend that, in certain circumstances, the sincere acceptance (or internalization) of the principle of social responsibility by the officer corps may lead them to feel that they should ignore, to some extent at least, professional perfection in order to participate in the solution of broader social issues. Even doctors or lawyers are sometimes required to extend their conventional circle of professional activities to emphasize the particular aspect of social responsibility which is fundamental to their profession. It is thus perfectly legitimate to distinguish between varying *emphases* and different *nuances* of military professional images.

One noteworthy condition involved in the emergence of the variations of the professional image entails a consideration of the changes in the structure of the military system which have occurred in this century. These changes reflect organizational requirements which force the military establishment to parallel large scale civilian organizations. As a result, the military assumes more and more elements characteristic of a government or a business organization. The differentiation between the military and the civilian is thereby seriously weakened. All these trends are changing the model of the professional soldier by "civilianizing" the military elite to a greater extent than the civilian elite is undergoing "militarization."[19] It seems, however, that, in the new nations, this particular process of civilianization of the military is still embryonic, and it may become further evident only with the passage of time. Owing to the low level of managerial and technological achievements of the economy and the civil bureaucracy in the new nations, efficient organization of the military comparable to that evident in more highly developed states is not yet apparent. It is also possible that the gap between the two sectors is actually *widening,* preventing the military from coming closer to the civilian.

A more pressing question is how this process will influence the delicate relationship between the two elites. Will it encourage acceptance of the principle of superiority of the civilian sector or will it further blur the division of functions between the two sectors? At present the answer is clear: it is almost indisputable that an "antipolitics" outlook of the military is accompanied by a negative view of and even hostility to politicians and political groups. This attitude involves an overemphasized positive affiliation with whatever at the time is embodied in the concept "nation" rather than an interest in anything expressing or symbolizing either the "state" or the "government."[20] Consciousness of mission and destiny is not untypical of many military elites, and this is helped by the fact that in the "public" eye they are often the embodiment of national unity. The anticorruption and puritanical outlook attributed to officers also contribute to this feeling of "national mission."

A rather protracted controversy is in progress in the literature about the impact of the process of professionalization of the military on politization and political activism. Huntington states unequivocally that professionalism of the military is linked with decreased military intervention.[21] One can, however, make many qualifications about this statement, largely to confine Huntington's generalization to more specific and definite conditions and circumstances.[22]

One should note these reservations, as civil-military relationships in developing countries reveal a very different pattern than that of Huntington. It may even not be exaggerating to say that in these societies a *reverse* trend may be discerned. Whether this be so or not, it is interesting that, while in Western societies professionalism is considered a *requisite* for upholding supremacy of the civilian sector, it is doubtful whether the same obtains for most developing nations. A plausible explanation of this lies in the different interpretations of the concept of professionalism by military elites in emerging nations. However, such an explanation does not account for the phenomenon in its entirety, for one may further hypothesize that, even in ideal circumstances—when the officer corps (in these new countries) have indeed fully internalized the "classical" concept of military professionalism and thereby have committed themselves to all its requirements—the propensity to exceed the definition of their role may be *intensified* rather than decreased. In other words, both *underprofessionalism* and *overprofessionalism* may lead to a number of similar consequences.

Two principal stages can be distinguished in this context. In the *first stage,* the uniqueness of the military profession is significant, despite the serious backwardness of its organization and technology. This backwardness is, of course, relative to the civilian sector, and the military always fares better than the civilian. Within developing societies, internalization of the norms of the military "profession" may bring a desire—even definite intentions—to mold the society at large as much as possible according to the features exhibited by the military establishment. In other words, the military seeks to create an apolitical society.[23] An apolitical society would supposedly release the executive from being harassed by interest groups through "compromise politics." The military's attitude here stems from the distorted development of an otherwise legitimate distinction between the *nation* and the *state* (or the *contemporary* regime). This distortion is manifested by an officer corps who consider themselves the exclusive embodiment of the will of the nation and view all other functional groups as expressing only partial and temporary interests. Their self-image as guarantor of the permanent interests of the nation provides (in their eyes) the necessary legitimacy for them to assume the right to rule. The officer corps in the European societies of the nineteenth and early twentieth centuries were often also faced with internal contradictions owing to their willingness to maintain simultaneously the image of the most objective bureaucrats while being the popular incarnation of the national conscience.[24] This kind of feeling appears, however, to be much rarer among officers in Asia or Africa, perhaps because, in the breakdown of traditional structures (brought about by modernization), these two elements neutralize—or complement—each other. One inevitable consequence is a growing *overlap* between membership in a distinctive status group and membership in a definable functional-operational framework, that is, the military. This situation is somewhat reminiscent of that which prevailed during the eighteenth century in some European countries, particularly in France, where each of the organs of the state (such as the legislature, the bureaucracy, and the army) became both the symbolic and political focus of different status groups. This "sectorial segregation" contradicts the requisites of modern social and cultural pluralistic society. Evidence of such sectorial segregation, particularly with regard to the military, may be found in officers' aspirations for optimal political and economic autonomy. Moreover, the officer corps constantly feel inclined to intrude into nonmilitary spheres of activity, thereby distorting the functional division of labor which the various branches of the polity seek to maintain. Only in the *second stage* of the development of the military profession, that is, when an optimum of civilianization is achieved, are the structural conditions more conducive to a decrease in the alienation of the civilian and military sectors.

We have dealt with some issues related to possible patterns of interaction between the internal structure of the military system and its social commitments to the society of which it is a part. This mutual interdependence is based on two fundamental facts.

First, the military establishment requires a certain amount (the precise amount is flexible) of external resources in order to guarantee a certain standard for the satisfactory accomplishment of its conventional role, namely, defense.

Second, when the quality of resources of their rate of flow "disturbs" (in this context, the concept is viewed subjectively, from the point of view of the officer corps) the military's fulfillment of its conventional role, several—not necessarily mutually exclusive—paths are open to the military elites. They can promote optimal autarky in order to secure a necessary supply of vital resources. A more conventional alternative solution is to take over the general societal resources and to channel distribution according to the military's needs.

To understand why officers prefer a particular course of action and in what circumstances, our analysis must not be confined to the military subsystem alone but must refer to the entire network of social processes considered "responsible" for the activity—or apathy—of the military in developing societies.

D. THE POLITICAL AND ECONOMIC BACKGROUND FOR MILITARY INTERVENTION

This responsibility may be attributed to many interrelated factors. We refer here in a very schematic way to several major factors or dimensions, that is, the political, the stratificational, and the economic. The order of their presentation is purely accidental and indicates nothing about their respective weight. Moreover, one can certainly expect to witness, in different circumstances, varying configurations in which each factor would carry more or less weight.

One can hardly find any issue that has been analyzed more extensively than the features of the political regimes where military takeovers have occurred. Finer's summary of the political regimes vulnerable to military coups is typical. He suggests a classification of the countries according to the maturity of their political culture. The level of maturity is determined by two criteria:

a. The extent to which there exists "a wide public approval of the procedures for transferring power and a corresponding belief that no exercise of power in breach of these procedures is legitimate."
b. "The extent to which the political public is wide and well mobilized into associations such as trade unions, churches, firms and industrial organizations, co-operatives and political parties."[25]

According to Finer, only countries with mature political culture—"those in which both consensus and mobilization are very high"[26]—are actually immune from military takeovers. All other types of countries, where there is some unevenness between mobilization and consensus, are vulnerable.[27]

Behind these general formulations, one can find some specific and concrete indicators that their presence or nonexistence reflects the level of maturity of the political culture, according to Finer's terminology, or the extent and type of praetorianism, in Huntington's. The manipulation of various indicators encourages the search for either quantitative or qualitative relations between those indicators and the frequencies of military coups. One conspicuous example of this trend is the study of party systems and the impact military intervention has on them. We mean the extent of political splitting, disunity, and subdivision as reflected in the number of political movements and parties.

The literature contains several statistical analyses concerning the relationship between types of party systems (one-party regimes, multiparty systems, etc.) and the frequency of successful or abortive coups. Huntington, Hopkins, and others supply evidence that demonstrates a positive correlation between multiparty systems—or so-called noneffective parties—and frequency of revolutions.[28] Theoretical confirmation of such empirical evidence is suggested by Apter, who contends that military coups are *less* frequent in what he calls "mobilization systems," which, in most cases, are one-party regimes (although not all one-party system societies need necessarily be mobilization systems). According to Apter, it is only at a later stage of their development, when mobilization systems take on the form of "modernizing autocracies," that a military oligarchy comes to power through the institutionalization and professionalization of the authority which had come to rely on the military as an organization. Thus it seems that one-party systems as such do not render the society immune to revolutions.[29]

The *number* of parties is a significant indicator, albeit only a formal and external one. Its contribution lies in its ability to provide a general notion of the society in question, particularly of the existence of channels through which the opposition may communicate its ideas to the government. In other words, the number of parties may be used as one indicator (among many) that makes it possible to assess the degree to which civilian channels of political change have reached a critical phase demanding the use or at least the threat of force.[30]

In their search for additional statistical evidence, Textor and others have not confined themselves to the number of political parties. They have tried to find a statistical relationship between the propensity of the military to intervene in domestic politics and more *general* types of social channels available for political expression. They have concluded that the military's inclination to intervene is significantly higher when interest articulation by *anomic* groups is frequent (or at least occasional) or in societies where interest aggregation by political party is negligible.[31] This conclusion in a sense confirms the relationship between noneffective parties and the frequency of coups within the society.[32]

The Role Expansion of the Military

We should also mention an additional complex of "independent" variables thought to be involved in the military's inclination to intervene in domestic politics. Hardly a paper dealing with military-civil controversies finds it superfluous to cite evidence showing crises of confidence, credibility gaps, and a decline of the symbols of authority. One would expect to note a direct relationship between such phenomena and the efforts of various ambitious groups (either within or outside the central political elite) seeking to exploit the current chaos and the waning authority of the ruling elite by displacing it. The army's officer corps has often been noted for self-generated concepts designed to undermine the bases of legitimacy of the civilian government. The distinction made by some officer corps between *unconditional* commitment to the nation, on the one hand, and reserved and *conditional* allegiance to the regime and ruling elite, on the other, is a striking example. However, the ideology prevailing within the society at large does not always find itself at odds with the military ideology. Huntington, discussing the professional ethic and political ideologies, distinguishes between ideologies favoring and sympathetic to military regimes and ideologies strongly deploring such an association. Among the former, he mentions the conservative ideology: "In its theories of man, society and history, its recognition of the role of power in human relations, its acceptance of existing institutions, its limited goals, and its distrust of grand designs, conservatism is at one with the military ethic."[33] In contrast, liberalism—and fascism and communism—are obviously, for different reasons, basically dissimilar to the military ethic.

This distinction certainly provides a useful clue for understanding the relations between the political and the military elites, especially the ideological motives promoting or preventing a direct confrontation between the two.

To make this point less abstract and render it more capable of accounting for variabilities, one must bear in mind that there are at least three possible forms of disharmony between the military and the civilian ethics.

The first is focused around the ultimate and most sacred values of the society, expressed, for example, in ideas about social justice, principles of equality or allocation of social resources, etc.

The second focuses around questionable ad hoc issues or policies, initiated by and large merely to deal with the current problems besetting the society.

The third focuses around constitutional elements which determine the rules of the political game. It centers around patterns of access to power, the limitations superimposed on formally available channels, and procedures of transferring authority to legitimate candidates.

The direct consequences of disagreements between the military and the attitudes prevailing in the civilian elite in connection with each of these three points may eventually result in a similar situation. One can, however, also hypothesize that the indirect and long-term effects may be very different, depending on whether the disputes center around ultimate values or refer to ad hoc policies. When the disagreement is over ultimate values, it is the very basis of legitimacy itself which is at stake; when the argument is over policies, the problem is "only" one of lack of confidence in the efficiency and ability of the ruling elite.

However, it would be fallacious to assume that a resort to violence need necessarily involve a legitimation crisis or the suspension of the "rules of the game." As demonstrated by a significant number of Latin American countries, the use of force has itself become partly institutionalized and, as such, constitutes an integral part of these rules. In other situations, where violence has not been institutionalized, the use of force indicates a collapse of the rules which determine the game of politics. It reveals that consensus over the norms governing the exchange of resources and social services between the various sectors involved has ceased to exist or is no longer effective. Here one may often discern the intention of a particular sector (advantageously placed with respect to valued resources) to promote or to enforce new principles of exchange which would not only alter the actual balance of power but also its bases of legitimacy.

Another notable trend in much of the research is the quest for a correlation between the frequency of military intervention in domestic politics and the level of current economic development. Two questions are particularly relevant to this: (1) can such a correlation actually be established; and (2) if it does exist, how should the economic factor be treated? Should it be considered an independent factor? Or are the indexes of the level of economic development only a reflection of more general social processes? When dealing with the reliability and validity of the established correlation itself, one must remember that, although ascertainment of GNP per capita is probably not the best index of the level of economic development, it does show a high correlation with the frequency of revolutions.[34] However, generally, statistical correlations indicate the direction of the interdependence between factors, without explaining its causes. The ambiguous status of the economic factor is reemphasized when one seeks to explain the significant number of *deviant cases*—for example, Argentina and Brazil, countries notorious for conflicts between civilian and military elites, despite their relatively high economic development. We may therefore ask whether an absolute level of economic development can serve as the most reliable indicator of a particular pattern of tension between military and civilian elites. It seems more judicious to inquire into the *relative* levels of economic growth. This relativity is apparently linked with the society's ability to ingest and digest the consequences, either directly resulting from or by-products of economic growth, or its setbacks, as manifested in structural changes and extent of social mobilization.[35] This hypothesis may sound plausible, but one must nevertheless be cautious about assuming that the propensity to military involvement is likely to decrease with greater social mobilization. The interpretation of social mobilization is very different when it applies to a society with a defective and impotent political center or to a society where the political center, if not able to command all of the ongoing processes, at least exploits some part of them in an effort to strengthen itself and to neutralize potential rivals. In other words, the political elite has the capacity to absorb dissension.

E. STRATIFICATION AND THE PROPENSITY OF THE MILITARY TO INTERVENE

Unfortunately, the interdependence of the stratification variable and the military's propensity to intervene in politics has been studied far less systematically than the political and economic variables. This may be because these variables have mistakenly been taken to cover the stratificational aspect. After all, there is definitely a significant empirical overlap between these sectors. The negligible knowledge accumulated can be summarized by the popular thesis that the rise of the middle strata is associated with the decline of military role expansion.[36] The most common explanation is that the middle class is motivated to create, and has the ability to sustain, stable civilian political institutions.[37] Also, the growth and the crystallization of a middle class indicate possibilities for social mobility as well as availability of alternative channels of mobility, outside both military and political institutions, and thereby prevent a concentration of frustrated people within the military system.[38]

The matter of mobility cannot be confined, however, to the question of exclusiveness of mobility channels. A close and related issue is that of the proportion of the scope of upward mobility vis-à-vis that of downward mobility. The question is concerned with the proportion between the out movement from the elites and the in movement to the elites.[39] Generally, there are four prototypes of societies. In the first, one can discern a *high* rate of both upward and downward mobility. In its opposite, a *low* rate of both upward and downward mobility is typical. The third prototype is distinguished by a high rate of upward and a low rate of downward mobility. The fourth has the reverse characteristics—a low rate of upward and a high rate of downward mobility. It is reasonable to assume that, in those societies where upward mobility and downward mobility are relatively balanced, there will be a less frustrated elite, since there would be less pressure for redistribution of status. This is not the case with the other types of societies, especially those whose upward channels of mobility are blocked more than the downward channels.

It is also fashionable to link the existence of a large middle class to conditions which favor the growth of democratic institutions and the internalization of a democratic model of interaction between political and military elites.[40]

We could thus assume that, if a middle class is absent or its growth and quest for self-expression are severely curbed, the stage would be set for the emergence of the military as an alternative political power. However, historical as well as contemporary evidence indicates that this assumption may hold true only in certain circumstances. It is not sufficient that a coup becomes feasible for the military, for all practical purposes, to be the sole or even the main channel to *rapid* mobility within the society. This condition is sometimes accompanied by an additional one: the officer corps must manifest *deliberately* the characteristics of a distinct status group and/or consider themselves the champions or representatives of a broader stratum which has found no proper and adequate channels of political expression.

However, we must still determine the extent to which military officers are qualified to represent and to realize what are deemed to be the central values of the middle class and to perform functions similar to those carried out by the middle class in the West during its modernization. This question is very difficult to answer, and there should be far more research on the alleged similarities (and discrepancies) of functions performed by the military in developing countries and those performed by the middle class in Europe.[41]

The need to pursue such research is further indicated by certain theses and hypotheses about the effects of modernization on stratification patterns. One states that the modernization of the "class" structure must be coupled inter alia with "encounter points" to guarantee the existence of structural and social circumstances for interaction and exchange of services among key groups. The puzzling question is when and to what extent the officers, as individuals and as a collective group, are able to accomplish this function adequately, since the officer's status in developing countries is quite different from the status of the officer corps toward the end of the absolutist period in Europe. In the latter, "the professional soldier finds himself in an anomalous position. His is perhaps the only prominent group excluded both by tradition and by design from making a positive welfare contribution. His professional affiliation commits him to the positive consent of the state. By tradition the officer corps was anti-commercial, nonentrepreneurial. In function it was nonproductive."[42]

Certainly, in some developing states the self-image of the officer corps and the prestige it has with opinion leaders are markedly different. Military personnel consider they possess the qualities enabling them to contribute both symbolically and empirically to the civilian sector. In some societies the military even demonstrates, in comparison with other sectors, significant entrepreneurial qualities. There can be no justification for the view that the military is excluded or that it plays anachronistic roles. It may well be said that, in this respect, circumstances make it theoretically easier for the officer to serve as an *intermediary* or broker among the various sectors and elites.

The situation becomes more complex when other groups—political parties,

The Role Expansion of the Military

trade unions, or voluntary associations—see themselves as entitled to fulfill this function. Nonetheless, the sheer willingness of the military to operate as a broker has a direct impact on the content, scope, and rate of the military's role expansion. This could alter the entire pattern of relationships with other elites and could urge (or halt) a seizure of power. Moreover, it may unintentionally fulfill the function of conserving and freezing the existing social structure. Some of the reasons are related to the built-in weaknesses of the military establishments per se. Others are associated with more specific and local historical circumstances.

Besides the political, economic, and stratificational factors, the literature shows additional factors to which importance is accorded depending on the particular circumstances and type of society. One of the most frequently named is the external security factor—as some may argue, the myth of external dangers which may have some unspecified impact on the military's propensity to intervene in domestic politics. An important element here is the army's actual battle experience, that is, its balance of victories over defeats. This balance (or rather imbalance) often serves as a very important and sometimes a direct activating factor for military revolution. Observers have contended that, in the absence of external danger, the army is inclined to engage in real or imaginary internal security problems, whose natural outcome nearly always is to emphasize political and nonmilitary considerations.[43] Currently, problems of both internal and external security can have repercussions on the international balance of power, as is manifested by the military aid policies pursued by the big powers. Therefore the hypothesis of a relationship between the behavior of the military in internal conflicts and institutional connections with other countries should not be completely discounted. This hypothesis can be formulated in another way: the less the military's actual dependence on the government for resources, the greater the likelihood—and the more serious the forms—of military "deviance from its obligation of responsiveness to governmental control."[44] Although the importance of this factor has been questioned, it would be worthwhile to follow it up in certain cases. The possibility that military cliques in neighboring states may emulate coups occurring in another country, thereby creating a chain reaction, should also be investigated.[45]

F. TYPES AND CONSEQUENCES OF MILITARY COUPS AND REVOLUTIONS

So far we have focused on the factors which may be considered as independent (or even intervening) variables. Let us now discuss some of the consequences (which may be seen as dependent variables) of military coups and revolutions.[46]

The concept of revolution has dozens of definitions, and, in most cases, the distinctions among them are semantic. Their common denominator is the lack of harmony between the social and political structures. This lack of harmony becomes intensified when some subsystems feel deprived as a result of radical changes, rapid economic growth and/or technological changes, or even significant transformation in metaphysical beliefs, etc. These circumstances, alone or in combination, need not lead to violence or to attempts at an illegal takeover. Much is contingent on additional conditions, such as the behavior of the entrenched and their intransigence, manifested, for example, by their blocking any means to express opposition. Other accelerators (or precipitating elements) are the emergence of a charismatic leader or the creation of secret revolutionary organizations. Trying to summarize the numerous factors involved, Chalmers Johnson states that "power deflation, plus loss of authority, plus an acceleration provide revolution."[47] Power deflation is caused mainly by pressures created by an unbalanced social system; loss of authority, by the inability of the leadership to offer changes which would prevent further deterioration. The accelerator—according to Johnson, the direct and last cause of the revolution— "is some ingredient, usually contributed by fortune, which deprives the elite of its chief weapon for enforcing social behavior (e.g., an army), or which leads a group of revolutionaries to believe that they have the means to deprive the elite of its weapons of coercion."[48] Some writers, although generally accepting these three conditions, do not feel revolution to be inevitable, even at that stage. They note various factors which could prevent it or mitigate its intensity.[49]

One must remember that the combination of conducive factors and mitigating mechanisms, which could change the potential, preconceived, and intended character of the revolution, can give rise to different types of revolution. The military coup is certainly only one possibility among many. Role expansions initiated by other groups—the government or the party, the bureaucracy, oligarchic elites, or a popular movement—are daily occurrences.

A distinction should be made first between "revolution" and "rebellion." One of the most erudite discussions of this is by Johnson. He accepts Hannah Arendt's concept that a rebellion is not involved in challenging authority or the established order but is always a matter of displacing the person holding the position of authority, either by replacing a usurper with a legitimate king or by replacing a "tyrant" with a lawful ruler.[50] Johnson also distinguishes between a simple rebellion and an ideological rebellion. The former is "not motivated by an ideology; the goal structure of such a movement is actually a fully elaborated structure of values that the rebels believe is still capable of organizing their communal life."[51] The salient feature of the ideological rebellion is that it espouses "the revival or reintroduction of an idealized society that allegedly existed in the society's own past. These movements advocate the creation of a pattern of social organization which the rebels justify by a claim to traditional values, although they may actually break with tradition in many of the institutions that they seek to establish."[52] The definition of ideological rebellion raises the question of its difference from the phenomenon of revolution. Johnson's answer is that only "when the goal culture of an insurrectionary ideology envisions the recasting of the social division of labor according to a pattern which is self-consciously unprecedented in the context of a particular social system, then we should use the term 'revolutionary'."[53] He further distinguishes between simple revolution and total revolution. In the former, the revolutionary ideologies are restricted to fundamental changes of only a few values. In total revolution, the aim is to supplement "the entire structure of values and to recast the entire division of labor."[54] The ideological criterion is central to the differentiation between the main types of revolutions but insufficient for specific typologies. Johnson contends that the concept and the wielding of force may be clarified if reviewed "in terms of the levels of socio-political organization upon which they impinge." He refers to three levels, the governmental, the regime, and the community, suggesting that the target of the attack be added to the ideological criterion.[55] Other relevant criteria are the duration of violent activities, and the ruling elite's position with regard to mass participation.[56] All these criteria are helpful in distinguishing among different forms of violence directed against the ruling elite. It is particularly important to distinguish the intensity, scope, and pervasiveness of the conflict. Our few examples show that the analysis is not restricted to revolutions sponsored and led by the military.

G. THE POSITIVE AND NEGATIVE QUALITIES OF THE MILITARY AS AN AGENT OF MODERNIZATION

The type of revolution eventually carried out or the kind of regime imposed on the population is not the sole variable to be sought in this context. A much more important variable for our study is the degree of success or failure of the revolutionaries in consolidating their power and in establishing, or reestablishing, an effective, dynamic political and cultural center. To understand the reasons for the military's success or failure, one must try to locate and analyze its main advantages and disadvantages as an agent engineering change and/or modernization.

The scope of either success or failure to serve as an agent of modernization is primarily a function of the scope of the problems being faced by the political center. In this respect, there is no difference between military or civilian elites. Other things being equal, the military has some advantages and disadvantages in comparison with other organizations. Moreover, both its strong and its weak points are magnified in the light of ongoing modernization.

What are the positive qualities attributed to the military which supposedly enable it to deal with social change and modernization more effectively than other organizations? First, certain achieved qualities, absent or very insignificant in other sectors (especially in pretechnological societies), are customarily found in or attributed to the military. For example, the military is considered to be a pioneer in the technological-logistic and administrative fields. Willingness to develop and maintain a modern army compels even small and rather primitive armies to promote a trained and efficient cadre equipped with technological know-how rare in other sectors. Such experience is usually acquired through training in more developed countries. One central result of graduation from a foreign military (or civilian) institution is probably the adoption (albeit a selective one) of the norms prevailing there. It is supposed to be only "natural" that the officers return, eager to inculcate in their soldiers at least some of the norms to which they have been exposed. They thus become agents of order, efficiency, and social change.[57]

Second, the military, as a social system combining traditional structural features (ritualism, rigidity, hierarchy, etc.) with a division of labor based on universalistic principles, is considered to be a very convenient framework for absorbing unorthodox norms by people raised in and accustomed to a traditional background.[58] In other words, the military is considered superior because its framework "is one of the characteristic ways in which traditionalism and innovation can be conveniently blended to restructure social life."[59] The innovative spirit is not merely a function of a different type of professional education. It is also linked, in the opinion of many, to belonging, both chronologically and mentally, to a younger generation. The officers can thus more readily capture the youth and identify with their impatience.

A third advantage, attributed particularly to the officer corps but also to the entire military establishment, is that, in fragmented societies, the military may serve as a new focus of solidarity and even as an embodiment of respected and sacred symbols. It would thus seem that the military is irreplaceable as a nation builder.

Finally, even in a society where the military is less respected or prestigious, it is still the most highly organized and efficient system within the society. The fact of having adequate resources and means to guarantee its establishment as an alternative elite enhances its likelihood to become a more productive elite, if only in terms of providing substantial security and stability.

These and other factors have been advanced to explain why, for the decades since World War II, the most potentially effective agent of modernization was considered to be the military. However, one can cite many cases where these alleged advantages did not lead to any gains. The dramatic failures of many military takeovers have actually forced the students of military coups to reexamine the data and admit that some of the myths associated with the military must be discarded.

One such a myth is that of the military's efficiency. An overwhelming number of armies in many developing countries are small and very far from being modernized. Their limited size and the lack of serious challenges to their security (which is also indicative of a lack of opportunity for testing their skills) are reflected in a rather simple, conservative, or even primitive administrative and logistic structure. The experience of the officers, whether acquired in field commands or in staff assignments, is limited even in comparison with that accumulated by administrators in civilian occupations. Often the officer corps is simply not able to handle complicated administrative problems efficiently —much less establish a more effective administration than the civilian bureaucracy.[60]

Collaboration between civilian and military administrators may temporarily ease the burdens on the officers. But in the long run, such collaboration undermines the already shaky administrative framework and the communication with key groups in the society. One inevitable result is a diminishment of information going upward, which eventually leads to a distorted view of reality. The inability to cope with economic and administrative problems stems from inadequate training or qualifications and also from the fact that military expenditures often represent a severe drain on an impoverished economy. A defense budget is a burden to any modern economy—let alone a backward economic structure. One may confidently assume that there is some correlation between a low rate of economic development and military role expansion, but we must be cautious about assuming a similar correlation between military rule and accelerated economic growth.[61]

Another myth views the military as mediator between opposed groups. Administrative and economic knowledge is achievable, and it does not contradict the basic tenets that activate the military bureaucratic network. This is not true of so-called political know-how. The weakness of the military's attitude is its inability to adjust to political bargaining. Analysis has revealed various direct and indirect factors attributed to this potentially debilitating characteristic of the military. Some scholars emphasize the psychological aspect or the type of socialization received by officers in their rather exclusive, closed training schools. The isolation of these institutions does not promote sensitivity to current public opinion. Rather, the typical graduate from such institutions is inclined toward authoritarian behavior and a lack of tolerance about "flexible interaction and interrelations of manifold power elements within the society."[62] As a complementary explanation, some also refer to structural causes. Janowitz, for example, asserts that those armies which have not yet achieved that level of technological, managerial, and logistic development which promotes a mental affinity between military and civilian sectors are less capable of dealing with civilian affairs and especially of promoting political communication.

Another weakness of armies caught up in the process of modernization is that, when they are eager to ensure that reforms will be pursued at a faster rate, without any serious interruptions, they may destroy the social networks vital to two-way political interaction.[63] On the other hand, officers confront almost insurmountable obstacles in their efforts to suggest alternatives to criticized networks and mechanisms. The military ruler would find it difficult to articulate ideas and mold the manpower into a new social movement intended to support military rule. Good examples of these suggested alternatives are what may be called nonpolitical models of power relations. They are nonpolitical in that they possess very little provision for mediating conflicts and reconciling incompatible interests. They promote *cohesion without consensus* by balancing social forces against each other. This kind of manipulation is by no means the monopoly of the officers. They do, however, seem to be predisposed to adopt it indiscriminately.[64]

When considering the potential deficiencies of military rulers in the technological-managerial sphere, and particularly in political communication, we find that skills acquired in the army are not easily transferable to civilian life. The training the officer has had makes him much more competent to prevent the exercise of political rule than to exercise it himself. In some cases, in the throes of revolution, the military is able to open bottlenecks within frozen and rusty social frameworks. New bottlenecks follow rapidly, however, either because of the military's ineptitude or because of unwillingness to provide new infrastructures designed not only to mobilize material assets but also to crystallize new "contractual relationships." The officers are more or less able to safeguard their professional identity as long as they are dealing with issues like technical reforms, guaranteeing basic defense, improving physical means of communication, etc. These matters have some indirect repercussions on traditional political and social patterns, but they do not frustrate or confuse the officers, who are still on familiar terrain. To the extent that the military slips, either voluntarily or pushed by circumstances, outside its domain into the realm of more fundamental decisions (which could effect important changes in the contractual principles uniting the society), it moves on foreign ground. The officers are most disturbed by circumstances that compel them to change their original professional image. This image was, in the first place, quite different from the so-called classical professional image, and in some cases it must undergo even more radical alterations in order to accommodate to the military's role, namely, to head a political system and provide a new kind of legitimation for contractual relations within the society.

Our brief survey of the potential advantages and shortcomings of the officer corps as a ruling elite has been aimed at underlining the fact that any analysis of the chances of success of military coups must take into account the ambiguity of this potential and test it against the background of the general conditions in which the coup occurs.[65] There is no guarantee that each of the advantages will materialize. By the same token, all the potential failings may not be revealed to the same degree or curb the army in similar ways. Coups are, after all, staged in different circumstances and their initial objectives are not all identical. Bearing in mind the "natural" capabilities and weaknesses of armies as agents of modernization, we can evaluate the chances of a particular military establishment in given circumstances. To improve predictability, a more sophisticated typology of armies is needed. The main conditions (and their variations) conductive to military interference in internal politics should also be further defined.

We may, perhaps, sum up this discussion by citing Willner's arguments against those who considered the military as one of the most promising agents of modernization. These optimistic observers were wrong, first, in that they "projected upon the military organization in one setting attributes they have been observed to possess in others." Second, there is no basis for assuming that the military is capable of preserving the positive qualities attributed to it in a nonmilitary context. Third, there is no assurance that the alleged positive qualities are indeed efficient and functional in the civilian sector.[66] In other words, one should expect that the army often will fulfill the role of a *pseudo-modernizer*. In some extreme cases, the army must be defined as a *deceptive* agent of modernization.

H. FROM MILITARY TO CIVILIAN RULE

Almost all types of military elites, moderate or radical, genuine or deceptive modernizers, must eventually deal with the transfer from direct military rule to various types of civilian rule. Theoretically, there are two major types of transfer: the first is *abdication* (or disengagement from overt military rule). Here the military (or the ruling junta) willingly—or unwillingly—hands the reins of power over to civilian elites. The second is *recivilianization*. The original military elite gradually becomes civilianized. This shift of emphasis is both symbolic (e.g., wearing civilian clothing) and constitutional. The new constitution is supposed to redefine the separation of functions and power among the military and other executive branches of government. It also should forbid soldiers and officers on active duty to participate in politics. The civilianized military elite itself takes over (with different degrees of success) the leadership of a civilian-political movement.[67]

These are two principal paths of "returning to the barracks." In practice, there are many in-between ways. For example, in one middle-of-the-road pattern, the military becomes, sometimes even formally, a *functional group* alongside other functional groups, such as political parties, trade unions, etc. In their new capacity, the officers take an active and *legitimate* part in partisan politics. Most often, the military becomes a partner in a coalition government. This pattern, also typical of a pre-coup situation, may prevail in the period preceding full restoration to civilian rule.

Under what conditions does this civilianization of military rule follow either the extreme patterns or some combination of them? Part of the answer lies in the character of the ruling military elite itself.

Four main types of military elites can be distinguished: (a) the entrepreneurial-ideological; (b) the nonideological entrepreneurial; (c) the ideological nonentrepreneurial; and (d) the nonideological nonentrepreneurial. This typology is based on two variables or aspects. The first, namely, the *entrepreneurial qualities* of the military, involves the degree of innovativeness inherent in the military's programs and actions when compared with the social structure as conceived by the civilian elites.[68] Innovative and entrepreneurial efforts may be exerted in different spheres, such as the political, the economic, or the educational. The second aspect refers to the degree of *ideologically articulated rationalization* evident in entrepreneurial activities. One can also see the ideological articulation in terms of a higher level of military politization, whose source may be either external or internal.[69]

From this, we can hypothesize that the military elite that evolved in the first place as an *entrepreneurial and ideologically* articulated system, while consolidating its power, will reveal more than any other type of elite a reluctance to relinquish political control and return it to civilian hands. Such an elite would rather civilianize itself and find proper ideological justification for doing so. It would often argue that there is no place for any alternative social theories or for competing social and economic programs. Its own programs appear, to this particular kind of elite, to provide the only way to redeem society from its agonies. The official and undeclared position, when encouraging such a policy, would be based on a strong belief in policy's diagnostic and therapeutic value.

Paradoxically, and for entirely different reasons, *the nonentrepreneurial and nonideological military* ruling elites will also probably prefer to become civilianized rather than give up their monopoly of power to civilian counterelites. Their major reasons would be dictated by the desire to continue the personal enjoyment of the various rewards involved in a monopoly of political power.

It is also reasonable to hypothesize that the two other types of military elites will be inclined to some kind of abdication or cooperation with influential civilian partners. The *ideological, nonentrepreneurial* elite is generally conservative. It tries to introduce social reforms very gradually and it thus needs civilian partners. It will be ready (in certain circumstances) to abdicate altogether when it feels that the civilian alternative would pursue more or less similar policies of gradual reform. In the opposite case, officers who de facto are *enterprising* in the economic and political spheres but happened to be *ideologically "sterile"* might seek an adequate ideology among civilians, who might then become the chief partners in the government.

Empirical evidence in support of, or which would disprove of, these hypotheses is unfortunately very meager. True, over the past twenty years there have been a number of instances, particularly in Latin America, of army withdrawal and "return to the barracks." These cases were however all of one type, namely provisional abdication. No sufficient evidence is available of military elites of all four main types who changed their constitutional status or who may be expected to do so. It seems nonetheless worthwhile to test these hypotheses even if only a limited number of case studies can be examined.

The prospects for the emergence of a particular type of civilianization is contingent also on the rate of institutional development. In other words it is contingent upon the expansion of political participation, the creation of durable political institutions, and the emergence of a leadership which is capable of bridging the gap between tradition and modernity. Another important condition is the existence of a closer compatibility between the political center and its periphery. Huntington states in this context that

> for a society to escape from praetorianism requires both the coalescence of urban and rural interests and the creation of new political institutions. The distinctive social aspects of radical praetorianism is the divorce of the city from the countryside; politics is combat among middle-class urban groups, no one of which has reason to promote social consensus or political order. The social precondition for the establishment of stability is the reappearance in politics of the social forces dominant in the countryside. The intelligentsia has the brains: the military have the guns, but the peasants have the numbers and the votes. Political stability requires a coalition between at least two of these social forces.[70]

I. PROTOTYPES OF SOCIETIES AND MILITARY ELITES

We have reviewed a number of current opinions about the direct and indirect causes and processes attributed to a growing inclination by various militaries to extend their role in society and the obstacles they face as agents of modernization. The various relevant factors have been divided into two main parts, those linked to the internal structure of the military system and those related to processes taking place in the overall society.[71] These two types actually consist of a complex of more specific factors, only a sample of which have as yet been presented here. However, we do not have any illusion that we shall be able to deal systematically even with the limited number of factors and variables mentioned. To make the analysis more acceptable, we should perhaps attempt to deal with a smaller, although more abstract, number of variables. A substantial number of the questions we have raised or hinted at may be summarized in an efficient—although simplified—way by examining the types of power relationships between the *center* and the *periphery*. We need not place particular emphasis on the significance of "center" and "periphery" since Shils has so ably dealt with them.[72] For our research, their prime importance is in the necessity to study the capacity of the center ("capacity" here is equivalent to political power) to cope with the problems of social mobilization in the periphery or within the center itself. The main challenge, from the center's point of view, is the emergence of new social groups or the recrystallization of older and disintegrated ones, which creates a new balance of power, and puts forward new types of demands to the political center. In other words, processes of differentiation in the periphery or at the center itself challenge the centers in many countries, including the developing ones. On a more abstract level, the interaction between the center and the periphery reflects the actual state of uneven development and low level of sustained growth, an issue which will be considered in the next chapter.

These two concepts—the power of the center and the intensity of demands from the periphery—suggest two main dichotomies.

a. The strength of the political center (strong versus weak), namely, its capacity to deal with the direct and indirect consequences of modernization and social and political change, in the center and especially in the periphery.

b. The degree of institutional differentiation as a result of which political, social, and economic subcenters emerge and become a focus of new or renewed demands and claims directed to the regional and national leadership (radical versus moderate demands). The demands may complement or contradict each other, according to the type of the periphery and its kind of internal differentiation.

These dichotomies give rise to four prototypes of societies, presented in Table 1.1.[73] Two basic assumptions are associated with these prototypes: (1) the extent of stimulation and temptation confronting the military (or other groups) to extend, de facto and/or de jure, its conventional roles differs according to the specific prototype; and (2) the ability of the military (or other groups) to give a new and enlarged definition of its role varies from one prototype to another, according to the military's character, magnitude, and power.[74]

The stimulus to intervene, the predisposition, and the potential and actual power to materialize the predisposition are thus the main independent variables. Some brief clarifications of these variables follow.

1. *The stimulus and impetus to intervene.* The built-in stimulus existing in the society will differ in each of the prototypes of power balance between the political center and the social forces of the periphery, because fundamental differences exist among the four prototypes.

The Role Expansion of the Military

TABLE 1.1

		Strength of the Center	
		+	−
Intensity of	+	A	B
demands	−	C	D

Prototype A: an *optimal* balance of power between the strength of the political center and the differential demands of the social forces of periphery has been reached.[75]

Prototype B: the power of the center is insufficient, i.e., the center cannot cope with demands and pressures from the accelerating process of differentiation, formation, and consolidation of new groups within the periphery or the center itself.

Prototype C: the strength of the center is relatively unchallenged because of apathy and lack of organization of the periphery.

Prototype D: the power relations between the center and the periphery are more or less balanced because of the weakness and retardation of both the center and the periphery.

2. *The propensity and the predisposition to intervene.* The propensity to intervene is contingent on the general atmosphere prevailing outside the military establishment. It is, however, eventually determined by the officer corps's interpretation of developments outside the military establishment. This interpretation is dependent, moreover, on the structural and functional features of the military as well as the personal characteristics of the interpreters.

We suggest four prototypes to deal with issues included under this heading. They are based on the assumption that many officer corps are faced with an acute choice—between emphasizing intensive pursuit of higher levels of technological, administrative, and logistic standards, and promoting a *separatist* ideological identity and sense of exclusive corporateness.

There is, perhaps, no internal logical contradiction between these spheres of activities. In developing countries, however, and probably not only there, the fact is that often the emphasis on internal cohesiveness, and especially an ideological exclusiveness and purity, inflicted many injuries to the professional standards of the military.

Our four theoretical prototypes may be presented schematically in Table 1.2.

Type A: there is an optimum coordination between technological-logistic achievements and the scope of social cohesiveness and normative identity. This is the attitude which characterized, for example, the Prussian army.

Type B: lack of internal balance is expressed by a large-scale effort by the

TABLE 1.2

		Cohesiveness–ideological identity	
		+	−
Technological	+	A	B
and logistic			
achievements	−	C	D

military to improve the professional level without paying special attention to maintaining internal cohesiveness and a satisfactory value system. This is the classical professional approach of the officer corps in democratic societies.

Type C: the integrative and pattern-maintenance aspects are overemphasized at the expense of the technological-logistic dimensions. Partisan units are an example, although this type can also be found in regular armies.

Type D: there is very low achievement in the logistic and technological spheres as well as in the cohesiveness-ideological sphere. These features were very typical of Latin American armies in the nineteenth century, of some Middle Eastern armies in the twentieth century, and probably also of a number of contemporary African armies.[76]

3. *The real and effective power of the military.* The focus is on the existence (or absence) of an absolute or relative advantage for the military as against other power centers. It results from the control of resources available for use against real or potential adversaries.[77]

In this chapter, we have tried to present what seem to be the most relevant variables in the study of the differential conditions conducive to the extension of military roles beyond maintaining internal and external security. We have also attempted to unfold some of the internal and external factors associated with the emergence of the impetus of the military to intervene in political and social matters. Moreover, we have tried to clarify some of the positive and negative traits which may explain the partial success of various militaries to reform their own societies, and the dramatic failures, in many other cases, of the militaries to become the chief agents of social change and modernization.

Finally, we have sought to present a preliminary theoretical framework, suggesting consideration of whether it is possible to interpret and explain some of the processes involved in the emergence of the military as a political power from the point of view of the capacity of the political center to cope with the pressures on it from the center itself and the groups composing the periphery. This is, as a matter of fact, one of the major issues of social change in general and of processes of modernization in particular. It, and the question of unevenness of modernization processes that result from distorted relationships between the center and the periphery, will be the center of the discussion in the following chapter.

NOTES

1. One may also approach the phenomenon of role expansion in terms of the type of *boundaries* existing between the civilian and military sectors. For a very important elaboration of this approach, see A. R. Luckham, "A Comparative Typology of Civil-Military Relations," *Government and Opposition,* VI, no. 1 (Winter 1971), pp. 17-20.

Luckham suggests that a distinction be made between "integral," "permeable," and "fragmented" boundaries. "Integral boundaries are assured to the extent to which the interchange between persons holding roles at various levels of the military hierarchy and the environment are under control of those with responsibility for setting the operational goals of the Armed Forces, that is, the higher command. Boundaries are permeated to the extent to which there is a complete fusion both in respect of goals and of organization between the possessors of the means of violence and other social groups. Boundaries are fragmented to the extent that in a military with distinctive military format and goals—the interactions of holders of military roles with holders of civilian roles escape the control of the military elite in a way that impairs its freedom to interact with the political and social environment as a single entity in a consistent manner" (p. 18).

The concept "role expansion," as a matter of fact, does include the phenomenon of "civil action." It seems to us that the latter concept is more narrow than the first, although in specific cases one can discern a great deal of overlapping. For a discussion of the concept of "civil action," see Davis B. Bobrow, "The Civic Role of the Military: Some Critical Hypotheses," *Western Political Quarterly,* XIX, no. 1 (March 1966), pp. 101-111; Edward B. Glick, *Peaceful Conflict* (Harrisburg, Pa.: Stackpole Books, 1967); H. Bienen, "The Background to Contemporary Study of Militaries and Modernization," in *The Military and Modernization,* ed. H. Bienen (Chicago and New York: Aldine & Atherton, 1971), pp. 25-28. For a more detailed list of "new incentive areas" in foreign and domestic policy, see B. Abrahamsson, *Military Professionalization and Political Power* (Beverly Hills, Calif.: Sage Publications, 1972), pp. 146-147.

2. For a preliminary attempt, see M. Lissak "Stages of Modernization and Patterns of Military Coups," *International Journal of Comparative Sociology,* XIV, nos. 1-2 (March-June 1973), pp. 60-75.

3. See, for example, Samuel P. Huntington, *Political Order in Changing Societies* (New Haven and London: Yale University Press, 1968), p. 193; Roslyn C. Feldberg, "Political Systems and the Role of the Military," *Sociological Quarterly,* XI, no. 2 (Spring 1970), p. 207; Luckham, "Comparative Typology," pp. 13-14; Charles W. Weatley, "The Military Coups and Political Development: An Exploratory Study of Overt Crisis in Political Military Relation," (Ph.D. diss., Columbia University, 1967), pp. 407-411.

4. Charles W. Weatley, "Political-Military Relations: Trends in the North American Republics," paper prepared for the American Sociological Association annual meeting, 1965, table A.

5. Morris Janowitz, *The Military in the Political Development of New Nations: A Comparative Analysis* (Chicago: University of Chicago Press, 1963), p. 17.

6. Ibid., p. 68; Keith Hopkins, "Civil-Military Relations in Developing Countries," *British Journal of Sociology,* XVII, no. 2 (June 1966), p. 174. What is clearer and more obvious is the fact that internal cohesiveness of the officer corps as a whole has an impact on the type of the coup. With regard to this aspect, one can distinguish between different types of coup groups—for example, the "general staff coup group," led by the commander-in-chief; conspiratorial groups within one or more branches of the armed forces;

and various partnerships between officers and civilians. For a systematic treatment of the question, see Weatley, "Political-Military," pp. 70-77.

7. Johnson rightly suggests that one must distinguish not only the "traditional" division of the military into army, navy, and air force. One also has to take into account the plausibility of further differentiation, for example, special or separate military units (or paramilitary units) such as the militia, special elite corps, and sometimes even the military police who may be serving as the watchdog of the political regime. See Chalmers Johnson, *Revolutionary Change* (Boston: Little, Brown & Co., 1966), p. 100.

8. The importance of this structural attribute should not, perhaps, be overemphasized. One should consider it as only one of the factors molding internal cohesiveness and shaping the behavior of the officer corps. However, no effort has yet been made to isolate the variables and to examine the circumstances in which they are operative factors and play an active role. It must thus be acknowledged that it is fairly difficult to measure the extent of internal cohesiveness and to enumerate the factors promoting it. The question of its potential impact on the attitudes and norms it determines remains unanswered.

9. Janowitz, *Military of New Nations*, p. 56. He states that "the rural, or, more accurately, the hinterland social background, coupled with petty middle-class bureaucratic occupational origin, contributes to a 'fundamentalist' orientation and to a lack of integration with other elites, especially the political elite." Janowitz gives considerable weight to the absence of a feudal tradition in the majority of new nations. He sees the feudal tradition as having a mitigating effect because "it inhibits direct intervention by the military in domestic partisan politics" (ibid., pp. 57-58).

10. Eric A. Nordlinger, "Soldiers in Mufti: The Impact of Military Rule upon Economic and Social Change in the Non-Western States," *American Political Science Review*, LXIV, no. 4 (December 1970), pp. 1142-1148. See also Robert E. Dowse, "The Military and Political Development," in *Politics and Change in Developing Countries*, ed. Colin Leys (Cambridge: Cambridge University Press, 1969), pp. 228-229.

11. In a comparative study of fourteen officers corps concerned with relationships between the recruitment basis of the officers and their political orientations, the authors concluded that "broadening the social base of recruitment has not been accompanied by a concomitant process of political democratization in the officers' political attitudes or political behavior. Indeed, this comparative analysis somewhat indicates the reverse to be the case. In some instances, broadening the base in officer recruitment has encouraged rather than deterred the propensity of the officer corps to actively participate or intervene in the processes of national and international sociopolitics." See George A. Kourvetaris and Betty A. Dobratz, "Social Recruitment and Political Orientations of the Officer Corps in a Comparative Perspective," *Pacific Sociological Review*, XVI, no. 2 (April 1973), p. 250.

12. See, for instance, Gerhard E. Lenski, "Status Crystallization: a Non-Vertical Dimension of Social Status," *American Sociological Review*, XIX, no. 4 (August 1954), pp. 405-413; Irving W. Goffman, "Status Consistency and Preference for Change in Power Distribution," *American Sociological Review*, XXII, no. 3 (June 1957), pp. 275-281.

13. For the potential impact of education on the political behavior of the military, see Janowitz, *Military of New Nations*, pp. 61-63.

14. S. E. Finer, "Armed Forces and the Political Process," *Penguin Social Sciences Survey 1968* ed. Julius Gould (Harmondsworth, Middlesex, Penguin Books, 1968), pp. 16-33.

15. Ibid., p. 21. For a summary of arguments against the validity of predictions of political behavior of the military on the basis of social background, see Abrahamsson, *Military Professionalization*, pp. 57-58. See also the criticism of the prediction power of social origin with regard to the officers' inclination toward modernization suggested by A. R. Willner, "Perspective on Military Elites as Rules and Wielders of Power," *Journal of Comparative Administration*, II (1970), pp. 271-272.

16. Samuel P. Huntington, *The Soldier and the State* (New York: Knopf, Vintage Books, 1957), pp. 11-13. Huntington notes also that "the peculiar skill of the military officer is universal in the sense that its essence is not affected by changes in time or location." Thus the military profession includes the basic elements of any other profession because it is a "specialized knowledge and skill in a significant field of human endeavor. His expertise is acquired only by prolonged education and experience" (ibid., p. 8). See also Joseph Ben-David, "Profession in the Class System of Present-Day Societies: A Trend Report, *Current Sociology*, XII, no. 3 (1963-64). For a clear, concise discussion of the concept of professionalism in general, and of the military profession in particular, see Abrahamsson, *Military Professionalization*, pp. 14-15. For a more comprehensive discussion, see ibid., ch. 3. See also ibid,. ch. 1, for a discussion of the historical background of the emergence of the military profession.

17. Abrahamsson defines this situation as follows: "The state is supposed to be both client and superior at the same time" (*Military Professionalization*, p. 66).

18. It is worthwhile to mention two additional dimensions suggested by McKinlay, namely, institutional autonomy and development of internal controls of effective neutrality. "The development of internal controls entails the development of self-controls of behavior which become internalized in the process of training or occupational socialization." R. D. McKinlay, "Professionalization, Politicization and Civil-Military Relations," in *The Perceived Role of the Military*, ed. M. R. Van Gils (Rotterdam: Rotterdam University Press, 1971), pp. 250-251. For the distinction between "corporate ideology" and other types of ideology, e.g., "operational ideology" and "political ideology," see Jacques Van Doorn, "Ideology and the Military," in *On Military Ideology*, ed. M. Janowitz and J. Van Doorn (Rotterdam: Rotterdam University Press, 1971), pp. xviii-xxiii.

19. This point has been intensively analyzed by Janowitz. He remarks that (1) the rate of technological change has been greatly accelerated and a wider diversity of skills is now required to maintain the military establishment; and (2) the complexity of warfare machinery and the requirements of research, development, and technical maintenance tend to weaken the distinction between the military and the non-military organizations. Janowitz, *Military of New Nations*, pp. 115-117. See also Charles C. Moskos, Jr., "The Emergent Military: Civil, Traditional, or Plural?" *Pacific Sociological Review*, XVI, no. 2 (April 1973), pp. 267. On the other hand, one should not go too far and blur the differences between the military profession and other professions. See, for example, Maury D. Feld, "Professionalism and Politicalization: Notes on the Military and Civilian Control," in Van Gils, *Perceived Role*, p. 270; and M. Feld, "Professionalism, Nationalism, and the Alienation of the Military," in *Armed Forces in Society*, ed. Jacques Van Doorn (The Hague and Paris: Mouton, 1968), pp. 55-59.

20. Finer notes that "the moment the military draw the distinction between nation and the government in power, they begin to invent their own notion of 'national interest' and from this it is only a skip to the constrained substitution of this view for that of the civilian government." S. E. Finer, *The Man on Horseback: The Role of the Military in Politics* (London and Dunmow: Pall Mall Press, 1962), p. 26. See also Feld, "Professionalism, Nationalism," pp. 65-66.

21. Huntington, *Soldier and State*, p. 84.

22. For example, Feld shows that the process of professionalism in certain European countries, like France and Germany (and in Japan), brought with it increasing alienation between the two sectors. The officer corps sought for exclusively national and political roles and thus became a focus of militant nationalism (Feld, "Professionalism, Nationalism," pp. 59-63). Luckham went even further, saying that professionalism does not increase civilian control on the military but even decreases it (Luckham, "Comparative Typology," p. 6). A similar extreme stand is taken by McKinlay, who states that "it has frequently been assumed

that the spontaneous developments of military controls mean that the military completely withdraws itself from politics. However, this assumption is largely fallacious, for not only does professionalization not exclude a political role but it may also precipitate such a role" (McKinlay, "Professionalization," p. 252). A similar thesis is elaborated by Abrams: one may find a great deal of alienation of the military from the civilian sector in democratic societies as well. He summarizes: "Isolation, powerlessness and meaninglessness in more or less intense forms are inescapable probabilities of the military predicament in peacetime in this type of society." P. Abrams, "Armed Forces and Society: Problems of Alienation," in *The Armed Services and Society: Alienation, Management and Integration,* eds. J. N. Wolfe and J. Erickson (Edinburgh: Edinburgh University Press, 1970), p. 34. A similar approach is taken by Abrahamsson, who presents some counterexamples to Huntington's argument. Abrahamsson rejects both theoretically and empirically the statement that professionalism involves political sterility (Abrahamsson, *Military Professionalization,* pp. 158-160).

23. It is important to emphasize that this feeling of alienation was apparent in European societies, too. The reasons, however, were the opposite: the backwardness of the military in terms of managerial progress in comparison with the civilian sector. See Feld, "Professionalism, Nationalism," p. 68.

24. Ibid.

25. Finer, "Armed Forces," p. 22.

26. Ibid., p. 22.

27. For a criticism of Finer's formulation, see B. J. Dudley, "The Military and Politics in Nigeria: Some Reflections," in *Military Profession and Military Regimes, Commitments and Conflicts,* ed. Jacques Van Doorn (The Hague and Paris: Mouton, 1969), pp. 211-212.

With a very different kind of formulation and terminology, although he is referring in fact to the same question, Huntington describes these societies: "In such societies, politics lacks autonomy, complexity, coherence and adaptability. All sorts of social forces and groups become directly engaged in general politics. Countries which have political armies also have political clergies, political universities, political bureaucracies, political labor unions, and political corporations. Society as a whole is out-of-joint, not just the military. All these specialized groups tend to become involved in politics dealing with general political issues: not just issues which affect their own particular institutional interests or groups, but issues which affect society as a whole." He calls these societies "praetorian societies" where one can find different types of praetorian armies (Huntington, *Political Order,* p. 194). See also Amos Perlmutter, "The Praetorian State and the Praetorian Army: Toward a Taxonomy of Civil-Military Relations in Developing Politics," *Comparative Politics,* I, no. 3 (April 1969), pp. 388-390.

28. S. P. Huntington, "Political Development and Political Decay," *World Politics,* XVII, no. 3 (April 1965), p. 427. Keith Hopkins, "Civil-Military Relations in Developing Countries," *British Journal of Sociology,* XVII, no. 2 (June 1962), p. 175.

29. For the African experience, see Bienen, *Military and Modernization,* pp. 14-15.

30. Dankwart A. Rustow, "The Military," in *Political Modernization in Japan and Turkey,* eds. R. E. Ward and D. A. Rustow (Princeton: Princeton University Press, 1964), p. 327. See Egil Fossum, "Factors Influencing the Occurrence of Military Coups d'Etat in Latin America," *Journal of Peace Research,* no. 3 (1967), pp. 235-236, for a statistical analysis of the positive correlation between election periods and frequencies of coups.

31. Arthur S. Banks and Robert E. Textor, *A Cross-Policy Survey* (Cambridge, Mass.: MIT Press, 1963), p. 132.

32. A detailed, systematic analysis of this very thesis in Latin America led to the conclusion that: "There is very little evidence linking political development in military abstention in any *straightforward way* [italics added]. Widespread participation in elections,

strong parties, pressure groups and freedom from political violence are neither necessary nor sufficient conditions for military abstentions." The key word here is obviously "straightforward," for a breakdown into indexes shows a *negative* correlation between frequency of military intervention and interest aggregation by parties or the stability of the party system. In other words, the more interest aggregation, the less frequent one may expect military intervention to be, and vice versa. Robert D. Putnam, "Toward Explaining Military Intervention in Latin American Politics," *World Politics,* XX, no. 1 (October 1967), p. 100. For correlations with specific indexes, see p. 98. For other illustrations, see Feldberg, "Political Systems," p. 208.

33. Huntington, *Soldier and State,* p. 93.

34. In the 1960s, the dividing line was apparently around an average of $500 per year. Approximately 50 percent of the countries whose annual average income per capita was lower than $500 experienced military interference, whereas this occurred only in about 8 or 9 percent of countries where annual income averaged higher. See Hopkins, "Civil Military Relations," p. 175.

Janowitz maintains that negative results were revealed by a correlation between economic development and the political role of the military in new nations. He states this because he disapproves of identifying economic development with political competitiveness (i.e., with democratic regimes). He is thus skeptical of the validity of the negative relationship between economic growth and the military's propensity to intervene in civil affairs (Janowitz, *Military of New Nations,* pp. 18-22). See also Fossum, "Factors," pp. 321-333, 237-238. Fossum contends that the lower the per capita GNP the more archaic and highly stratified the social structure and consequently the less mobilized the population.

35. Putnam, "Toward Explaining," deals with this issue and tries to corroborate the hypothesis with statistical evidence. Indirect evidence revealing the importance of economic growth came from data compiled by Tanter and others, who note that it is more a sudden setback in economic development, not necessarily the gradual regression to a previous stage, that intensifies the probability of violence.

36. Ibid., p. 88. See also Gino Germani and Kalman Silvert, "Politics, Social Structure and Military Intervention in Latin America," *Archives Europeennes de sociologie,* II, no. 7 (1961), pp. 62-81.

37. Germani and Silvert, "Politics."

38. Edward Shils, "The Military in the Political Development of the New Nations," in *The Role of the Military in Underdeveloped Countries,* ed. John J. Johnson (Princeton: Princeton University Press, 1961), p. 17.

39. S. M. Miller, "Comparative Social Mobility," *Current Sociology,* IX, no. 1 (1960), p. 51.

40. According to Janowitz, "Under the democratic model the civilian and military elites are sharply differentiated. The civilian political elites exercise control over the military through a formal set of rules" (*Military of New Nations,* pp. 111-112). Huntington defines this type of control as "objective control" and describes the situation thus: "Civilian control in the objective sense is the maximizing of military professionalism. More precisely, it is that distribution of political power between military and civilian groups which is most conducive to the emergence of professional attitudes and behavior among the members of the officer corps." See Huntington, "Soldier and State," p. 83.

41. For a critical analysis of this issue, see Amos Perlmutter, "Egypt and the Myth of the New Middle Class: A Comparative Analysis," *Comparative Studies in Society and History,* X, no. 1 (October 1967). See also Irving L. Horowitz, *Three Worlds of Development* (New York: Oxford University Press, 1966), p. 267. See also Dowse, "Military," p. 215.

42. Feld, "Professionalism, Nationalism," pp. 64-65.

43. Horowitz, *Three Worlds,* p. 26.

44. C. W. Weatley, "Some International Dimensions of the Role of National Military Forces in Internal Political Conflict," paper presented for the 1965 meetings of the American Sociological Association, p. 2. Weatley's paper includes one of the most systematic developments of this subject. See also William Guttridge, *Military Institutions and Power in the New States* (London and Dunmow: Pall Mall Press, 1964), ch. 9. For a negative opinion about the importance of external military aid as a relevant factor, see Huntington, *Political Order,* pp. 191-193.

45. For the opinions of two researchers who find this relevant, see Fossum, "Factors," pp. 238-240; Huntington, "Patterns of Violence in World Politics," in *Changing Patterns of Military Politics,* ed. S. P. Huntington (New York: The Free Press, 1962), pp. 44-45.

46. Focusing on coups and revolutions should not divert our attention from more indirect and less spectacular forms of military role expansion, such as lobbying, public statements, collusion with groups appeasing the government, etc. See Abrahamsson, *Military Professionalization,* pp. 142-144; Finer, "The Man on Horseback," ch. 10.

47. Johnson, *Revolutionary Change,* pp. 103-106.

48. Ibid., p. 91. For the three types of accelerators, see p. 99.

49. Studies on internal war have enumerated some of these factors. Eckstein, for instance, names the following: (a) ruthless, efficient repressions; (b) diversion of energy (foreign war or religious movements may serve "as the opiate of the people"; bread and circuses); (c) timely political concessions. See Lawrence Stone, "Theories of Revolutions," *World Politics,* XVIII, no. 2 (January 1966), p. 159. For a further discussion and definition, see Raymond Tanter and Manus Midlarsky, "A Theory of Revolution," *Journal of Conflict Resolution,* XI, no. 3 (September 1967); Huntington, *Political Order,* ch. 5.

50. Johnson, *Revolutionary Change,* p. 176.

51. Ibid., p. 137.

52. Ibid., pp. 137-138.

53. Ibid., pp. 138-139.

54. Ibid., p. 176. In addition to the general distinction between the two types of revolution and the two types of rebellion, there is another typology consisting of six types: (1) the Jacquerie; (2) the Millenarian rebellion; (3) the anarchistic rebellion; (4) Jacobin Communist revolution; (5) conspiratorial coup d'etat; and (6) militarized mass insurrection. See Stone, "Theories," pp. 162-164. Other typologies are suggested by William Kornhauser, "Revolutions," in *A Survey of Military Institutions,* ed. Roger W. Little (Chicago, Illinois: Inter University Seminar on Armed Forces and Society, 1969), ch. 14.

55. C. Johnson, *Revolution and the Social System* (Stanford: Hoover Institution Studies, 1964), cited in Stone "Theories," p. 159. See also "Theories," p. 162, for criticism of this approach.

56. Tanter and Midlarsky, "Theories of Revolution," p. 226; Peter Calvert and John Simpson, "Attributes of Revolution," paper prepared for the International Sociological Association Group Conference on Armed Forces and Society, London, September 1967.

57. Pye described the leadership of the new militaries of the fifties as "dynamic and self-sacrificing military leadership committed to progress and task of modernizing transitional societies that have been subverted by the 'corrupt practices' of politicians." See Lucian W. Pye, "Armies in the Process of Political Modernization," in J. J. Johnson, *Role of the Military,* pp. 69-70. Levy went further and argued that the armies are the "most efficient type of organization for combining maximum rates of modernization with maximum level of stability and control." See Marion J. Levy, *Modernization and the Structure of Societies: A Setting for International Affairs* (Princeton: Princeton University Press, 1966), II, 603.

58. For a detailed analysis of these unorthodox means, see Pye, "Armies," pp. 69-70.
59. Ibid.
60. Hopkins, "Civil Military Relations," p. 172; Janowitz, *Military of New Nations,* pp. 31-40; A. Daalder, *The Role of the Military in the Emerging Countries* (The Hague: Mouton, 1963), p. 22.
61. For statistical data about the relationships between military coups and defense budgets, see Nordlinger, "Soldiers in Mufti," p. 1135. Serious doubts about the military's capability and willingness to engage in economic development are expressed by Willner, "Perspective," pp. 273-274.
62. Hopkins, "Civil Military Relations," p. 117.
63. For an interesting attempt to prove that officers whose origins were in a flourishing middle class, reluctant to share resources with the lower classes, will resist social and economic reforms, see Nordlinger, "Soldiers in Mufti," pp. 1132-1148. See also Willner's discussion about the capacity for political brokerage, "Perspective," pp. 269-270.
64. For more shortcomings and reasons for the failure of the military as modernizer and leader of political development, see Perlmutter, "The Praetorian Army," pp. 403-404; and Weatley, "Military Coups," pp. 387-388, 405-407.
65. For additional analysis of some of the arguments presented here in favor of or against the military as an agent of modernization, see Bienen, "Background," pp. 14-24.
66. Willner, "Perspective," pp. 261-263.
67. Finer, "Armed Forces," pp. 30-32.
68. Moshe Lissak, "Modernization and Role-Expansion of the Military in Developing Countries: A Comparative Analysis," *Comparative Studies in Society and History,* IX, no. 3 (April 1967), pp. 250-251. This is not the place to discuss the historical and sociological circumstances of the emergence of entrepreneurial military elites. Bobrow's paper has some interesting hypotheses on a related subject—civic action. He notes five relevant variables for the analysis of civic action: the social composition of the military, the skill level, the image the public holds of the military and the military's opinion of that image, the relations to civilian authority, and the standard of self-evaluation (Bobrow, "Soldiers," pp. 104-109).
69. Following McKinlay, we suggest making a distinction between "overt politicization" and "induced politicization." The first "represents the deliberate or overt drive by the polity to inculcate extra-military political values in the armed forces," whereas the latter "has the same end-product as overt, i.e., the acquisition of an enlarged sphere of political reference, but differs in the process of acquisition of the political values" (McKinlay, "Professionalization," p. 255).
70. Huntington, *Political Order,* p. 240.
71. We have not tried systematically to link the internal structural factors with the external political factors. This task deserves a special and independent work. Weatley's work advances a limited number of hypotheses concerning linkages between aspects of the initial coup situations and attributes of the emerging coup groups. Weatley, "The Military Coups," pp. 395-398, 407-411.
72. Edward Shils, "Center and Periphery," *The Logic of Personal Knowledge* (London, 1961), pp. 117-130. See also Luckham, "Comparative Typology," pp. 12-13.
73. For additional suggestions of typologies, see Huntington, *Political Order,* pp. 408-411; S. M. Lipset, "Some Social Requisites of Democracy, Economic Development and Political Legitimacy," *American Political Science Review,* LIII, no. 1, pp. 87-90. There is no doubt that the scheme suggested here can be further elaborated by adding more variables (such as the tempo of consolidation or the rate of decay of the central power center) or by adding more dimensions to avoid dichotomization.
74. See also Nordlinger, "Soldiers in Mufti," p. 1145.

75. We are ignoring the fact that each prototype may have some variations here.

76. In addition to these typologies, the literature includes some other classifications, like those dealing with functions and orientations of military elite(s) in connection with general issues and particularly with problems of development and changes. (a) Huntington's typology is based on the distinction between military elites subjugated to a "subjective control" and those subjugated to an "objective control" (see Huntington, *Soldier and State*, ch. 4). (b) Janowitz's typology classifies all civil-military relations in four major models: aristocratic, democratic, totalitarian, and garrison state (see Janowitz, *Military of New Nations*, app.). Janowitz also distinguishes among the military as the instrument of sovereignty, the military as a partner in a political bloc, and the army as a ruling group (ibid., p. 10). (c) Finer suggests four levels of military intervention: influence, blackmail, displacement of the civilian government, and the supplantation of the civilian regime (see Finer, *Mann on Horseback*, p. 139). For other typologies, see Huntington, *Political Order*, pp. 195-237; I. L. Horowitz, "The Military Elites," in *Elites in Latin America*, eds. S. M. Lipset and A. Solari (New York: Oxford University Press, 1967), p. 168; Davis B. Bobrow, "Soldiers and the New States," *Annals of the American Academy of Political and Social Science*, CCCLVIII (March 1965), pp. 56-57; David C. Rapport, "A Comparative Theory of Military and Political Types," in Huntington, *Changing Patterns of Military Politics*, pp. 71-100; Luckham, "Comparative Typology," pp. 20-25. The propensity of the military to intervene in government may also be better understood by taking into account the a priori entrepreneurial qualities of the officers and their degree of articulation.

77. A distinction between structural and quantitative aspects of potential power resources of the military is suggested by Abrahamsson. Among the variables of the first, he notes the location of the military in relation to executive, legislative, and judicial positions in the state; the existence of paramilitary forces and the relationship between them and the military; and the relative unity or disunity of the military establishment. With regard to the quantitative, he notes the proportion of the gross national product spent on the maintenance of the military; the military participation ratio; and the proportion of industrial production devoted to the manufacturing of military goods (Abrahamsson, *Military Professionalization*, pp. 141-142).

Chapter 2

THE MULTIDIMENSIONALITY OF MODERNIZATION AND THE ISSUE OF UNEVENNESS

A. THE MULTIDIMENSIONAL DEFINITION OF MODERNIZATION

The subject of this study, as indicated by its geographical and historical location, is directly and deeply involved with the complex social process known as modernization. No comprehensive proposition about modernization will be presented, as it would but add to the dozens of existing schemes or paradigms of which only a minority appear to be of interest. We must, however, survey the most important propositions and definitions found in the literature. Tentative conclusions, especially about *evenness or synchronization* of processes of modernization in developing countries, will be sketched.

There are literally dozens of definitions of "modernization" in the literature concerned with this topic. Most definitions, however, tend, diliberately or accidentally, to emphasize only a few basic variables either simultaneously or by stressing one variable and neglecting all others. The four most important variables are as follows:

a. Structural change involving further *institutional differentiation,* functional specialization, and increasing complexity in the stratification order. These developments necessitate the creation of a social and economic infrastructure —governmental, public, and private administrative complexes to ensure the efficient operation of the manifold roles and tasks.[1]

b. *Sociodemographic changes.* These are allegedly responsible for the circulation of manpower and assets (material resources) both on the "horizontal" level (movement from rural to urban areas, etc.) and on the "vertical" level. The latter, mobility from a lower social group to a higher one, often results in significant changes within the status hierarchy itself. This flow of resources is sometimes described as "social mobilization."[2]

c. *Changes in the value system.* However, there is no consensus about which of these changes are specifically related to or even synonymous with the process of modernization.[3] In any case, modernization in this respect clearly does not refer to secondary changes in the value system but to qualitative changes in basic symbols and cultural premises, especially in the political and cultural tradition of the society. Toward the second decade of intensive research into modernization, attention was drawn to the phenomenon of *neotraditionalism* (or retraditionalism) in developing societies, whose importance and consequences are still ambivalent. The presence and influence of this phenomenon are, however, unquestioned.[4]

d. What Eisenstadt calls the capacity for *sustained growth,* the ability of the society to absorb changes "beyond its own initial institutional premises."[5] This element refers to the ability of the societal center to be conscious, attentive, and capable of absorbing the demands directed toward it from various groups within the "periphery."[6]

The assumption concerning sustained growth does not suppose uninterrupted growth. Development is not—as Rostow seems to have hinted[7]—self-maintaining once takeoff has been achieved. A sustained process clearly requires constant reevaluation and innovation, or stagnation or breakdown of development is bound to occur.[8]

Many definitions take for granted a clear-cut distinction between a traditional and a modern social system. Although it is now apparent that it is fallacious to speak about either totally traditional or totally modern social systems, the argument over the more precise boundaries of each continues. Clearer distinctions must be made between those social changes which are of no consequence for the process of modernization and those which do promise or even ensure modernization—be it political, cultural, or economic.[9] Moreover, one must avoid the chronological connotation which creeps into many of the more conventional definitions and results in the mistaken impression that the more "ancient" the social system the less modern, and vice versa. Finally, caution is necessary when analytically comparing modernization with Western patterns of development. The construction of a more complex and sophisticated typology of patterns of modernization should be encouraged.[10]

Definitions of modernization are thus *multidimensional.* They refer to sociodemographic, structural, and value changes as well as to the capacity to adjust to new situations. When dealing with a multifaceted phenomenon, we must check and verify the compatibility and internal harmony or synchronization of its indicators carefully. Nevertheless, the positive correlation between the various indexes, such as economic differentiation, communication, urbanization, and political development, has long remained unquestioned, despite the somewhat conflicting findings of numerous qualitative and quantitative studies.[11] In subsequent research, doubts have become more prevalent.[12]

The Multidimensionality of Modernization

Skepticism has been greatly enhanced by the new concern with retraditionalization and the breakdown of political systems in various developing countries. These two phenomena—which are by no means causally connected—show that the indexes of modernization do not necessarily follow a linear, parallel development. Uneven development, in fact, is one of the crucial factors determining the stability of developing countries. The extent of this unevenness can be examined at several levels. It can be assessed by considering the status of individuals or small groups, by comparing the rate of modernization in specific institutional spheres (the polity, the economy, etc.), and by analyzing the relationship between more generalized and diffuse entities, such as the "center" and the "periphery." Within the framework of this study, the emphasis will largely be on these last two levels.

B. UNEVENNESS AND LOPSIDED DEVELOPMENT

Disparities in the rate of development and growth of the various institutions composing the social system of the center and of the periphery are undisputed historical facts. They have been characteristic of several Western societies, some of which are suffering or benefiting from the consequences to this day. There are many reasons for such *lopsided* development. Some are of a specific and local character, others more general. One of the more general causes seems to be the fluidity of society's resources—their freezing and unfreezing. Thus K. Polanyi, describing the industrial revolution and the growth of the market economy in England, pointed to the legal, formal, and informal changes in the principles regulating the relations among labor, land, and money as mainly responsible for creating the necessary precondition for the emergence of a modern market economy in general, and the modernization of England in particular.[13] Thus, the unfreezing of manpower and of land and the increasing importance of money and other fiscal mechanisms have played a crucial part in the rapid economic growth of England. Social change and modernization may, however, be related to other resources as well, and we shall use more general concepts, such as manpower (or labor force), material assets (or resources), and loyalty frameworks (normative, political, and social).[14]

For various reasons, the process of thawing, both quantitatively and qualitatively, is usually not the same in all institutional spheres. A backward economy may coexist with a pseudomodern political organization and vice versa, or structural differentiation may be more intensive in the center than at the periphery. We may fairly conjecture that societies with differential unfreezing rates will be likely to have very different social and political configurations. These, in turn, will probably lead to different types of instability and different solutions by the ruling elites.

To clarify this issue, let us consider the potential or real impact of unevenness in the fluidity and mobility of human, material, and normative resources on the various aspects of modernization. There is and can be no rigid formula to describe the destructive or constructive effect of one pattern or another on the institutional development of either the social or the political sectors. However, when the various institutional spheres are changing at a markedly different rate, the political center has far greater difficulty in adequately distributing the available resources among them and in coping with social mobilization in general.[15]

Now, social mobilization is regarded as one of the central aspects of modernization.[16] Mobility and fluidity of wealth and natural resources, the rate of internal and external migration, demographic changes, and opportunities to recruit and rally potential supports around ultimate and middle-range values—in sum, all the changes implied by social mobilization—profoundly affect the smoothness of the exchanges among the various sectors of the society. The military, for example, need candidates able to function in a more universalistic and achievement-oriented system than had been in force previously. The principal reservoir for such manpower is the institutions of secondary and higher education. Again, parties that want their supporters to adopt a more positive attitude toward larger social and political frameworks—typically societies where the political center is striving to promote the climate of a participant society [17] —depend on the various socialization units that encourage a less narrow and introspective orientation. At the same time, the economy as a whole needs people with entrepreneurial qualities, which must be inculcated by both the traditional and the modern frameworks.

The lack of harmony between the process of political and economic differentiation is a much-discussed, fashionable topic. Some interesting quantitative analyses have been made that indicate a fairly significant correlation between the levels of political competitiveness and of economic development.[18]

This correlation has been frequently interpreted as meaning that the greater the economic growth, the greater the chances for political competition. This is true for either extreme of political and economic development. However, it is doubtful whether this relationship obtains for the various intermediate levels, especially over a short period. Economic growth leads to the crystallization of new functional groups, with their own demands, who may frequently clash with an impatient elite, unable to respond to the simultaneous demands that are constantly made on it. The elite commonly reacts by suppressing all other political power centers which threaten its position and trying to establish an authoritarian or totalitarian regime of one kind or another. The peripheral power centers generally remain helpless onlookers of a chain of rapid events. Only the ruling elite controls the independent economic resources necessary to maintain

The Multidimensionality of Modernization [51]

cadres of professional politicians and continue to recruit potential supporters. Semiindependent power centers are consequently destroyed. This, coupled with the overpoliticization of society, leads to modifications in the rules of competition. The political channel of mobility retains its predominance, having the most prestige and yielding the highest returns for an individual's investment, in comparison with the educational or occupational channels.

Also typical are the frequently disharmonious cognitive, affective, and expressive interpretations of the concepts of state and nation. Almond and Verba ascribe this to lack of congruence between the political system and the political culture.[19] One may go still further, as Pye has done for Burma, and blame it on an underlying disharmony among personality, culture, and polity.[20] At certain stages in the modernization process, modern elites are sincere in their intention to copy and imitate some modern political institutions. Unfortunately, they are usually not aware of the need for adjusting these to local conditions. Thus the rate at which institutions are built is not matched by the rate at which the images and concepts pertaining to their operation and manipulation are internalized. Social stratification is out of gear with economic realities. Merchants and other entrepreneurs have a lower social status than persons with political authority or higher education—by whom they are also vastly outnumbered. There are many historical reasons for this. For example, political intellectuals, or intellectual politicians, appear on the scene long before anyone has dreamed of economic growth. In the absence of a middle class such as had existed in Europe, the political elite becomes the initiator and bearer of social change. However, in the usual caste or tribal structure of society at large, there is no breeding ground for an ideology that espouses economic mobility and entrepreneurship and regards economic position as a marketable status attribute. In societies where mobility aspirations have always been to some extent legitimized, they are generally realized through one of two channels—through the possession of cultural traits typical of particular ethnic minorities living in sociogeographical enclaves, like the Chinese in Southeast Asia or the Indians in East Africa; or through the adoption of the new images of stratification and mobility by an indigenous sector of society. Few social systems, however, are able to activate incumbents of these new roles and images. Potential entrepreneurship is paralyzed by the backwardness of the economy and its excessive politization and centralization.[21]

Notwithstanding far-reaching flexibility of exchange and considerable interchangeability of means and resources, strong obstacles to mobilization may eventually arise and the channels of exchange may become clogged. The resulting vacuums and bottlenecks are a challenge to those political entrepreneurs who consider themselves able to abolish them. In extreme but nonetheless fairly frequent cases, they try to construct a full-fledged political system for the principal—if not exclusive—purpose of rigidly controlling the mobilization process.[22] But the chances of success are rather poor. The ruling elite, civilian or military, is simultaneously confronted with a welter of fundamental and urgent problems: the shaping of the national identity and numerous basic economic issues.[23] Attempts to set up an order of priority so as to escape the nightmare of "simultaneous solutions" generally fail because of the enormous pressure exerted on the center by the various groups interested in staving off radical structural changes for as long as possible. Then there is the prevailing discrepancy between the prestige awards available exclusively to the post-independence elite and the number of those eligible to receive them, which leads to a measure of internecine strife. Moreover, although most elites in developing countries try desperately to find substitutes for rare or "frozen" resources by developing a surplus of manpower rather than of wealth, or by replacing economic incentive with intensive ideological indoctrination and the like, consensus about what constitutes an adequate substitution is rarely attained.

C. POLITICAL MODERNIZATION AND POLITICAL DEVELOPMENT

We have referred in very general terms both to the concept of modernization and to the phenomenon of uneven institutional development without specifically emphasizing the complicated and diversified network of processes in many different institutional spheres that are involved in modernization. These processes affect and may create further difficulties for any requisite interaction and exchange of services and resources among those spheres. It is therefore important to refer, if only briefly, to some of the main definitions of political, cultural, stratificational, and economic modernization and to illustrate the character of their interaction.

Vagueness prevails in the more specific and limited segments of this topic. Conspicuous examples are the difficulties of defining modernization in the political, cultural, and stratification spheres. It seems to us that the most logical point of departure for more accurately defining *political modernization* is to consider it as only one specific type of political development. Political development, a more generalized concept, may be defined, following Huntington, as the institutionalization of political institutions, mainly through introducing constitutional and legal organs to cope with ongoing social change.[24] However, few of the students of political modernization try, or even consider it necessary, to distinguish between political modernization and political development—a fact that is clear in many definitions of political modernization.[25]

The typical components of political development mentioned in the literature are national integration and the institutionalization of political organization.[26] Another component frequently cited is the attitudinal aspect of the political system, which is alleged to be an attribute of the prevailing political culture. A famous typology in this context is that of Verba and Almond, namely, the "parochial," "subject," and "participation" orientation toward political activities.[27] Huntington and others, referring to the attitudinal aspect, have made suggestions about sensitivity to principles of equality and acceptance of universal law.[28] Similar concepts, such as "intensive social mobilization" and "mass participation," are mentioned by Pye,[29] Huntington,[30] and many others. Efficiency and ability to control the social process are also often offered as concomitants of political development.[31] What, then, is left in the arsenal of variables applicable to the phenomenon of *political modernization* as distinct from *political development*?

We do not intend to suggest here any unequivocal answer, if such a thing exists, to this question. It seems, however, that any suggestion about the uniqueness of political modernization will have to resort to a number of criteria which can isolate the most characteristic features of this central phenomenon of our generation.

There are at least three criteria that should probably be used to deal with this issue. The first concerns the "changes in both the distribution of power within a political system and in the amount of power in the system." These changes may be discerned in the concentration, expansion, or dispersion of power.[32] In other words, as Eisenstadt has put it: "on the one hand continuous development of a high extent of differentiation, unification and centralization of the political system, and on the other hand, continuous development of a high extent of 'free-floating' (i.e., non-committed to any ascriptive group) political power and resources."[33]

The second criterion refers to the ability to deal with continuous change in political demands.[34]

The third criterion is the extent and integrity of political and social mobilization typical of modern political systems, for example, the "participation of the ruled in the selection of the rulers, in setting up the major political goals and, to a smaller extent, in the formulation of policies,"[35] in various forums, either parliamentary or extraparliamentary.

D. THE MODERNIZATION OF CULTURE

Three important issues have captured the attention of those concerned with the capacity of traditional value systems to adapt to new political, economic, and technological frameworks: (1) the definition of a "traditional culture" (as opposed to a "modern culture"); (2) adequate criteria for the examination of the adaptation capacity; and (3) the circumstances in which new traditional ideologies emerge and their compatibility with the new social order.

The attempt to define traditional culture eventually led to an interesting distinction between its two most prevalent types. Shils named the first one "traditionalist," the other "traditional."[36] "Traditionalism" is characterized by an all-embracing religious legitimation: It is a type of system in which "society, the state, authority and the like are all parts of elaborately sustained high-solidarity structure in which religion is pervasive as a cognitive guide."[37] The implication, tacit or explicit, is that this value system is the antithesis of that which underlies a more modern culture, such as Western (democratic) societies. The second traditional-cultural approach refers to a society where attitudes are more instrumental and pragmatic. Here, despite the profound appreciation of and respect felt toward customs, norms, and recognized virtues—because of their ancient origin—the range of permissiveness accorded to personal and collective interpretation of those norms is much broader. It would be an error to assume that these characteristics apply to one society on an all-or-nothing principle. These cultural elements *coexist* in varying proportions in all traditional societies. The capacity to adjust and to contribute to (or to impede) the process of regulated modernization may be determined by the proportional predominance of either attribute. (The emphasis is, of course, not on the quantitative aspect.) The particular institutional sphere and its centrality in which either type of traditional values is dominant are also important. The tendency and willingness to adopt and accommodate to new principles of action are greatly reduced where most normative regulation is based on "consummatory" rather than "instrumental" principles.

During recent years, students' attitude toward the transformative ability of various value systems has undergone interesting developments. The general trend has been from a rather deep-seated pessimism[38] to a reserved and quiet optimism.[39] The optimism is based primarily on the assumption that a traditional culture is not totally monolithic and that, consequently, the more the key institutional spheres are regulated by instrumental and pragmatic traditional values, the more easily they can take advantage of their own internal transformative capacity.[40] It is true that colonial regimes could and did serve as an external accelerated force, and traces of gentle—or brutal—Western intrusion are to be found among all the elites and pseudoelites of developing states. Nevertheless, "the mobilization of the motivational forces embedded in the cultural and religious subsoil is open to deliberate manipulation only to a degree. It is only fully possible when activated from the inside, from the well-spring of religious life itself."[41] The transformative capacity of a society must be examined against the attitudes toward work, time, money, decision making, resolution of conflicts, functioning within large impersonal social organizations, etc., and also in the changes in concepts, beliefs, and images of power exchange and power hierarchy within the society.

Our attention should not, however, be diverted from a rather reverse phenomenon, the *retraditionalization* of various roles and institutions, which, because of exposure to Western civilization, became at least pseudo-modern. Traditionalization in this sense means "the process by which traditional, indigenous elements of belief and behavior became reinvigorated within the modern organization inherited by new states from their colonial predecessors."[42] This phenomenon indeed adds another dimension to the problem of synchronization in developmental processes. Not only is the process of modernization of various value systems by and large not synchronized, but there is also a process of "regression" to previous points of departure. Some consider this as a blessed process and even as a prerequisite to "take off to modernization that can be generated and sustained from within."[43] If this assumption is partially or even totally true, the simultaneous existence of traditional, neotraditional, and pseudo-modern norms and values impinges heavily on the ability to solve problems of personal and/or collective identity.

E. THE MODERNIZATION OF THE STRATIFICATION SETUP

Despite all the defects evident in the literature dealing with modernization in general or with its more specific issues, the level of systematization and sophistication already achieved is very impressive compared with achievements in the field of stratification. True, it is widely asserted that modernization of the "class" structure means a transfer from a system in which affiliation and belonging are based on ascriptive and particularistic criteria to a system where these criteria are more achievement oriented and have a universalistic flavor. It is unnecessary to explain in detail why this belief, albeit essentially true, is inadequate. Chiefly, it is unsatisfactory because it refers only to two rather fictitious poles without any concern for the problems involved in the movement of individuals and groups between these two ideal types. Processes of modernization in the stratification setup eventually involve radical changes in the system of interaction between topdogs and underdogs. These changes are clearly related to the differentiation and specialization manifested by the creation of new roles, whose emergence and crystallization do not mean that all—or even most—of them have broken out of or dissociated themselves from the traditional framework. Many new roles are actually "accommodationist in nature,"[44] i.e., traditional frameworks that adopt new functions or give fresh nuances to old and obsolete functions. Typical examples are the tribal unions in Africa, the organization for mutual help of ethnic minorities, etc. Only a few new roles (although their number increases rapidly) are created in more or less new types of social systems, such as the governmental bureaucracy or the military. Moreover, a significant number of social roles are not only activated in traditional frameworks but defined traditionally. To be sure, the confrontation of the two types of roles may eventually create tension and anxiety (no less for the group than for the individual), and the source of this tension lies in the *pluralistic* character of the society. Pluralism is based on a configuration of many types of roles performed in variegated social systems by various social groups differently exposed to specific aspects of modern role behavior. When the possibility of enclaves, organized on separate linguistic, ethnic, and religious bases, is added, the resulting picture is a complex and problematical stratification system.

It is customary to call this kind of society "heterogeneous" and pluralistic. Yet societies like that of the United States are also frequently called pluralistic. The fact that such entirely different stratification orders are described and defined by the same term makes it necessary to specify much more accurately the discrepancies between various types of pluralistic societies. For example, we may distinguish institutional, cultural, and social pluralism.[45]

Institutional pluralism is characterized by the coexistence of institutional systems opposed to and estranged from each other. Any encounter between them occurs exclusively on the instrumental level. Poignant examples of institutional pluralism are provided by former colonial societies and developing societies in our times, where a capitalistic market economy and an exchange or subsistence economy coexist. Different legal frameworks and marriage patterns and contradictory stratification criteria are further examples of institutional pluralism.

Cultural pluralism refers to the differences as basic value orientations and socialization patterns, consumption norms, and religious rituals. The existence of cultural pluralism as a sociological fact does not imply acquiescence to it by the political and cultural leadership. The model of cultural pluralism can be accepted as a guiding rule for relations among the different cultural groups only if other possible models are rejected—e.g., the "conformity model" and the "melting-pot model."[46]

Social pluralism is characterized by the existence of latent normative restrictions, especially on informal contacts (marriage, membership in exclusive clubs, etc.) among the different groups. These restrictions are usually a result of a free decision of the potential partners to the contact. On the other hand, the contacts on the formal-instrumental level are many and of a very diverse character. In other words, the scope of social pluralism is a function of the degree of openness of the stratified structure. The stratification system in a socially pluralistic society differs from the one in an institutionally pluralistic society. In the latter, the stratification structure is imposed and totalistic, and its bases of evaluation are collectivistic and ascribed. In a socially pluralistic society, the system is less hierarchic and more permissive, and its evaluation criteria tend to be more achieved and individualistic, even if the ethnic principle is firm and abiding.

The Multidimensionality of Modernization [57]

History shows that social antagonism is a rather integral part of all sorts of pluralistic societies. However, its severity depends on the presence or absence of certain conditions and mechanisms of integration. From many points of view, the factors contributing to integration in pluralistic societies are not different from the conditions found in less pluralistic, more homogeneous societies. A common value system, external pressures from political or military adversaries, consensus about the rules of the struggle for political and economical interests—these are only a few examples of the univeral mechanisms of integration. However, socially or culturally pluralistic societies must, more than others, encourage the development of two mechanism. First, conditions must be created which will facilitate voluntary partial insulation and segregation of the different status groups. This depends on the more or less voluntary readiness of each group to be different and to possess a separate and unique identity, but, at the same time, on its acceptance of the rules which regulate intergroup contact. It is not the same, therefore, as the rigid segregation and the exclusive frameworks of institutional pluralism; rather, it is a form of preferential voluntary association.[47]

Following Williams, we define the second mechanism as the existence of multiple, though partial, overlappings of status groups and social categories. Such a situation can help blur the sharp edges of potential and real cleavages.[48] Multiple group membership and orientation toward various reference groups help to develop crisscrossing allegiances. The higher the number of relevant status dimensions (education, income, political power, profession, etc.), the greater the number of crisscrossing allegiances.[49] These individual and collective overlapping points may constitute potential convergence points and vital communication links among different status groups and/or groups with different cultural identities. The central function of these convergence points is to enable the partners in an encounter to exchange resources. In order to allow for fair bargaining, however, there should not be extreme asymmetry in their "possession" of status assets. The partners at these encounters should have more or less balanced but not necessarily equal forces. Moreover, the status assets should not be fixed and unchangeable, since this could effect an interrelational standstill and a departure from the rules of the game, which could lead to the use of violence. From society's point of view, this implies the need for an optimal institutional dispersion—a dispersion of the population in multiple and diverse occupational and economical categories.[50] In terms of the individual's status profile, this implies the multiplication of individuals with inconsistent status of a certain kind.[51] The strengthening of this type of status ensures the existence of convergence points and social exchange principles suitable for multiscaled stratification. It also practically eliminates the possibility of a clash between polar groups, i.e., between those holding a total monopoly and those lacking everything. There are increased possibilities of encounters in which the partners will enjoy partial advantages, but only for limited periods of time and only in the status dimensions. Under this type of constellation, we can conceive possible encounters between possessors of economic advantages and others with advantages on a political level, or between the latter and others with intellectual or social preferential assets. More complicated configurations are obviously possible. Although these kinds of contact do not completely eliminate the possibility of conflict, they soften and neutralize potentially violent changes.

Status images of a certain kind contribute to maintain this partial balance of power which paradoxically results from the convergence of inconsistent status. Flexible and differential images concerning the stratification system imply openness, flexibility, and a more rational regard toward the means and the use of resources for personal advancement. People with these types of status images will usually have weaker ethnocentric feelings. They will also be less vulnerable to anxieties and fears of failure. It follows that aggression directed toward scapegoats will also be lower or even minimal. If the development of cultural and social pluralism cannot be avoided, people with differential and flexible status images potentially constitute its most efficient and favorable element. They are psychologically more capable of acting as mediators in the complex exchange structure which results from heterogeneous stratification units. (The units are heterogeneous in their status dimensions, given their partial monopoly of different kinds of resources.) These people can usually be found in democratic societies, since in many ways they are the most loyal bearers of the basic values of democratic tradition.

Social pluralism and cultural pluralism are a challenge for every society. If pluralism crystallizes into a crisscross of convergence points, and if communication avenues among the central social categories (religious, ethnic and cultural groups) facilitate contact, it is easier to overcome. It is decisively important that contact channels be institutionalized, and that any steps taken in order to change the position of a group be accepted by the whole. The degree of consensus in these areas depends considerably on the stature of the group leaders and their social orientations.

The importance of these types of encounter points in developing countries is obvious. First, a heterogeneous population is a cradle for separatist tendencies which could repeatedly bring these societies to the verge of collapse. Second, in some societies the existence of an inflexible, crystallized, and nonegalitarian system of stratification may lead to a violent confrontation between the topdogs and the underdogs. Even where a less crystallized, more egalitarian stratification prevails, tension is not at all uncommon. The social mechanisms of encounter might be able to cope with the intensive and unregulated process of upward social mobility, one of the most severe problems confronting pluralistic socieites. The desire to rise in the social order is very strongly felt, and this endangers the political center with probable "floodings," as many strive to gain access to it as well as to the economic field.[52]

F. THE SYNCHRONIZATION OF DEVELOPMENT AMONG SUBSYSTEMS

We have seen that no parallel movement, in the long run as well as in the short run, need be observed in either the direction or the rate of development of various institutional spheres. If this issue is to be considered in greater detail, it would be expedient to break each institutional sphere into *subsystems* and to trace more specifically the discrepancies in the rate and synchronization of development among themselves. Earlier, in dealing with political modernization, we emphasized the occurrence of radical changes in the norms regulating socialization, recruitment, and the organization of decision making. In almost all cases, these changes result in the emergence of new groups seeking an opportunity to use political power resources that are relatively untrammelled by particularistic interests. As a rule, such free-floating political forces emerge more rapidly within the central political, administrative, and cultural spheres than in the outlying fields. Apart from accelerating the politization of life in the center, they tend to bring about far-reaching changes in the fundamental norms governing most spheres. Though the periphery may also be subject to intensive politization, its political articulation and socialization usually occur within the traditional framework. When there are no unmanageable and ardent pressures from the periphery, the political elite is able to cope with the political problems and forces impinging on the center. However, it can no longer do so once it becomes swamped by unrealistic demands from the periphery—unrealistic because the periphery, under these conditions, lacks the necessary mechanism for sifting and preselection. An instance in point is when the electorate actually avails itself of the privilege of universal suffrage. It is, therefore, imperative to maintain a delicate balance of prestige, authority, and power between the political framework responsible for absorbing the various specific or diffuse demands and the groups and collectivities articulating and presenting them. Such frameworks should be at least partially institutionalized at as early a stage as is possible, so as to be able to cope with the emerging of peripheral groups. Here lies one of the central paradoxes that developing societies must face. Fulfillment of the national elite's pre-independence pledge to grant universal suffrage provides a lever for various groups to seek satisfaction of their particularistic needs and to gain direct access to decision making and the sharing of real power. New political roles are frequently articulated within tribal and communal ethnic organizations which are at least initially left intact. When, as often happens, a process of revivalism is thus set in motion, the gap between the center and the periphery is widened still further.

Other imbalances within the political sphere are due to the uneven growth, crystallization, and institutionalization of the various branches of government. Bureaucracies with a long tradition of public service often operate alongside and in sharp contrast to weak and corrupt executive and judicial organs, or vice versa. Consequently, the division of functions among the military, judicial, and executive organs becomes blurred. Hence the roles of the elite frequently overlap and its authorities are vague and ill defined.[53]

Disparities in the rate, direction, and content of the consolidation of classes and status groups are another factor to be considered. They may be bound up or quite unconnected with political developments. The slow emergence and crystallization of formal and informal social interaction between new and older status groups in most developing societies are typical. Societies with a traditional, inflexible, and hierarchical stratification system and societies without any clear and definite social hierarchy both seem to lack adequate mechanisms for regulating such interaction. In the rigidly stratified societies, their absence may exacerbate and strengthen the tendency toward polarization and culminate in a violent confrontation between the two opposite poles. In less stratified societies, where efforts to establish patterns of arbitration and selective dealings of undifferentiated groups are obstructed, the way is left open for demagogues and political agitators, and the elite is easily enticed into making irresponsible commitments. Another facet of the same problem is the discrepancy between an intensive urge for or expectation of upward mobility and the structural potential for absorbing prospective candidates. Modifications in status symbols and social stratification, which are no longer adequate to the requirements, scope, direction, and range of the effective social mobility, may also result in disharmony. For example, in colonial times in many countries four years' schooling was a sufficient qualification for white-collar jobs which apparently carried considerable prestige; this qualification has been greatly raised during the last decade. The prestige of elementary education has thus automatically declined.

The focus of prestige has, moreover, frequently shifted from the educational or occupational to the political sphere. Yet these modifications in the rates of exchange of status components do not always coincide with actual mobility.

Developmental imbalances also have economic repercussions. In some countries the standard of living has risen with economic growth and improved health services. The cumulative effect is an increased life expectancy. When there is no concomitant drop in the birth rate, the population increase is accelerated and the demand for food, work, social services, and the like may be doubled or trebled. To be able to meet this demand, the infrastructure must be expanded.[54] Otherwise, channels of mobility would become blocked.

The ambition to establish modern industries often stems from noneconomic considerations. As a rule, the educational system is unable to supply the required skilled cadres, partly because of a real lack of economic resources and partly because of mistaken, politically inspired priorities. The tremendous gap between the level of urbanization and the very gradual increase in labor resources in the cities, characteristic of the major part of the less developed world, is another example.

Eagerness to establish a modern economic system is not only an emergent necessity but also a function of espousing a modern system of status symbols. Modern industry confers a prestigious status and power on the local and on the international scenes. Nevertheless, even when the political elite adopts the aim of economic modernization, the elite itself, as well as those groups which are to be the objects of change, are often reluctant to adopt a position favorable to the structural and psychological modifications called for by incipient industrialization. This particular phenomenon is of great importance: the norm of change has been adopted but those involved have not fully realized that change in one sphere logically entails and brings about some changes in others.

The most significant manifestation of imbalances in the cultural value orientations is clearly the discrepancy between the high level of national consciousness within the elite (and other affiliated social groups) and tribal or ethnic loyalties which, despite extensive exposure to external indoctrination, retain their original inconceivable vitality.

In conclusion, we must warn against the dogmatic view that an uneven course of development is necessarily dysfunctional and destructive. However, if uneven development is to play a positive role, two important conditions must be met. The first is that a substantial measure of institutional autonomy must be assured. Where the society is permissive about the independent development of symbols, values, and norms, the political, economic, and educational elites are not exposed to negative sanctions from other social groups in developing their transformative capacities. Such autonomous development may be restricted on the symbolic level and by the amount of resources and services that can be drawn from other institutional spheres. It is, however, essential that the range of manipulation be such that the elites are free from strict and rigid outside regulation. The second condition relates to the character of the social group or elite. The aristocracy, the military, the bureaucracy, the intelligentsia, or other groups participating in the political modernization of a country use different means to overcome the problems they encounter and respond differently to potential or actual breakdowns.

Breakdown is a situation where the mechanisms for maintaining the boundaries of a society, including its internal and international territorial boundaries, and the consensus on its basic and ultimate values, are suspended or destroyed.[55] Both values as such and the rules regulating the interaction of those concerned in adhering to them are affected. The breakdown of these mechanisms may remain latent for a long time before its symptoms become manifest. The symptoms are not necessarily indicative of the type of breakdown that has occurred, which is, rather, determined by the type of mechanisms that are disrupted and the extent and duration of their malfunction.

The general hypothesis about the condition leading to breakdown stipulates that modernization manifests itself in a thawing of resources or a change in the norms regulating their mobilization. In practice, this is not a straightforward process; there are many obstacles in its way. At one stage or another, both those who oppose and those who favor radical change find themselves stymied by events. A positive outcome depends on the flexibility of the social system, especially on the extent to which the society is able to seek and discover provisional or permanent substitutes for frozen or unavailable resources. This flexibility is not an abstract attribute of the society's value system but a structural characteristic of its elites and the personal property of its members. The elites must be able to interpret new situations and adapt traditional values accordingly. When this integration and transformative capacity are missing, the dissonance between the society and its political core becomes increasingly strident. An entrenched elite, blind to the demands of emergent groups, that flagrantly and systematically blocks all channels of expression induces polarization or antagonizes an already polarized society and provokes direct confrontation with potential political power centers. As no intermediate groups are left, alternative channels of communication cannot be used. Eventually, the national symbols, the boundary-maintaining mechanisms that had hitherto protected the physical framework of the society, also lose their validity and impact.[56]

G. PROTOTYPES OF CENTER AND PERIPHERY INTERRELATIONS

It is possible to conclude that the particular relations between the center and the periphery play a very important part in bringing about those conditions which are conducive to the breakdown of the system. This is also true when the breakdown occurs, as it often does, only within the boundaries of the center itself, leaving the periphery untouched and uninvolved.

In the first chapter we described four prototypes of interrelations between the center and the periphery. They were based on the interaction between a strong and effective (or weak and ineffective) center, on the one hand, and the high (or low) intensity of demands, on the other hand—demands which are mainly the result of the extent of social and political differentiation of the periphery.[57]

It is certainly rather difficult to place one of the various societies into one of the four prototypes. This difficulty stems not only from the hard task of defining a strong or weak center but also from the fact that in many cases it is rather speculative to define the boundaries of the center or its centrality as well as the boundaries of the periphery and the extent of its marginality.[58]

The Multidimensionality of Modernization

Furthermore, the dichotomization of the variables does an injustice to other aspects of association between the center and its periphery, especially with regard to the mutual commitment to social change and modernization.[59] Nevertheless, despite the simplicity of the prototypes, they may help to suggest some basic assumptions about the relationship between the character of specific prototypes and the emergence of conditions conducive to various forms of power usurpation by the military.

We have assumed that the amount of temptation and inducement toward institutional or noninstitutional, legitimate or illegitimate role expansion put in the way of such elite groups as the bureaucracy, the military, etc., varies with the prototype, as does the ruling elite's ability to cope with the predisposition of the various groups to expand their roles.

The validity of these assumptions may be gauged from the following description of two prototypes. Prototype B has been defined as having a rather *weak center* politically, socially, and economically, and a highly *differentiated periphery*. Applied to developing countries, this means that, first, the central political framework is at a low level of institutionalization and has not yet reached a high degree of complexity, specialization, and rationalization. At the same time, there is a considerable growth of free-floating political elements eager to participate in all levels of government and politics, although, contrary to their official statements, they are not always prepared to rise above regional religious, linguistic, and tribal differences.

Second, in spite of these floating political elements, there is a conspicuous shortage of politicians capable of and interested in integrating and consolidating the dispersed forces of the modern and the traditional sectors. If there are such men, they lack the necessary instruments, organization, or economic resources. The imperfections of the political elite, especially its personal and administrative inefficiency and impotence, prevent it from dealing properly with the increasing number and variety of economic, political, and cultural demands. It is usually not too successful in setting up firm institutions (cabinet, parliament, administration, etc.) and strong associations (political parties). The potential opposition, on the other hand, tends to organize in nonassociational and sometimes anomic groups.[60]

Third, because of its structural differentiation, specific and functional organizations emerge in the social periphery. At the same time, however, its tribal and communal organization is resurrected—and shows much ingenuity in adapting to new conditions by redefining its former, now obsolete, functions and taking on new ones.[61] The general development of the periphery, which contains enclaves with a participant social orientation, is such as to speed its access to the political arena. The elite is frequently unable to regulate and direct the masses that flood it with their demands and threaten to sweep away the power center.[62] Typical of most of these countries is the emergence of big new social enclaves consisting of incongruent status groups. The older enclaves consisted of ethnic minorities that monopolized key economic positions but were socially despised, while the new enclaves consist of the educated and semieducated. Yet despite the debility and passivity of the political center in relation to the vitality of the periphery, there still remains a substantial gap between the central and local levels of development.[63] The very fact that the new groups of the educated and semieducated tend to amalgamate indicates that their access to administrative, economic, and political positions is barred, either because positions are overstaffed or for political reasons.

Finally, the political, stratificational, and economic obstacles—especially the differential rate and quality of development in these and other spheres—interfere with the mobilization of national resources. Under these circumstances it is hardly surprising that the process of mobilization, which is supposed to promote national cohesion, in fact often enhances destructive social and political divisions and threatens the common national interest.[64] These and other weaknesses ultimately bring most of these societies to the verge of breakdown, because of the instability of the political center and the unsatisfactory relationship between the elites and the population at large.[65]

Prototype C has been defined as a social system with a relatively *strong political center* and relatively *little social differentiation at the periphery*.[66] First, the center derives most of its strength from one of two sources. There may be a small elite or a single dominant figure whose power derives mainly from traditional sources (an aristocracy or a king) that may nevertheless be an effective agent of modernization. This type of elite is fast disappearing. Strong political centers based on personal charisma and exclusive political organization are becoming far more common. Here, strong government does not necessarily mean that the political system has become institutionalized and has reached a high standard of complexity, specialization, and rationalization. A parochial or subject orientation may be no more or less dominant than where authority derives from traditional sources, though in some countries of this type large enclaves oriented toward a participating society and culture may be found.

Second, because the structure of the center and particularly of the periphery is undifferentiated, these societies lack substantial floating votes detached from particularistic and regional allegiances. While there may be small privileged cliques within the main political circle, they lack public support and represent only themselves or definite particularistic groups. Because of the low level of occupational, economic, and educational differentiation, elites lack an ideal of accomplishment, although in contrast to type B they do have the necessary instruments. The common result is that they misuse their political talents in intrigues within the dominant circle.

Third, in this kind of society politics and administration, civilian and military, are the main, if not the only, pathway of mobility in the early stages of modernization. Being practically exclusive, it is easily regulated, but may soon become heavily overloaded. Frustration and bitterness may be the result. Here the effects of unbalanced development are different from those described in type B. The political and administrative sectors flourish while the periphery fails to develop. The natural function of the body politic and of the administration is impaired. They do not cater properly to the demands of the populace and provide the necessary services. In the absence of clients, they become an end in themselves. The gap between the central and local level becomes still wider than in type B. Despite the limited scope and penetration of institutional and noninstitutional groups, their activities tend to be very intense. Sometimes the use of force receives legal sanction.

Fourth, the number of young, semieducated people, small businessmen, and trade unionists who are under strict surveillance and become frustrated politicians is smaller than in the previous type. Since there are few alternative ways of moving up the social ladder and the political structure is monolithic, access to political and bureaucratic position is, however, no less difficult than in type B. Government is often able to deal with frustrations, usually by selectively doling out patronage to a few leaders of the small, potentially disaffected groups. Here the problem is more easily solved on a personal level, while in type B a more radical structural solution is required that imposes a great strain on the weak political center.

In type B, the main problem of the political leaders is to regulate and slow down social mobilization. In type C, the central issue is to thaw out frozen economic, manpower, and normative resources. Failure to do so may expose the political elite to rival political and administrative factions that have better relations with the periphery.

Fifth, compared wtih type B, in type C the rate of economic and social change is more moderate, although frequent changes of personnel may occur in the center. Theoretically, this slow rate of change is a major asset of the elite, affording it an opportunity to prepare the political and normative instruments and to take the steps necessary to anticipate future change. In fact, few elites have made a successful attempt in this direction. In many type C countries, the political center has broken down or is about to disintegrate, less as a direct result of social processes in the periphery than of personal power struggles within the elite.

We have tried to deal with modernization as a multidimensional issue and examine the compatibility and harmony of its different facets. Uneven development has been regarded as one of the most crucial problems of developing countries, mainly because of its impact on the fluidity of the unfreezing and refreezing of resources. We have presented some illustrations of discrepancies in the rate of development in the intra- and interinstitutional sphere. Unevenness as such has not been considered as a pathological symptom, and the conditions under which it could play a positive role have been discussed. We have tried to summarize the issue of unevenness and nonconcurrence by relating to two prototypes of societies.

In the following chapters the military, political, and social features of Thailand and Burma will be presented as an illustration of only some of the issues discussed. The focus will be on the presentation of basic facts (as far as they were available) which seem to be vital for the more comprehensive, analytical analysis in the last chapter.

NOTES

1. Typical examples may be found in the following: S. N. Eisenstadt, "Modernization: Growth and Diversity," (Bloomington: Carnegie Faculty Seminar on Political and Administrative Development of Government, Indiana University, 1963), pp. 2-6; Eisenstadt, "The Development of Socio-Political Centers at the Second Stage of Modernization—A Comparative Analysis of Two Types," *International Journal of Comparative Sociology* (March 1966), pp. 119-122; Eisenstadt, *Modernization: Protest and Change* (Englewood Cliffs, N.J.: Prentice-Hall, 1966); Reinhard Bendix, *National Building and Citizenship: Studies of our Changing Social Order* (New York: Wiley, 1964), p. 5; Marion J. Levy, Jr., "Pattern (Structures) of Modernization and Political Development," *Annals of the American Academy of Political and Social Science,* CCCLVIII (March 1965), pp. 29-40; Samuel P. Huntington, *Political Order in Changing Societies* (New Haven and London: Yale University Press, 1968), pp. 17-20.

2. Karl W. Deutsch, "Social Mobilization and Political Development," *American Political Science Review,* LV, no. 3 (September 1961), pp. 493-514; Amitai Etzioni, *The Active Society* (New York: The Free Press of Glencoe, 1968), ch. 15.

3. For different definitions and suggestions, see Arthur L. Stinchcombe, *American Sociological Review,* XXXI, no. 2 (April 1966), p. 267; David E. Apter, *The Politics of Modernization* (Chicago: University of Chicago Press, 1965), p. 56.

4. See, for example, Fred W. Riggs, *Thailand: The Modernization of a Bureaucratic Polity* (Honolulu: East-West Center Press, 1966), p. 376; Apter, *Politics,* p. 6; Ann R. Willner, *The Neotraditional Accommodation to Political Independence: The Case of Indonesia* (Princeton: Princeton University Center of International Studies, 1966), pp. 3-8.

5. Eisenstadt, "Modernization," p. 2.

6. Eisenstadt, "Development of Socio-Political Centers," p. 119. For an attempt to systemize what is called the "capacity" approach to modernization," see Chong-Do-Hah and Y. Schneider, "A Critique of Current Studies of Political Development and Modernization," *Social Research,* XXXV (1968), pp. 147-156. This brief survey of variables does an injustice both to the variety of research in modernization and to the historical dimensions of growth and development of research in the field. See Chong-Do-Hah and Schneider. See also A. R. Desai, "Need for the Reevaluation of the Concept," *Essays on Modernization of Underdeveloped Societies,* ed. R. A. Desai (Bombay: Thacker & Co. Ltd., 1971), I, pp. 464-474; R. Bendix, "Tradition and Modernity Reconsidered," *Comparative Studies in Society and History,* IX, no. 3 (April 1967), pp. 294-307; R. A. Nisbet, "Developmentalism: A Critical Analysis," *Theoretical Sociology,* eds. J. C. McKinney and E. A. Tiryakian (New York: Appleton-Century-Crofts, 1970), pp. 168-177.

7. We say "seems," since Rostow does not say so explicitly. See W. W. Rostow, *The*

Process of Economic Growth (New York: Norton, 1952). For a brief review of Rostow's approach, see Hah and Schneider, "Critique," pp. 134-137.

8. D. Weintraub, M. Lissak and Y. Azmon, *Moshava, Kibbutz, and Moshav* (Ithaca, N.Y.: Cornell University Press, 1969), p. 315. See also Henry Bernstein, "Modernization Theory and the Sociological Study of Development," *Journal of Development Studies*, VII, no 2 (January 1971), pp. 143-154.

9. See Apter, *Politics*, pp. 67-68, where he tries to distinguish among "development," "modernization," and "industrialization."

10. One of the most fruitful approaches to a more sophisticated typology involves distinguishing more systematically between modernization per se and other types of social change, for example: growth, transformation, development, etc. For an attempt, see Dov Weintraub, "Developmental Change: Towards a Generalized Conceptualization of Its Basic Dimensions and of the Relations Among Them," *Development and Change*, III (1971-72), pp. 7-15. For a critical view of the ideological bias concealed in the concept of modernization and especially its identification with the concept of Westernization, see Desai, "Need for Reevaluation," p. 459. For a critical review of the evaluative approach to the study of modernization, see Bendix, "Tradition and Modernity," pp. 309-313.

11. For the relationship between urbanization and exposure to mass media, see Daniel Lerner, "Communication Systems and Social Systems: A Statistical Explanation in History and Policy," *Behavioral Sciences*, I, no. 1 (January 1956), p. 271. For education and the rate of urbanization, see ibid., pp. 269-270; Arthur S. Banks and Robert B. Textor, *A Cross-Polity Survey* (Cambridge, Mass.: MIT Press, 1963), Matrix 45/29. On education, income, and industrialization, see Lerner, "Communication Systems," n. 6; Karl W. Deutsch, "Toward an Inventory of Basic Trends and Patterns in Comparative and International Politics," *American Political Science Review*, LIV, no. 1 (March 1960), p. 44. On the rank correlation between technological, economic, and demographic indicators of modernization and the extent of urbanization, see Leo F. Schnore, "The Statistical Measurement of Urbanization and Economic Development," *Land Economics*, XXXVII (August 1961), p. 234. On economic and political development, see, for example, *The Politics of the Developing Areas*, eds. Gabriel A. Almond and James S. Coleman, (Princeton: Princeton University Press, 1960), pp. 532-576; Seymour M. Lipset, "Some Social Requisites of Democracy, Economic Development and Political Legitimacy," *American Political Science Review*, LIII, no. 1 (March 1959), pp. 87-90; Lerner, "Communication Systems," pp. 271-273.

12. Apter, *Politics*, p. 61. See also Samuel P. Huntington, "Political Development and Political Decay," *World Politics*, XVII, no. 3 (April 1965), pp. 387-393; Deutsch, "Social Mobilization," p. 495. A more or less complete list of those who oppose the previous approach can be found in C. S. Whitaker, Jr., "The Dysrhythmic Process of Political Change," *World Politics*, XIX, no. 2 (January 1967), pp. 193-199.

13. Karl Polanyi, *The Great Transformation* (New York: Farrar & Rinehart, 1944), ch. 6.

14. Moshe Lissak, "Social Change, Mobilization and Exchange of Services Between the Military Establishment and the Civil Society: The Burmese Case," *Economic Development and Cultural Change*, XIII, no. 1, part I (October 1964), pp. 2-3.

15. Deutsch, "Toward Inventory," p. 495; and Lipset, "Social Requisites," p. 81.

16. Deutsch, "Social Mobilization," pp. 493-494. See also Etzioni, *Active Society*, pp. 418-421; J. P. Nettl, *Political Mobilization* (New York: Basic Books, 1967), pp. 32-35.

17. Sidney Verba and Gabriel A. Almond, *The Civic Culture: Political Attitudes and Democracy in Five Nations* (Princeton: Princeton University Press, 1963).

18. Almond and Coleman, *Politics*, tables 2, 3, 5, pp. 540-542; Lipset, "Social

Requisites," p. 3; Irma Adelman and Cynthia T. Morris, *Society, Politics and Economic Development: A Quantitative Approach* (Baltimore, Md.: Hopkins Press, 1967); Dick Simpson, "The Congruence of the Political Social and Economic Aspects of Development," *International Development Review*, VI (June 1964), pp. 21-25.

19. Verba and Almond, *Civic Culture*.

20. Lucian W. Pye, *Politics, Personality and Nation Building: Burma's Search for Identity* (New Haven: Yale University Press, 1962), ch. 3.

21. In a discussion which is partially related to the issue concerned here, Weintraub distinguishes four main types of society building: (1) the "lag" profile, which "refers to a situation in which change in one major element lags considerably behind the others"; (2) the "associated" profile, in which "a close parallelism [exists] among the dimensions of the process of change"; (3) the "dissociated" profile, where the components of change form an incoherent or minimally "balanced" profile; and (4) the "great leap forward" profile, "a relation in which the process of change proceeds by a dramatic spurt—or a series of dramatic spurts—in which advances are made into new areas and enterprises before earlier or antecedent projects are consolidated" (see Weintraub, "Developmental Change," pp. 16-23). More generally and within the context of a discussion about convergence of industrial societies, Weinberg deals with various potential profiles of development. See Ian Weinberg, "The Problem of the Convergence of Industrial Societies: A Critical Look at the State of Theory," *Comparative Studies in Sociology and History*, XI, no. 1 (1969), pp. 1-15. See also Gino Germani, "Secularization, Modernization and Economic Development," in *The Protestant Ethic: A Comparative View*, ed. S. N. Eisenstadt (New York: Basic Books, 1968), pp. 343-344. Deutsch introduces two concepts of thresholds. The first is "the threshold of significance, S, that is, the numerical value below which no significant departure from the customary workings of a traditional society can be detected and no significant disturbance appears to be created in its unchanged functioning." The second is the threshold of criticality, which refers to significant change in the side effects, actual or apparent, of the process of social mobilization. See Deutsch, "Social Mobilization," p. 497.

22. Apter calls this a mobilization system. See *Politics*, ch. 10.

23. One reason that many countries of the third world are forced to cope simultaneously with social and political problems is that they are "late starters" in comparison with countries like England, the United States, etc. In some cases this chronological fact is supposed to facilitate the rate of growth, but usually it does not. For an interesting elaboration of this, see R. P. Dore, "The Late Development Effect," a paper submitted to the Seminar on Modernization in Southeast Asia, Institute of Southeast Asian Studies, Singapore, 16-21 January 1971. In this context, Nordlinger suggests the following: "With respect to time sequences, it is argued that the probabilities of a political system's developing a nonviolent, nonauthoritarian, and eventually democratically viable manner are maximized when a national identity emerges first, followed by the institutionalization of the central government, and then by the emergence of mass parties and a mass electorate." See Eric A. Nordlinger, "Political Development: Time Sequences and Rates of Change," *Politics and Society*, ed. E. A. Nordlinger (Englewood Cliffs, N.J.: Prentice-Hall, 1970), pp. 332-333. Desai has paid special attention to the specific problems of the "late starters" or the "late modernizers." He states that "conscious mass participation called the 'mass aspect' is a peculiar feature of these underdeveloped societies which took to active modernization after World War II in contrast to the earlier modernizers" (Desai, "Need for Reevaluation," p. 466).

24. See Huntington, "Political Development," pp. 384-39. See also J. S. Nye, "Corruption and Political Development: A Cost-Benefit Analysis," *American Political Science Review*, LXI, no. 2 (June 1967), p. 418; H. Bienen, "The Background to

Contemporary Study of Militaries and Modernization," in *The Military and Modernization,* ed. H. Bienen (Chicago: Aldine-Atherton, 1971), p. 23.

25. See, for example, Lucian W. Pye, "Introduction: Political Culture and Political Development," in *Political Culture and Political Development,* eds. L. W. Pye and S. Verba (Princeton: Princeton University Press, 1965), pp. 11-14.

26. Huntington, "Political Development," pp. 384-438. See also Leonard Binder, *Iran: Political Development in a Changing Society* (Berkeley: University of California Press, 1962), p. 47.

27. Verba and Almond, *Civic Culture.*

28. Huntington, "Political Development."

29. Pye, "Political Culture," pp. 11-13.

30. Huntington, "Political Development."

31. Binder, *Iran.*

32. Huntington, *Political Order,* p. 145; C. E. Black, *The Dynamics of Modernization: A Study in Comparative History* (New York: Harper & Row, 1966), p. 13.

33. S. N. Eisenstadt, "Political Modernization, Some Comparative Notes," *International Journal of Comparative Sociology,* V, no. 1 (March 1964), p. 4.

34. Ibid., p. 8.

35. S. N. Eisenstadt, "Modernization and Conditions of Sustained Growth," *World Politics,* XVI, no. 4 (July 1964), p. 577.

36. Edward Shils, "Tradition and Liberty: Antimony and Interdependence," *Ethics,* XLVIII, no. 3 (1958), pp. 160-161. Apter refers to "consummatory traditionalism" and "instrumental traditionalism." See *Politics.*

37. Ibid. Shils, "Tradition and Liberty."

38. Daniel Lerner, *The Passing of the Traditional Society* (Glencoe, Ill.: The Free Press, 1958).

39. Eisenstadt, *Modernization;* also Everett E. Hagen, *On the Theory of Social Change* (Homewood, Ill.: Dorsey Press, 1962); David McClelland, *The Achieving Society* (Princeton: Van Nostrand, 1961); Dov Weintraub and Frieda Bernstein, "Social Structure and Modernization: A Comparative Study of Two Villages," *American Journal of Sociology,* LXXI, no. 5 (March 1966), pp. 509-521; E. Shils, "Tradition," *Comparative Studies in Society and History,"* XIII, no. 2 (April 1971), pp. 144-159; Apter, *Politics,* p. 83.

40. This issue is directly related to the much discussed and famous Weber thesis and its validity for the developing countries. For a summary and a survey of the main opinions, see Eisenstadt, "The Protestant Ethic Thesis in an Analytical and Comparative Framework," in *The Protestant Ethic and Modernization,* ed. S. N. Eisenstadt (New York: Basic Books, 1968), pp. 3-45.

41. Soedjatmoko, "Cultural Motivations to Progress: The Exterior and the Interior Views," in *Religion and Progress in Modern Asia,* ed. Robert N. Bellah (New York: The Free Press of Glencoe, 1965), p. 7.

42. Willner, *The Neotraditional Accommodation,* p. 1.

43. Ibid., p. 6.

44. Apter, *Politics,* p. 123.

45. M. Lissak, *Social Mobility in Israeli Society* (Jerusalem: Israel University Press, 1969), ch. 1. See also Michael G. Smith, *The Plural Society in the British West Indies* (Berkeley: University of California Press, 1965), p. 80; Leo Kuper, "Plural Societies: Perspectives and Problems," in *Pluralism in Africa,* eds. L. Kuper and M. G. Smith (Berkeley: University of California Press, 1969), ch. 1.

46. See M. Gordon, "Assimilation in America: Theory and Reality," *Daedalus,* XC, no. 2 (Spring 1961), p. 263.

47. Robin M. Williams, Jr., *American Society* (New York: Knopf, 1952), pp. 523-524.

48. Ibid., p. 531. For a theoretical development of this issue, see John Galtung, "Rank and Social Integration, A Multidimensional Approach," in *Sociological Theories in Progress,* eds. J. Berger, M. Zelditch, and B. Anderson (Boston: Houghton Mifflin, 1966), I, pp. 145-198.

49. Galtung, "Rank"; and J. Galtung, "A Structural Theory of Aggression," *Journal of Peace Research,* I (1964), p. 111.

50. S. N. Eisenstadt, *The Absorption of Immigrants* (London: Routledge & Kegan Paul, 1954), pp. 11, 13, 260 ff.

51. Moshe Lissak, "Occupational Choice, A Theoretical Model and Research Hypotheses," *Megamot,* XI, no. 3 (April 1965), pp. 321-330 (in Hebrew).

52. Huntington, "Political Development," pp. 419-421.

53. Max F. Millikan and Donald L.M. Blackmer, eds., *The Emerging Nations, Their Growth and United States Policy* (Boston: Little, Brown, 1961), pp. 74-75.

54. Ibid., p. 41. For a systematic analysis of the relationship between education and economic growth, see Mary Jean Bauman and C. Arnold Anderson, "The Role of Education in Development," in the Brookings Institution, *Development of the Emerging Countries: An Agenda for Research* (1962), pp. 153-180. See also M. J. Bauman and C. A. Anderson, "Concerning the Role of Education in Development," in *Old Societies and New States,* ed. Clifford Geertz (New York: The Free Press of Glencoe, 1963), pp. 247-280; and *Social Structure and Mobility in Economic Development,* eds. Neil J. Smelser and S. M. Lipset (Chicago: Aldine, 1966), ch. 1.

55. Talcott Parsons, *The Social System* (Glencoe, Ill.: The Free Press, 1951), pp. 45-50.

56. One interesting question is, what happens after a breakdown? What sort of regime emerges after political, social, and economic reforms have failed? Eisenstadt is of the opinion that neopatrimonial societies emerge. For the major characteristics of neopatrimonial regimes, see S. N. Eisenstadt, *Traditional Patrimonialism and Modern Neopatrimonialism,* Beverly Hills and London: Sage Research Papers in the Social Sciences, 1973, pp. 13-15.

57. In defining the strength of the political center, we should refer to mechanisms of political control and government. See the definitions and ranking of countries (or cluster of countries) according to these variables in Almond and Coleman, *Politics,* tables 1-6 (in the "Conclusions"); Fred R. van der Mehden, *Politics of the Developing Nations* (Englewood Cliffs, N.J.: Prentice-Hall, 1964), pp. 54, 65. See also Phillip M. Gregg and Arthur S. Banks, "Dimensions of Political Systems: Factor Analysis of a Cross-Polity Survey," *American Political Science Review,* LIX, no. 3 (September 1965), pp. 602-614; Banks and Textor, *Cross-Polity Survey,* pp. 78-79, 85-86, 101-105. The extent of control over manpower and economic assets by the political center should also be referred to. See Bruce M. Russett et al., *World Handbook of Political and Social Indicators* (New Haven: Yale University Press, 1965), pp. 69, 72. See also Gregg and Banks, "Dimensions," pp. 605-612; and Deutsch, "Social Mobilization," pp. 493-514. In addition, reference should be made to institutional-constitutional stability. For more information about definitions of these concepts and the ranking of countries accordingly, see Deutsch, "Social Mobilization"; Russett et al., *World Handbook,* p. 101; Ivor K. Feierabend and Rosalind L. Feierabend, "Aggressive Behaviors within Politics, 1948-1962: A Cross-National Study," *Journal of Conflict Resolution,* X, no. 3 (September 1966), pp. 260-262; Raymond Tanter, "Dimensions of Conflict Behavior within Nations, 1955-1956: Turmoil and Internal War," *Peace Research Society (International) Papers,* III (1965), pp. 176-178; Banks and Textor, *Cross-Polity Survey,* pp. 84-85, 171-172. The periphery should be divided into subspheres: (a) Economic differentiation. See Deutsch, "Toward Inventory" and "Social Mobilization"; Lipset, "Social Requisites,"

pp. 76-77; Mehden, *Politics,* pp. 16-18; Banks and Textor, *Cross-Polity Survey,* pp. 63-64. (b) Differentiation in the field of communications. See Russett et al., *World Handbook,* pp. 213-226; and works just cited. (c) Political differentiation. See Gregg and Banks, "Dimensions"; Almond and Coleman, *Politics,* Introduction. (d) Occupational differentiation. (e) Primordial and particularistic differentiation.

58. Elsewhere we have tried to elaborate on this subject. See D. Horowitz and M. Lissak, "The Origins of the Israeli Political System," in *Political Institutions and Processes in Israel,* eds. M. Lissak and E. Gutmann (New Brunswick, N.J.: Transaction Inc., forthcoming).

59. For a suggestion, see Weintraub, "Rural Periphery, Societal Center, and Their Interaction in the Process of Agrarian Development: A Comparative Analytical Framework," *Rural Sociology,* XXXV, no. 3 (September 1970), pp. 367-376.

60. Almond and Coleman, *Politics,* pp. 33-34, 536-637.

61. See, for example, James S. Coleman and Carl G. Rosenberg, Jr., eds., *Political Parties and National Integrity in Tropical Africa* (Berkeley: University of California Press, 1966), Conclusions; Aiden Southall, ed., *Social Change in Modern Africa* (New York: Oxford University Press, 1961), part 1; M. N. Srinivas, *Caste in Modern India* (New Delhi: Asia Publishing House, 1964), ch. 1.

62. G. Germani, "Social and Political Consequences of Mobility," in Smelser and Lipset, *Social Structure,* p. 390.

63. S. N. Eisenstadt, "Sociological Aspects of Political Development in Underdeveloped Countries," *Economic Development and Cultural Change,* V, no. 4 (July 1957), pp. 293-298.

64. Deutsch, "Toward Inventory," p. 501.

65. Excluding, perhaps, the possibility of differentiation on a particularistic basis.

66. Thailand is a case in point.

Chapter 3

THAILAND: THE PERMEABLE BOUNDARIES OF A MILITARY ESTABLISHMENT

PART I. THE MILITARIZED POLITICAL CENTER

A. Introduction to the Political History of Thailand

Thailand's modern political history is so closely bound up with the history of the interrelationships between the military establishment and the civilian administration that any discussion of current political affairs in Thailand that omits reference to the sociopolitical and professional profile of Thailand's armed forces becomes difficult and unrewarding.[1]

The best point of departure for our analysis is 1932, when the first army coup occurred.[2] While the personal imprint of the coup's promoters was felt at least until the middle of the 1960s, their impact on the institutional structure of Thailand will be felt for many years to come.

The June 1932 coup was carried out by a group of young civilians and military officers who subsequently organized into a political circle called the People's Party, which later became better known as the Promoters.[3] Many of them had been educated abroad with the financial and moral aid of the king of Thailand. Their leader and theoretician was Nai Pridi, a lawyer and lecturer at the local university. The motives for the coup may be traced partially to the republican and socialist radical tradition to which they had been exposed while studying in Europe, especially in Paris, and in part to dissatisfaction with the system of appointments and promotion, the heavy taxes, the salary levels, and, finally, the cutbacks in the military budget. This last was a consequence of an economy gravely damaged by a severe international economic crisis. The immediate result of the military coup was the eviction of the king and the royal aristocracy from all positions of political power (such as the decision-making roles in the military and civilian hierarchies). Beyond this, very few changes occurred. The military officers among the Promoters opposed Pridi when he attempted to initiate radical changes in the economic sphere. The changes envisioned included the nationalization of land, industry, and wealth, as well as the conversion of the entire labor force into hired labor.[4]

A year later this coup was followed by a second, in which the military partners of the earlier coup ousted the radical elements of the left and the conservative elements of the right. This coup was led by two people, Phahon (phonpha Yuha), who later became prime minister and commander in chief of the armed forces, and Field Marshall Phibun (Songkhram), who was nominated minister of defense. The official explanation for this second coup was the threat of communism. Since June 1933, repeated use has been made of this.[5] In its first years of existence, the revolutionary government had to deal with several crises: in October 1933, a countercoup was led by several royal princes; in 1935, the abdication of King Prachatipok was followed by the coronation of young King Ananda Mahidol (Rama VIII). In December 1938 Phibun became prime minister. A tightening of the political and cultural ties between Thailand and Japan made the regime's militaristic character increasingly pronounced. An ultimatum and the invasion of Thailand by Japan were followed by an alliance between the two countries which swept Thailand into the military and political orbit of the Axis. In that period pan-Thaism—an ideology of territorial expansion—flourished and, with Japan's aid, was partially realized (at the expense of Indochina, Malaya, and some border provinces of Burma).

On the eve of Japan's defeat in 1944, pressure from certain groups in the National Assembly compelled Phibun to step down as prime minister and commander in chief.[6] His resignation was accepted by the military without comment. A peace treaty with the Allies was signed, and Thailand was to be placed under a civilian regime. In March 1946 the country held its very first elections. Pridi was appointed prime minister.

The central political crisis in the short period of his ministry (March-August 1946) arose from the mysterious death of the young king, for which Pridi's rivals accused him of being directly or indirectly responsible. In addition, some financial scandals in which several ministers of his government were involved became publicly known during this period. Pridi resigned and Vice Admiral Thamrong (Navasawat), one of the original Promoters, was nominated prime minister. Thamrong's adminsitration became notorious for its scandals, economic corruption, violence, and even political assassinations (especially victimized was the opposition Democratic Party). A coup headed by Phibun[7] in November 1947 terminated the rule of the vice admiral. This third military coup was explained as justified by the corruption of the regime and the damage it did to Thailand's image.[8] Phibun, denying political ambition, invited Khuang (Kowit Aphaiwong), the leader of the party that had opposed Pridi's regime, to form a new government.[9] In the ensuing elections of January 1948, Khuang was elected prime minister. However, after three months in office, he was notified by officer delegates of Phibun that the armed forces were not satisfied with the government's achievements in dealing with Thailand's economic and social problems. Moreover, the government was accused of corruption and of weakening the armed forces. Thus Phibun returned as prime minister after four years of compulsory absence.

Within a very short time after taking office, Phibun had to deal with several attempted countercoups.[10] The most dangerous, in February 1949, was directed by Pridi's supporters with the aid of certain marine units and the navy.[11] Following this many of Pridi's supporters were purged and some were executed without trial. After this period, General Sarit (Yuthasin) and the commander of the police, General Phao (Sniyanonda), consolidated their positions in the army and police respectively. These two generals were responsible for dissolving the existing constitution and for reenactment of the original constitution of 1932. While the emergence of these two personalities marked the beginning of an intensive interpersonal conflict at the top of the political hierarchy, there was a diminution of the threat to the regime from outside groups.[12] To counteract the influence of Sarit and Phao, Phibun made symbolic gestures toward democratizing the regime. He even proposed general elections, which were actually held in February 1957. Out of the twenty-three parties participating in the elections, the only effective oppositon was the Democratic Party (Khuang's party). Attacked for rigging the elections, Phibun and Phao lost much of their earlier popularity. Since, for certain reasons, Sarit was not involved in this scandal, he gained prestige. Shortly afterward, in September 1957, Sarit headed a military coup, terminating Phibun's second period of power, which had lasted ten years. Sarit's two main aides were Thanom (Kitikachorn), a future prime minister, and Praphas (Charusathien), the minister of interior in Sarit's government.

Immediately after his self-appointment to the position of prime minister in October 1958, he nullified the constitution, dissolved the parliament, and declared martial law. Thailand regressed to a regime typical of the period prior to World War II. Not even the façade of democracy remained. When Sarit died in December 1968, his loyal aide Thanom was nominated prime minister. In the second half of the 1960s, the rule of the armed forces, especially the army, was stabilized and consolidated, a development which permitted the military elite to extend its cooperation with civilian groups.

B. The Structure of the Political System

A penetrating treatment of the political center rather than its periphery is warranted more for Thailand than for most Southeast Asian or other developing countries. This is due to the relatively vast power of Thailand's political center as opposed to the kinds of political organizations found at the margins or in the periphery in the fifties and sixties. The first part of our discussion will thus be concerned with the image of the center, the extent of its internal differentiation, and the character of the political manipulations within it. Until 1932, the center of political power rested in the king and the royal court. From 1932 to 1957 it rested with varying combinations of personalities drawn from the military faction of the Promoters of 1932; from 1957 to the beginning of the seventies its locus has been senior officers drawn especially from the army and from the armored units.

The position of the king and the royal court. Before 1932, the royal court was the backbone of the traditional political structure. In the period of absolute kingship, this structure was rooted in both a symbolic hierarchy and an institutional hierarchy. The basis of the symbolic hierarchy was the balance of merits and demerits which eventually determined every person's position in terms of his Karamic state. At the apex of this symbolic hierarchy stood the Buddhist priesthood. The king, princes, and other senior officials formed the apex of the institutional monarchy. The king's personality reflected the intersection of the two hierarchies. As *Bodhisattva,* the king was considered as one in a state of incipient Buddahood who had nevertheless, out of compassion, elected to serve his fellow creatures instead of proceeding to Buddhahood. The king's power and authority stemmed not only from his strategic position at the pinnacle of the symbolic and institutional hierarchies but also from his becoming the center of a redistributive economic structure. The income from services given to the king was available to him for redistribution, especially to nobles or officials in his court and to the Buddhist order. The patron-client interaction system originates from this arrangement. In turn, each official was patron and client, rendering services and receiving benefits. The whole of the social structure was legitimized through the association of Karamic states with worldly positions.

The shift from the sacred-royal basis of authority to a parliamentary structure based on popular sovereignty was achieved through the Chakri rulers. They transformed the popular image of the monarchy from that of a divine being, ruling by supernatural right over a subject population according to Brahmanic rites and doctrines, into that of a great man serving his people by promoting true religion and morality. A viable basis was thus introduced for legitimizing the Siamese polity in a time of secularism and populism.[13]

The shift to constitutionalism involved a new definition of the monarchy, an alteration in the identity of the political elite, and a change in the basis for holding political power—achieved through the selective borrowing and interpretation of Western models and it was initiated and imposed from above. Much of the available national elite was incorporated or linked with the various cliques constituting the political elite, and material rewards and mercantilist values supplemented attitudes of respect as a basis for maintaining compliance and allegiance.

The institutionalization of the new principles of legitimacy was confronted with many difficulties, owing to the unstable personal status of King Prachatipok, the main victim of the coup.[14] His personal security and the continuation of the monarchy as an institution were seriously threatened after the abortive attempt of Prince Bavaradej to execute a promonarchy counter-coup. After this attempt, the mutual suspicion between the king and the Promoters resulted in an atmosphere where it became impossible for the king to realize even the limited rights provided him by the new constitution. Thus in 1935 he abdicated and went abroad. The young prince, Ananda Mahidol (Rama VIII), became head of state; and during the entire period of his studies abroad, a committee of regents fulfilled his functions. Thus during the critical period of the consolidation of the military regime in Thailand during the 1930s and the 1940s, the Promoters were not confronted by any opposition from the monarchy. The irrelevance of the monarchy as an autonomous political power center was clearly symbolized in the fact that Pridi became regent of Thailand.

Some changes in the status of the monarchy occurred after World War II. The constitution of 1946 removed the restrictions on political participation imposed on the royal family, and the short-lived civilian regime attempted to establish a more meaningful system of relationships with the monarchy. However, the mysterious death of the young king during Pridi's rule abruptly cut short these nascent tendencies.

A substantial change in the monarchy's status occurred when Sarit became prime minister of Thailand. Sarit deliberately exploited the personal prestige of King Bhumipon and of the monarchy in general to enhance the regime's popularity.[15] The new status of the royal court was consolidated by the many political and economic scandals during Phibun's rule, the increasing patronage of the king and princes by different voluntary organizations, and, finally, the exaltation by the politico-military leadership of the king's name and the monarchy as the embodiment of the unity of the nation and the Buddhist religion in counteracting the threat to the regime from subversive elements guided by foreign political forces.[16] Thus, for the first time since the 1932 coup, it seemed that a king would be able to fulfill his role as constitutional monarch, that is, to reign but not to rule. This trend was further strengthened during the prime ministership of Thanom. The king was not given any real share in the decision-making process. This privilege remained the exclusive monopoly of the cabinet, which had become the heart of Thailand's political center after 1932.

The cabinet—heart of the political center. During the general reforms of the governmental apparatus in 1892, King Chulalongkorn (Rama V) established a cabinet on the Western model. This was a turning point and the beginning of the process whereby the absolute king was replaced by a functional bureaucratic body. Some scholars go so far as to argue that what happened in 1892 had more far-reaching implications than the coup of 1932.[17] At any rate, after the 1932 coup the council of ministers was the summit of Thailand's political power structure. This is reflected in the fact that the council secured for itself, both formally and informally, almost an absolute monopoly on the state's major political resources. The other branches of government—the legislature, to the extent that it was active at all, and the judiciary—were for all practical purposes subordinate to the executive branch.

Within the cabinet, the prime minister unequivocally held the most powerful position. Usually he was the supreme commander of the armed forces and held the portfolios of defense and/or internal affairs. Formally—and this was not changed in any of the constitutions—the cabinet was nominated by the king with the recommendation of the prime minister. According to some constitutions, the prime minister was to be endorsed by the National Assembly.[18] However, in actuality the cabinet was nominated by the leader of the coup or his successor.

Except on certain rare occasions, all the ministers have been recruited from the military or civil services. The military members of the cabinet have belonged mostly to the Promoters of the 1932 coup or to the instigators of subsequent coups. Very few ministers have represented social forces beyond these two groups. In a political culture where the principle of patronage and the allocation of rewards to the different promoters of coups have reached an uncommonly high degree of institutionalization, there is only narrow room for experts—and even then they are coopted only when their nomination is irrelevant to the internal balance of power within the cabinet. Only very rarely and over very short periods of time in the constitutional history of Thailand have the revolutionary coup members not been represented in the cabinet.[19] It is thus no accident that the struggle between the different bureaucratic cliques has always been focused in the cabinet, which has in fact been a coalition of bureaucratic officeholders with powerful positions in the various branches of the military and civil services. Furthermore, the internal conflicts neither possess an ideological background nor directly involve any wider social groups. The main, if not the exclusive, motive behind these interclique conflicts is the preservation of political and economic vested interests or the willingness to change the criteria for allocating benefits.[20] When rivals are unable to agree on a compromise formula for these criteria, the chances for an overturn or for a realignment of the government increase. However, even when one does occur, most of the factions will remain in the cabinet, and the only real change will have been a shift in power. In this respect, the capacity of the ruling groups to absorb rival cliques has always been impressive.[21]

Summarizing, we may say that, even compared with the absolute monarchy, the cabinet following the 1932 coup was an extremely oligarchic institution. The oligarchy, which has dominated the various cabinets since then, has been almost totally free from accountability to public opinion. Its activities have always been legitimized post facto. It has never been obliged to give any account to any body other than its own members—the delegates of bureaucratic groups in the army, the civil service, and the National Assembly.

The civil bureaucracy. In this context the civil bureaucracy, one of the two components of the political military oligarchy, comprises the senior bureaucrats.[22] The lower and upper echelons of the civil bureaucracy are linked both by formal conventional channels and by a system of patrons and clients.[23]

The most outstanding feature of this bureaucracy is its self-serving orientation. This orientation was initially encouraged by the civil bureaucracy's superiority over the other civilian organizations, both organizationally and in terms of their internal crystallization. The basic reforms enacted between 1892 and 1900 were directed mainly toward extending control over the periphery by administrative means and the creation of modern ministries with a Western type of division of labor. The most important ministries created in this period were the ministries of the interior, of justice, of defense, and of finance.

After the 1932 coup the bureaucratic apparatus became the central focus of the political structure. This is not to say that previously the higher echelons were not involved in political affairs, but as the whole apparatus was less institutionalized, the level of politicalization was more restrained. The main changes in public administration between the 1930s and the 1960s were expressed in the quantitative growth of its manpower.[24] The government became the largest employer in the nontraditional economic sector of the population of Thai origin. Moreover, since the civil and military bureaucracies (in this context, one may also add the Buddhist bureaucracy) had monopolized the employment of the labor force in the more modern economic sector, there were in fact very few people, apart from the Chinese, who belonged to the modern sector and who had the capacity to become an opposition power center independent of the bureaucracy. The major works of research in this field have given us a more or less comprehensive picture of the different aspects of the bureaucracy's activities concerning the decision-making process, selection policy, training programs, salaries, etc.[25] The principal conclusions of these works are:

a. A great portion of the quantitative growth of the bureaucracy is a function of the rivalries among the different ministries. The drive for empire building within the administration is aimed at enlarging the power base of each political clique, and this is realized by the allocation of positions and other rewards to the members and followers of the different cliques.[26]

b. Extreme centralism and sensitivity to the differentiated authority of each grade of the bureaucracy coexist with a de facto autonomy of the lower echelons. The extreme centralism is an option adopted by the senior echelons; it is frequently achieved in practice, usually arbitrarily. Whereas senior officials deal with issues and problems which are usually supposed to be within the sphere of authority of the lower echelons, authority is delegated to the lower echelons and violations of rules by lower officials are systematically overlooked.[27]

c. Administrative inefficiency and corruption have been strongly criticized. One cannot expect a great deal of efficiency when rewards are by and large a function of relationship to superiors rather than of performance or achievement.[28] One scholar studying the extent of corruption concluded that the extent of bribery and "prebendalism" in Thailand is responsible for "the reduction of about 40% of the effective utilization of development expenditures."[29] While the accuracy of this quantitative evaluation may be debated, it is beyond all doubt that the different types of corruption—legal, illegal, institutionalized, or noninstitutionalized—play a major role in the crystallization of the different cliques dominating the armed forces and the civil bureaucracy. Next to kinship and friendship, indirect rewards resulting from service in the bureaucracy are the best guarantee for loyalty.

d. Although there is no law to prevent it, the Thai bureaucracy is not generally or intensively involved in political conflicts. While the bureaucracy as a whole does not constitute a pressure group, pressure groups may nevertheless be organized within specific ministries.

Parliament and political parties. The unique position of the bureaucracy, especially of its higher echelons, is a function of the absence in the period in question of almost any political power outside it. After forty years of constitutional regimes, both parliament and political parties are still limp—almost without responsibilities and functions. The military elite has never permitted them to go beyond ritual and symbolic functions. Moreover, while constitutionalism in Thailand has never formally ceased, it has always been subjected to many changes because each military regime has felt it had the right to proclaim a constitution of its own.[30]

What were the implications of constitutional instability on the position of the country's National Assembly and its political parties and movements? The first parliamentary framework and the first political organization which called itself a party were established after the 1932 coup. The People's Party comprised a small group of revolutionaries, civilian and military, without any social backing. Nevertheless, this political clique left its imprint on the political structure of Thailand for forty years. All the regimes adopted the two principles established by the Promoters of 1932. The first was that, though theoretically supreme power is vested in the people (through the National Assembly), it is in fact the revolutionary body which should nominate or at least control the nomination of the assembly's members. Second, democratization of the parliament should proceed through a shift from two types of members (nominated and elected) to one type (elected).[31] However, it is important to note that the application of this principle was curbed from the beginning. In 1933, the officers executed a new coup, ousted the conservative civilians, and took over all the key positions in the cabinet including the post of prime minister. The new cabinet prohibited all political activity and even the People's Party was reduced, at least officially, to a mere social club. This development almost completely eliminated most of the basic functions of the National Assembly as they were formulated in the constitution of 1932. Although up to World War II Thailand experienced two series of elections of the members of the National Assembly, the candidates never formally—much less de facto—represented any organized political groups. Furthermore, the nominated representatives came partially from the military officers and partially from ex-members of the National Assembly of 1932. The power of the elected and the nominated members of the National Assembly was based on their relationship to patrons in the cabinets—only the smallest fraction was derived from the support of their constituencies. Thus in the National Assembly there was no affinity discernible to any extraparliamentary or national parliamentary movements. The National Assembly thus did not fulfill any functions in terms of the aggregation and articulation of interests beyond those of a local and particularistic nature. The parliamentary institution in Thailand never could dissociate itself from the pattern which had crystallized in the 1930s and, more specifically, since 1938 when Phibun was nominated prime minister.

C. Political Participation

The curbing of the National Assembly for over forty years has had a crucial impact on the quality and range of political participation in Thailand. Until the 1960s, no significant extraparliamentary organization had emerged. This was reflected in the nature of the elections and the type of organizations which participated in them. Surprisingly enough, between 1932 and 1969 twelve elections and by-elections were held—about one every three years.[32] Although this number may be construed as evidence of intensive political participation, examination of the type of participants and the percentage of voters would reveal that the situation was the reverse. In the first election immediately after the 1932 coup, only 10% of the electorate voted. In 1937 it increased to 20%.[33] These two elections occurred when practically, and later theoretically, no political organization, either national or local, existed in Thailand. This situation lasted until the end of World War II. The first three years after the war were actually the first period in which it was possible for the "public" to form pseudopolitical organizations. Personal and parliamentary cliques organized themselves for the postwar elections, the first to be held after the toppling of Phibun's military regime. In the elections in 1946, the two parties which supported Pridi gained the upper hand.[34] According to official sources, only 32% of the electorate voted in these elections.

After the elections, the opposition reorganized itself. Various opposition groups, including the Progressive Party, established the Democratic Party *(Prachatipat)* headed by Khuang Aphaiwong. Despite internal splits which damaged its strength, this party became the main opposition in the following years. These political activities, as the first steps toward the institutionalization of political parties, were brought to an abrupt halt by Phibun's coup in November 1947. In January 1948, new elections were held in which only 16% of the electorate participated. The defeat of the ruling Justice Party *(Tharmathipat)* encouraged the military clique to strip the National Assembly of its functions, which they did after having forced the resignation of Khuang, the leader of the Democratic Party which received a large proportion of parliamentary seats. The National Assembly was reorganized and new elections were held in March 1949 to ensure a cooperative parliament. A short while after the bloodless revolution in 1951, the interim constitution was replaced by the 1932 "Permanent Constitution." Again the members of the National Assembly were divided into the categories of elected and nominated members. This development still further limited the possibilities for political manipulation within the National Assembly. The years between 1955 and 1958 were marked by intensive political activities very similar to those of the period from 1945 to 1948. The main focus of these activities was the two elections held in 1957.[35] This renaissance in Thailand's political life was made possible by the Party Law of 1955, which removed the legal restrictions on the existence of political parties.

The election of 9 February 1957 has been analyzed and described by scholars and journalists perhaps more than any other elections in Southeast Asia.[36] We may therefore examine only some of its most salient characteristics and attempt to point out its significance for Thailand's political culture. Two main characteristics of this election are noteworthy. First, there was a relatively high percentage of participation—about 40%. This phenomenon was certainly due to the relative liberalization of both the legal status of political parties and of the possibilities of communication and articulation of political interests. Another index of participation was the large number of lists (about twenty-eight) and candidates competing for the one hundred sixty seats in the National Assembly (about eight or nine candidates for each seat). Second, one can discern in these elections a thoroughgoing effort by the government to exploit its machine in order to ensure its victory. Typical techniques were the police intimidation of political rivals, physical violence, and extensive rigging of the ballots and of the lists of candidates.

In spite of the ruling party's victory, the results, by and large, were not disappointing for the opposition. The ruling party won eighty-three seats. The opposition was split and divided into small factions and thus could not challenge the ruling group, which was backed by the majority of the nominated members of the National Assembly. Nevertheless, the achievements of the opposition, and especially the Democrats (about twenty-eight seats), were evidence of significant potential opposition around the margins of the political center. However, even these elections and the general excitement that they aroused caused, except in the northeast part of the country, no reverberations in the periphery.

In December 1957 a new election was held. The circumstances and the climate in which it occurred were entirely different from those of the previous elections. It was held after Sarit's military coup, and in ten months almost a total change had occurred on the political map of Thailand. The greatest concentration of members of the National Assembly were independent. Many of them were ex-members of the *Seri Manangkhasila* Party, which had collapsed and disappeared. The most well-organized party was the Unionist, backed by Sarit. After the election, in which only 30% of the electorate participated, Sarit established a new political party, the National Socialist Party, whose first secretary general was General Praphas, the minister of the interior. However, shortly after this election, Sarit executed another "coup," nullified the constitution of 1932, and dissolved the parliament and the cabinet. Furthermore, he proclaimed a new provisional constitution, whose main clause established a National Assembly composed of twenty-four nominated members. Thus ended the period, beginning after World War II, when experiments with a more liberal policy were attempted. Ten years later a new era of political experimentation was embarked upon.

Before the adoption of the constitution of June 1968, new laws concerning elections and political organizations were ratified. These laws were, however, only variations of the 1955 election laws. The new constitution did not provide for large-scale political participation. It reestablished the bicameral legislature composed of an elected lower house and a senate nominated by the king.[37] Nevertheless, the adoption of a new constitution—which was actually a result of ceaseless pressure, especially from educated Thais—and the fixing of a new election date triggered off a new wave of political activities. Thirteen parties registered. The chief competitors were the United Thai People's Party (UTPP) and the Democratic Party headed by Seni Pramot. Many independents later joined the UTPP. In this election, 49% of an electorate of fifteen million went to the polls—the highest rate of participation in the country's voting history.[38] Although there were some complaints of rigging and bribery, the election of February 1969 has been described by all observers as the most organized and honest in Thailand's history.

We have been focusing on political participation within the central circle of political power in Thailand. The marginal political groups have not been ignored by accident. The disproportionate weight of the political center as compared with that of the periphery was more pronounced in Thailand during the fifties and sixties than in most if not all the countries of Southeast Asia. The peripheral political power groups are those political organizations which are not dominated by the establishment and which may or may not abide by the rules of the game of the particular country concerned. Typical sources of recruitment to these peripheral groups in Southeast Asia are students, monks, trade union members, journalists, manipulators of mass media, and—obviously—underground and subversive organizations. As far as Thailand is concerned, there is no doubt of the identity and attitude toward the establishment of the clergy, on the one hand, and of the pro-Communist underground, on the other hand. For other groups, the situation is more complicated and ambiguous.

The clergy. In sharp contrast to the Buddhist clergy of Burma, South Vietnam, and Ceylon, the Buddhist church of Thailand is an integral part of the political establishment. It has a significant impact on the social sphere but is almost entirely lacking in political power. The Thai monarchy has a long tradition of control over the sangha. This control was never considered irregular; on the contrary, it was considered an integral part of his functions. The first modern version of the legal status of the Buddhist church was published in 1902 by King Chulalongkorn (the Buddhist Order Administration Act). The act required that every monk be affiliated with a specific monastery. Through the aid of the patriarch, whose nomination is controlled by the government and the abbots of the monasteries, the administration was able to exercise efficient control over the monks' activities. Another channel of control was the government-sponsored examinations.[39] This bureaucratization of the relationships between the church and the government fits very well into the general bureaucratic pattern of Thailand.

The church adjusted itself without any difficulties to the constitutional regime that followed the 1932 coup, not least because the new regime did not introduce any change into its legal status. In 1941 a new law was formulated that aimed chiefly at democratizing and decentralizing the internal structure of the Buddhist church. However, in 1962, largely owing to continuous internal bickering between the two major ecclesiastic orders, Sarit abrogated this law and reimposed a centralized structure.[40] These reforms were received acquiescently and without public protest. One reason was the church's crucial economic dependence on the government.

The social power of the Buddhist church finds expression not only in the more purely religious sphere but also in the intensive use the regime makes of Buddhist tradition to keep down internal and external rivals. This means, of course, that the Buddhist church is used as an instrument of popularizing the regimes. In this respect, General Sarit outdid most of his predecessors. It seems that one of the reasons he initiated structural reforms within the Buddhist church was to facilitate such manipulations. In this sense, the Buddhist church and the royal court fulfilled similar roles—as symbols of national identity. The military regime on the other hand, did not show any intention of sharing any of its political power with the church.

Subversive activities. It has been quite a long time since Thailand has been troubled by underground activities directed by external Communist centers. The extent of these activities until 1965-66 was rather limited, demonstrating Thailand's uniqueness. Furthermore, they never really threatened the power center itself.[41] There was always a great gap between a regime's warnings about the Communist threat and the actual threat. The relatively greater influence that the various Communist organizations had on the minorities (the Chinese in Bangkok, and the northeast, and the southeast) was exploited, especially by Phibun's administration, to persecute the Chinese and, in many instances, to neutralize the personal rivals of the ruling clique. Thus the Chinese fulfilled an important function in the political life of Thailand, for Communist activities were concentrated chiefly within Chinese urban trade unions and to a lesser extent within the organizations of Thai students.

Because the divisions within the Communist groups were along ethnic lines[42] and the main recruitment was among non-Thais, the government's attempt to locate subversive activities within a certain population and within specific geographical areas was made easier. Moreover, the government was able to identify communism with anti-Buddhism and antipatriotism.

Trade unions. Ethnic division, with its implication for political identity, is also pronounced within the trade unions. Like the activities of political parties, those of the trade unions were curbed or even forbidden. Even in the relatively liberal periods, the trade unions, especially the Chinese ones, were frequently harassed by the secret police. Only after World War II, with the establishment of the Central Labor Union in 1947, did political potential within the trade union begin to evolve.[43] The 50,000 to 70,000 members of the Central Labor Union came mainly from the Chinese labor organizations and were dominated by functionaries of the Communist party. As a counterforce to this union, Phibun's military government established the Thai-dominated Thai Labor Union, later called the Thai National Trade Union. Moreover, the Central Labor Union was officially dissolved and could function only illegally. To take its place, General Phao of the police organized the Chinese progovernment trade union—the Free Workers Association.

Until 1957, no legal procedure or constitutional act existed which legitimized or organized the activities of either the government- or the nongovernment-sponsored trade unions. The Labor Act of 1957, enacted during the "democratic" period of Phibun, did for a short time create a legal basis for the existence of trade unions.[44] However, with Sarit's emergence as political leader, this act, along with the entire constitutional framework, was dissolved. Only at the end of the 1960s, with the proclamation of the new constitution, were trade union activities once again legal.

The exploitation of trade unions by the various regimes was made possible by the structural weaknesses within the trade unions and the labor force. The vast number of government officials in the labor force were forbidden to strike. The remaining salaried workers were largely associated with small shopowners, which made effective organization difficult. Ethnic division contributed much to weakening the organizational basis of the trade unions. Finally, we should also mention the deleterious effects of high rates of geographical mobility on job turnover and thus on effective unionization. All these factors determined the features of the Thai trade unions and enabled the political administration either to exploit the unions for its own purposes or to neutralize their potential influence as a political force.

The mass media. Thai newspapers exercise a fairly extensive influence on the public. Given the low level of literacy, the heavy government censorship, the limited circle of a politically active public, and the low quality of the newspapers, this influence is rather impressive. It is mirrored by and large in the articulation of the general mood of personalities and organizations located on the fringe of the political center or even in marginal opposition groups. Frequently the newspapers also reflect internal conflicts within the ruling circle, largely in an indirect way. Most of the journals and newspapers are basically opposition platforms reflecting almost the entire ideological spectrum from the left to the antigovernment right. Some of the dailies (like *Siam Rat*) had close relations with the court.[45]

During Pridi's regime and the more liberal stage of Phibun's administration, the mass media enjoyed their golden period. However, even during Sarit's administration, when many newspapers were banned and the others were severely censored, the press still served as almost the sole public critic of the government.

The students. In contrast to the relative stability and continuity so typical of the relationships that evolved between the social and religious groups and organizations and the political-military leadership, new and unconventional trends among the students were discernible. True, the students in the fifties and the sixties were, by and large, conservative, docile, and compliant—although by no means apolitical. In this respect, their attitudes were almost unique in Southeast Asia. One probable reason was the almost unlimited capacity to absorb university graduates into the government bureaucracy. The formal affiliation of most university departments with specific government agencies and the drawing of the university curriculum to conform to bureaucratic requirements further contribute to this absorptive capacity.[46] Only such a radical change that would reduce the bureaucracy's ability to absorb students, and the students' exposure to more radical views, could change their general conformity and passive attitude toward political affairs.

Indeed, such changes began to take place in the late sixties. Some indications of the potential power of the students could be discerned even earlier. One was the students' demonstration against Phibun and Phao for rigging the elections of February 1957. Another was the demonstration opposing the government's intentions, as proclaimed in the constitution of 1968, to continue with the emergency regulations.[47]

The real, even dramatic, transformation of students' political status became salient after the 1971 coup and the abolishment of the constitution. The students, together with a substantial part of the academic community, became the backbone of the Movement for the Early Promulgation of the Constitution, which accused Thanom of systematically stalling in order to stay in power. Eventually, in an astonishing turn of events followed by a bloody showdown in the streets of Bangkok, the students overthrew Thanom's military regime. A civil government headed by Sanya Thammasah, the highly respected dean of Thammasat University, was nominated by the king.

D. The Range and Intensity of Political Activities

A description of the organizations used for political manipulation could not alone produce complete comprehension of a society's political culture. Knowledge of the main political issues is also inadequate for full understanding. For this, knowledge about the style of politics in the society concerned is necessary. One important indicator of political style is the range of political activities within different institutional spheres—the range of social groups, organizations, and different collectivities in which internal regulation is influenced voluntarily or nonvoluntarily by power considerations on behalf of external power centers and especially of the political elite. A second indicator of political style is the intensity of the usage of power.[48] This includes the norms and practices by which political power is converted into other resources, and these resources back into political power. This indicator is thus concerned both with different degrees of coercion and with the exchange rate of political power. We shall present only a generalized survey of the subject, since some evidence concerning the analysis of political style in Thailand has previously been presented and further evidence will be offered in the discussion on the civilianization of the military.

The potential involvement of government agencies in different institutional spheres has been, in the period in question, reflected in the fact that very few roles and functions are not, at least nominally, defined as part of an official commitment of the various extensions of the civil service or of some independent government corporation. Furthermore, besides the conventional governmental departments, in Thailand there are dozens of public corporations and organizations which are supposed to deal with economic, financial, and social tasks.[49]

The administration's degree of involvement in economic, social, and cultural affairs is mainly a function of the particular attributes of the political system. The most salient of these attributes is the lack of political competition beyond the very limited and defined circle of the higher echelons of the military and civil bureaucracy and recently also the intelligentsia. Until the 1960s, there was no internal motivation on the part of the government to initiate a large-scale mobilization at the periphery, nor was there any serious pressure from the periphery to force the government to initiate such a policy. However, from the second half of the 1960s some changes have occurred in this area, and they have been due chiefly to the expansion of subversive activities in the northwest and southeast regions.

The relative lack of potential political competition may also be attributed to the fact that, once a certain political clique has assumed power, it is not unusual for some of the ousted leaders to be absorbed into the new ruling elite by being coopted into minor positions in the political hierarchy. This is made possible by the almost complete absence of an ideological basis for the conflict between the different factions of the military elite. As a result, the intensity of political conflict is generally lower in Thailand than in any of the neighboring countries.[50] Nevertheless, this situation by no means excludes arbitrariness and the use of violence against political rivals, as is seen in the administrations of Phibun and Sarit and in the "students' coup" of October 1973. The arbitrariness reflects a serious lack of accountability on the part of the various governments to any public body, apart, of course, from the cabinet.

Though the general intensity of political activities and especially the frequency or the threat of violence against political rivals have been moderate, Thailand's modern history does have symptomatic cases which clearly reflect the ruling elite's inclination to impose its will far beyond the political sphere. This type of behavior was especially characteristic of Phibun's regime. During his rule, the governing elite not only persecuted a marginal and limited opposition but also attempted to initiate cultural reforms through the National Institution of Culture. These so-called reforms and the government's inclination to impose its will on the public can be considered as amateurish in comparison to Phibun's second period of rule. Then, the regime relentlessly exploited all its legal and illegal resources in order to ensure its own continuity in the critical days preceding the election of February 1957. Besides "conventional" activities, such as rigging lists of candidates and bribing, it did not hesitate to use force and even to assassinate opposition leaders. However, in spite of all these manipulations, Phibun's regime maintained a democratic façade and refrained from imposing overt military rule on the country. In contrast, Sarit ensured, by means of emergency laws, an overt military regime which gave him, even from a legal constitutional point of view, a free hand for extensive intervention in all areas. Sarit used this option for imprisoning political rivals, especially those from the left, for extensive censorship of mass media, and for imposing a total cessation of all kinds of political activities. This kind of interference, despite the continued functioning of the military regime, was tempered to a great extent from the time Thanom assumed premiership in Thailand.

Most of our illustrations have referred mainly to activities with some constitutional and legal backing and only to a few acts which were illegitimate even under the particular constitutions and were intended to serve the selfish needs of its formulators. However, very important aspects of the intensity of the country's political activity found diverse expression in corruption and illegitimate activities. A distinction may be made between corruption in the political field and the use of political power to commit crimes in the economic sphere. Typical examples of the first kind of corruption are the rigging of ballots, double voting, and the bribery of voters and candidates.[51]

Corruption in the economic field, as we shall have occasion to see, was much more systematic, comprehensive, and institutionalized than these sporadic forms of political corruption linked chiefly with elections. Thus the exploitation of the economic sector by the monopolists of political power for the advancement of their personal interests was intensive both in the depth of its penetration as well as in the number of people involved. But, in addition to unequivocally illegal activities, border cases have occurred which have done violence to the public ethics—the partnerships formed between the politicians and Chinese merchants, imposed by the former after the Chinese tried to evade anti-Chinese laws whose sole purpose was to undermine their monopoly in certain vital sectors of the Thai economy.[52] However, anti-Chinese legislation was not limited to the Chinese middle class. The Chinese trade unions were persecuted with varying degrees of pressure and success. On the other hand, all progovernment trade unions were essentially apolitical. Save for some extremist groups, the only role trade unions played in the political competition between the different cliques was that of pressure groups to be manipulated by their leaders in the political elite. A similar pattern of government subsidizing of such other voluntary associations as the scout movement, various cooperatives, social welfare associations, and others may also be discerned.[53]

The pattern of government control of the Buddhist church is an additional example of the scope of politicalization of social organizations. This control is based on a variety of regulations, whose essential purpose is to limit the freedom of movement of Buddhist monks and—more important—to restrict the freedom of interpretation of Buddhism. Freedom of movement is restricted through the obligatory affiliation of each monk with a specific monastery. Freedom of theological interpretation is indirectly curbed through obligatory state examinations for all candidates for monkhood. The tight control over political organizations which deal with cultural functions has also been exercised over secular institutions, such as the universities, the press, and the radio and television stations. For example, in the 1960s the president, vice president, and other members of the University Council of Chulalongkorn University were military officers.[54]

The one-way political communication between the power center in Bangkok and its periphery is such a salient feature of the country's political system that one could almost analyze Thailand's power structure solely in terms of events in Bangkok. While such an analysis would not be without some justification, we should remember that the rural periphery is not entirely homogeneous or static. Not only have there been substantial developments in certain areas of the rural periphery since the 1960s; the extent of compatibility between political activities in the center and those in the rural periphery is an important issue. This is true despite the hitherto marginal role played by the periphery.

Between the villages or small towns and the central administration, the principal means of communication has always been through the district officer *(nai amphur)* and his staff.[55] This mechanism of arbitration is thoroughly bureaucratic in terms of contacts between nominated officials and an unorganized and powerless population and in terms of the formal, sporadic, and indirect nature of these contacts. The growth of the district officer's power as the focual point of contact between the rural periphery and the central administration stems from the weakness of the politically elected representatives on the national level and of the elected government on the local level and hence their inability to serve this function. Even though some of the National Assembly members have been successful, especially after World War II, in representing the demands of their rural constituents, these types of contact, though very personal and noninstitutionalized, have suffered from a high turnover of National Assembly members. The tradition of suspicion on the part of the villagers to any intervention into local affairs has discouraged any attempt by the government to foster the development of local government.[56]

The government since the mid-sixties has taken steps to encourage some gradual changes in this sphere. The tempo of these changes has been uneven in the different regions of the country. Moreover, this new development was not a result of inter-systemic processes within the ruling circles but, rather, a consequence of external pressure and the threat from minority groups in the rural periphery.[57] The minorities have for centuries been persecuted and deprived. Their lot has been much worse than that of the central plain Thai people, who have received only a minimum of consideration by the central government. The increasing attempts of these minorities to express their discontent through violent means have compelled the central government to initiate some reforms to prevent a full-scale deterioration of its relationship with the minorities. The serious attempts to mobilize the farmers for economic and community development should be viewed in this light.

PART II. THE CIVILIANIZED MILITARY

A. The Beginnings of the Professional Army and Its Development

Despite Thailand's many wars, especially with Burma and Cambodia, and although the foundations of a professional standing army were laid in the second half of the nineteenth century, it was not until the 1920s that a more or less full-fledged army emerged. It started with the establishment, in the second half of the 1800s, of a military cadet school and later a naval cadet school. In 1894 the ministry of defense was formed and the armed forces were finally given a recognized and respected position within the government hierarchy.

In the spirit of absolute monarchy, the king and princes had full control over the armed forces. According to a law of 1904, the crown prince served as the commander in chief of the armed forces and the king headed the National Defense Council.[58] This situation continued until the almost total eviction, following the 1932 coup, of the king and princes (although no nobles of middle and lower ranks) from senior positions within the armed forces. This dramatic act was followed by a change in the recruitment bases of the military elite. For example, during the absolute monarchy, officers from the royal family and nobility of high rank made up 87% of the military elite. Moreover, even among the rest, there was not a single commoner. In an unspecified period after the 1932 coup, commoners became the majority (52%) while the percentage of high nobles and princes diminished to 18%.[59]

Nevertheless, the recruitment bases remained rather narrow. Military families became the most important single source for military officers. A comparison between military cadets and students at the faculty of political science in Chulalongkorn University in 1965 shows that 30% of the naval cadets, 42% of the air force cadets, and 27% of the students at the military preparatory schools were sons of officers, while only 8% of the regular students were officers' sons. On the other hand, 39% of the latter were sons of businessmen and government officials.[60]

The quantitative and qualitative growth of the armed forces since 1932 reflects its crucial role in Thai political life. From 30,000 in 1920 they grew to 60,000 during World War II, with the most impressive growth occurring in the ranks of officers and generals.[61] At the end of World War II, the armed forces were reduced to about 30,000 in the army, 3,000 in the air force, 10,000 in the navy, and about 25,000 men in the national police.[62] However, with the return of General Phibun to the helm of government and especially with the inauguration of the United States' aid program, the expansion of the armed forces was once again resumed. Of the estimated 100,000 to 150,000 troops[63] in the armed forces during the 1950-60 period, 80% belonged to the army; 25,000 both to the navy and air force, and an estimated 40,000 to 50,000

TABLE 1: MILITARY PARTICIPATION RATIO IN THAILAND

	Army				Navy			Air Force	Total Armed Forces	As % of Total Population	Total Population (1,000s)
Year	Enlisted Men	Officers	Ratio	As % of Total Armed Forces	Enlisted Men	Officers	Ratio				
1933	16,000			77	4,800				20,800	0.16	12,819
1934	24,486	1,933	13	78	4,800			2,486	33,705	0.26	13,198
1955	30,000			66	10,000	1,200	8	4,000	45,200	0.20	22,762
1958	50,000			58	19,200	2,130	9	15,000	86,330	0.35	24,873
1961	90,000			67	22,000			22,000	134,000	0.50	26,000

SOURCE: J. Vibhatakarasa, "Military in Politics," Table 15, p. 131.

to the police.[64] In addition to the regular armed forces and police, the various governments in Thailand established auxiliary services. One such service is the Volunteer's Defense Corps which, according to official statistics, was composed in the sixties of 120,000 troops. This force was established in 1954 and is under the control of the minister of the interior.[65] On the whole, it is estimated that, from 1950 through the 1960s, the armed forces were composed of about 0.5% of the total population, and of about 0.9% of the population between the ages of 15 and 65. In 1961, Thailand was rated forty-ninth out of eighty-eight countries with respect to the percentage of total population in the armed forces and forty-fourth with respect to the percentage of population between the ages of 15 and 65 in the armed forces.[66] (See also Table 1.)

In Thailand there is compulsory military service. But only part of the entire eligible population is actually drafted.[67] Those exempted are transferred directly to the reserves of the second category. Drafted service personnel who completed their term are transferred to the first category.[68] Exempt from all military service are monks, career teachers, naturalized citizens, and any person whose father is an alien. These last two categories are directed mainly against the Chinese population. There is also a custom of exempting other ethnic minorities from military service. Thus the military establishment is in fact a monopoly of the Buddhist Thais.

Though very little is known about the criteria of promotion and the scope of annual turnover within the officer corps, we may assume that, at least during certain periods, the turnover was rather high. The various coups and counter-coups in the 1950s and 1960s were followed, on the one hand, by purges of rival officers and, on the other hand, by the promotion of officers who supported the new leaders. Another source of personal mobility was the flow—although limited—between military and police positions and between military and civil bureaucratic positions. Some high officials in the civil service became generals without receiving any military training or without being promoted gradually through the military hierarchy. These generals usually filled administrative posts.[69]

The Supreme Command Headquarters, which is subordinated to the minister of defense, is responsible for the operations of the three branches of the armed forces.[70] In this context, two other bodies involved with defense should be mentioned. The first is the National Security Council. It is composed of nine members and headed by the prime minister.[71] The second body is the Defense Council, composed of twenty-three members headed by the defense minister. Most of the members are senior commanders and deputies in the armed forces. While the National Security Council is the supreme political layer in the decision-making process, the Defense Council is the senior professional military layer.

The United States has done much to raise the professional level of the Thai armed forces since the end of World War II.[72] Thailand was considered an anti-Communist stronghold and, starting in the 1950s, the United States sent military missions to aid in training Thai soldiers. The 1954 location in Bangkok of the general headquarters of SEATO was a clear indication of Thailand's importance for the United States. This importance has been translated into impressive investments by the United States in the development of the Thai army and economy. It has been estimated that, between 1946 and 1966, economic and military aid to Thailand reached the one-billion-dollar mark.[73] The question of whether or not this extensive aid has actually altered the quality and effectiveness of the Thai military organization is beyond the scope of this work. However, the limited level of the Thai military's combat experience may be mentioned. Its experience in modern warfare is confined to some skirmishes with the French Vichy army in Indochina during World War II, the participation of one battalion in the Korean war, and more recently also some regiments in the Vietnam war. The accumulation of some experience in antiguerrilla warfare should also be noted.

Since the 1960s, subversive activities have been increasing in southeast and northeast Thailand. Generally, information about the extent of these activities and effectiveness of the response to them has been faulty, usually suffering from biases. After 1965, when a Peking-inspired union was established between the Patriotic Front of Thailand and the Thailand Independence Movement, the political situation worsened. The new body, the Patriotic Front, called for an armed revolt through a people's war. It is estimated that the union of these two bodies enabled them to mobilize about a thousand men.[74] Their union also increased the scope of skirmishes and the number of casualties. Subversive activities, though on a slightly smaller scale, are to be found also in the southeast, on the frontier with Malaysia. In 1965-66 the number of guerrillas in the southeast was estimated at between five hundred to one thousand.[75]

Regardless of the real threat—which, in any case, cannot be adequately estimated—the fact is that a rather large number of military and police units are engaged in the war against the guerrillas. Their measures include bombing of suspicious villages, the evacuation of village populations, and continual searches for guerrilla bases. Let us emphasize, however, that, in spite of the escalation of subversive activities in the period of our study, the "conventional" activities of the military were much more limited and marginal than those in the "nonconventional" areas—i.e., in the political, ideological, economic, and educational-cultural spheres.

B. The Competition for Political Power

The unchallenged dominance of the military in politics in the period concerned has been rooted in the 1932 coup. The changes in the nature and style of political intervention by the military in the years following that coup have been conditioned by two major factors. Of these, the first involves changes in the international political constellation, such as World War II and the Vietnam war. The second involves internal changes within the military establishment itself. Our concern will be mainly with the second.

Intensive intervention by the army in politics is a clear indicator of the weakness of the civilian political elite. On the other hand, conflicts within the armed forces, coups and countercoups, reflect the weaknesses and inefficiency of the military high command's ability to provide military and political leadership for the state. These weaknesses, conspicuous in the 1950s, were, with Sarit's military leadership, largely overcome in the 1960s. Though it is not entirely true to attribute Sarit's success to constitutional formulas or administrative reforms aimed at ensuring better feedback and control, the value of these types of mechanisms should not be underestimated. As may be recalled, the formal mechanisms of control have been embodied in the "civilian"-controlled National Security Council and in the military-controlled Defense Council. Officially, the main function of these two is to instruct and guide the Supreme Command on security matters. In fact, however, since both are at least partially staffed by the same personnel, the distinction between them is fictional. The importance of informal mechanisms of control is manifested in the simultaneous incumbency of key positions in the army and the civilian executive. In the early 1960s, General Sarit, then prime minister, was both the supreme commander of the armed forces and commander in chief of the army. General Thanom, his defense minister, served as first deputy supreme commander of the armed forces. The president of the constituent assembly also held the post of second deputy supreme commander. After Sarit's death in 1963, his successor, General (later Field Marshal) Thanom, served simultaneously as prime minister, defense minister, and supreme commander of the armed forces. The title "commander in chief of the army" was given to General Praphas who also served as minister of the interior. The minister of agriculture in this cabinet was nominated assistant supreme commander, and the air chief marshal became assistant defense minister.

To this phenomenon of multiple roles should be added the interchangeability between high-ranking officials of the civilian and military institutions. However, the importance of this practice should not be exaggerated. It is clear that the weight of the professional officers, especially of the army, is greater than that of officers coming from outside the military framework. The army's unduly heavy influence may be attributed mainly to the fact that they alone can ensure the loyalty of military units in cases of internal conflict between different cliques or branches of the army and police. At any rate, this concentration of authority in the hands of very few people not only underscores the dominant position of the military officers within the cabinet but makes it certain that the minister-officers do not lose contact with their political constituencies. Close operational relations with key units in the Bangkok area are not only a necessary condition for political mobility but also ensure the consolidation of power in the summit.

Legalization and institutionalization of coups. Military coups may or may not be followed by changes in the nature of the economic and political regime. However, they are almost always succeeded by intensive constitutional activities designed to provide ex post facto legitimacy for the military regime. The formulation of new constitutions and the calling of general elections may be viewed as typical examples. The Thai officers corps has distinguished itself in such legitimizing maneuvers no less than it has in the sphere of military coups.

Typical examples of what Wilson calls "faction constitutionalism" are the "permanent" and "provisional" constitutions of 1947, the two constitutions of 1948, and the constitution of 1957.[76] In short, coups and constitutions are Siamese twins in Thailand. The relatively large number of elections there reflects the variety of constitutions, whose purpose was to lend legality to at least part of the political manipulations connected with coups. Efforts to legitimize coups were encouraged by the Supreme Court of Appeal *(Di ka)* which extended a priori legality to a successful coup. The law states:

> The overthrow of a previous government and the establishment of a new government by the use of force is perhaps illegal in the beginning until the people are willing to accept and respect it. When it is a government in fact, which means that people have been willing to accept it, any person who attempts by rebellion to overthrow the government violates the criminal law.[77]

The number of coups (both unsuccessful and successful) have decreased in the fifties and sixties.[78] This trend may be due chiefly to the consolidation of army and police rule in that period in Thailand. Though this consolidation was undermined for a short period after World War II, it was quickly restored through United States economic and military aid which provided, among other things, rapidly increasing rewards and benefits for the military. Along with personal and collective instrumental interests in the continuation of the aid from the United States, the political and military challenges presented both by the war in Vietnam and the underground subversive activities have further intensified the internal cohesion of the armed forces. In this situation, more subtle and surreptitious systems of competition have been preferred.

The occupation of power positions. The capture of the whole power basis of a society by the army depends largely on the army's operational capability. One condition for such comprehensive control is the expansion of the army itself—its budget must be increased and its officer corps enlarged.[79] In Thailand, such changes in the balance of power between the armed forces and the civilian sector since 1932 are mirrored in the military budget. For instance, the budget rose from 19% of government expenditure in 1932 to some 27% in 1937, enabling the general staff to enlarge the officer class.[80] The opportunity for a further increase came with the royal princes' ousting from the army after the 1932 coup. In 1939 the military budget consumed 32% of the national income. Its share increased still further during World War II, though between 1944 and 1947 it was reduced by the civilian regime. With the return of Phibun and the expansion of United States military aid, the military budget once again increased, although it never officially reached the level of World War II or even of the late thirties. The main reason is that the official military budget was supplemented by the huge U.S. military aid.[81]

The proportion of officers to civilians in the cabinet. For obvious reasons, cabinet posts are among the most coveted rewards of coup promoters. Every cabinet since that of 1932 has included a number of military officers. According to Riggs,[82] between 1932 and 1958, i.e., between Manoprakorn's first cabinet and until Sarit's death, Thailand was ruled by thirty-two cabinets, with a total of two hundred thirty seven ministers. Of these, 34.5% were from the armed forces, 42.2% were civil service professionals,[83] 16% belonged neither to the officer class nor to the bureaucracy, and the remaining 7.3% were unidentifiable. Of the one hundred eighty four ministers from the military or civilian bureaucracies, as large a proportion as 45.6% were military men. These figures provide clear evidence of the predominance of ministers belonging to the bureaucracies and of the very close cooperation between the civilian and military bureaucrats.

The number of officers participating in the different cabinets varied greatly. Between 1932 and 1944, during what Riggs calls the "first ruling circle," 50% of the ministers were officers. Between 1944 and 1947, during the "second ruling circle," the proportion of officers in the various cabinets was rather small. In this period, some civilian ministers belonged to the original promoters of 1932. Even in this period of civilian rule, most of the ministers came from the bureaucracy. The most significant presence of the military in the cabinet was between 1947 and 1957—in Phibun's second administration. Quite surprisingly, during the period of the most direct military rule—Sarit's administration—the number of officers in the cabinet was reduced and there were always more civilian than military ministers.[84] This pattern was reinforced after Sarit's death until 1968. However, in the cabinet which took office following the election of 1969, the military and police increased their representation to parity with the civilians.[85]

Apart from cabinet posts, the senior positions in the civil service and its various extensions are the most important source for allocating power positions and prestige. There is no systematic information about the proportion of military and policy officers in the civil service. In general, it appears that there is no full-scale "exploitation" of the civil service as a source for positions for military and police officers. Such exploitative activities are limited to senior positions.[86] Membership in the National Assembly serves as another, though secondary, source for benefits. Indeed, among the officers nominated or elected to the National Assembly, there are many young ones, mostly captains and majors, and some lieutenants. The senior military officers in the National Assembly were largely retired or nearly retired.[87]

The crucial role of the military and police officers is at least an indirect reflection of the rather *selective* and *limited* efforts of the ministers, many of whom are themselves military officers, to court public support through political organizations. This pattern was institutionalized immediately after the 1932 coup. The presence of a "party"—the People's Party established by the promoters—deducted nothing from the fact that the focus of rivalry was in the bureaucracy.

The need for public support gained urgency after World War II, when both the ruling circle and the opposition were dominated by civilians. Both sides established political parties which were supposed to run in the coming elections. The officers who, in this period, conducted subversive activities against the civilian regime also used the political party as an instrument. Such use of political parties lasted until the military's seizure of power and the subsequent banning of civilian political activities. The ban was removed because of internal conflicts which induced each military clique to become interested in broader public support. During this period, the generals became very active in party politics. This was the first time in the modern history of Thailand that high-ranking officers used the political party as an instrument of power. They exploited their power to eliminate competitors among the different military cliques and to resolve conflicts between the military as a whole and various political civilian bodies.[88] Thus the role expansion of the armed forces—that, until this point, was either absent or very marginal—gained new momentum and dimension.

The ruling elite's instrument of party politics in that period was the Seri Manangkhasila Party. General Phao was the party's secretary general and strong man. All the promoters of the 1947 coup belonged to this party, which had at its disposal newspapers, radio stations, and legal as well as illegal economic resources. It had the support of more than half of the elected members of the National Assembly (eighty-three out of one hundred sixty) and of one hundred of its nominated members. Though General Phao's rivals publicly maintained their allegiance to the party, they clandestinely sought support beyond it. Thus General Sarit, for example, was active in the establishment of the national Democratic Party (the Unionists) and other political factions which collaborated with the main opposition party, the Democrats. Even Prime Minister Phibun was forced to follow this pattern. His name was associated with several lists put up for the election of 1957 (for example, the Labor Party, the Might Is Right Party, and the Hyde Park Movement Party). Phao was also connected with the establishment of "auxiliary parties," among which were the Free Democrats and the Nationalist parties.[89] The phenomenon of "auxiliary parties," through which patrons who belong to the same ruling circle and party fight each other by means of smaller parties, is one which, though found to some degree in other countries, is peculiar to Thailand. In Thailand, it may be viewed as one of the basic patterns which has dominated the power structure of the country since the earliest coups; namely, a *ruling circle* which meshes rival factions of patrons and clients, both of whom try to maximize ad hoc interests.

With the fall of Phao and Phibun at the end of 1957, the Seri Manangkhasila Party disintegrated and many of its representatives as well as those of the auxiliary parties reappeared as independents in the December 1957 election. Later these auxiliary parties joined the Unionists, who were supported by Sarit, and established the Nationalist Socialist Party. This new political organization gave the government and its prime minister, Thanom, an absolute majority in the assembly (two hundred twelve out of two hundred thirteen members).[90] The issue of political parties and activities was raised once again in the election of 1969. A new party was established, the United Thai People's Party (UTPP), whose leaders were senior cabinet members and commanders of various branches of the army and police.[91]

The intensification of subversive activities in some of the districts of Thailand has added a new dimension to the army's political involvement. Historically, such involvement had been confined to the Bangkok area. However, the urgent need to ensure the peasants' loyalty in suspect areas necessitated new concepts and instruments of control. These centered primarily around so-called civic programs. The best example is the Mobile Development Units program (MDU). This project was controlled by the army but conducted with the cooperation of the civilian administration.[92] The principal task of the MDU was to provide very selective and limited aid to the peasants in the form of road construction, public housing, public works, and health services.

The potential political repercussions of the MDU project are worth our attention. First, it should provide the armed forces with the opportunity of supervising the district officers more closely. Also, such bodies as the MDU were expected to open the way for new political bodies which could mediate between the peasants and the political center. A more balanced, two-way communication between the periphery and the center could thus emerge. Second, there were indications that the activities of the MDU could promote some economic and organizational initiative within local government—perhaps adding a new dimension of political power to that government. Third, MDU activities could promote more coordination between various government departments, especially on the local level. It is clear that the realization of the MDU's potentialities could provide the central government and the armed forces with a more efficient instrument for the social and political mobilization of the peasants. But there were some dangers involved as well. The chief danger was that new emerging local institutions, such as local councils and corporations, would become an ideal target for subversion by guerrillas. This can best be understood through considering the difficulties that both the guerrillas and the central government have had in gaining a foothold in the peripheral areas with a lack of clearly defined organizational frameworks through which to operate.[93]

C. The Military and Its Activities in the Economic Arena

Except for the political, no other sphere can demonstrate so effectively as the economic one the scope of the symbiosis and the permeability of the boundaries between the civilian and the military segments of Thai society. Though this phenomenon is found in quite a few developing countries and in a number of developed ones, the degree of symbiosis in Thailand was perhaps greater than that prevalent elsewhere.

The activities of the armed forces in the economic sphere may be grouped under two major types. The first involves illegal activities as defined by the Thai criminal code itself—though not necessarily by the accepted social norms. The other involves those economic activities that do not particularly diverge from legal norms.

Another distinction is that between activities initiated by military men and policemen as individuals (or as tentative groups especially organized for the purpose) and those initiated by unit commanders, by one or another of the various branches of the armed forces, or by the supreme command itself. There is only a *partial* overlap between illegal activities and their individualistic character and between activities that are legal and institutionalized and those carried out in formal and collective frameworks (whether these be the various branches of the armed forces or the armed services as a whole). True, presently available data sometimes make it difficult to distinguish and to classify the various phenomena according to the simple categories just proposed. For instance, the fact that many army officers receive or have sometimes in the past received two kinds of payments does not facilitate a simplified classification of income sources.[94] However, no difficulties arise in defining the nature of the income sources reported in the fifties and sixties. We refer here to the trade in opium, which at the time became a monopoly of the police, headed by General Phao.[95]

The opium trade was perhaps the most important source of illegal income, though by no means the only one. Many observers report that police officials were partners in houses of prostitution, in illicit gambling, and in illegal trafficking in gold. Phao has even been accused by the Democratic Party of printing notes to the sum of 14 million baht.[96] Nor were such activities confined to police officers. Army officers often outdid their police counterparts.

Thailand's Military Establishment

For instance, the embezzlement of welfare funds by army officers in 1948 is well known.[97] The best-known evidence is that uncovered after General Sarit's death. The officially estimated value of his known property amounted to $150 million. Of this total, about $30 million was defined as money taken in one way or another from the state treasury.[98] Considering the enormous sums involved, we cannot be surprised to read, in one of the estimates of corruption in Thailand, that in 1954, about 12%(!) of the total national income flowed into the pockets of Phibun, Phao, Sarit, and their favorites.[99] Since the Sarit scandal, a series of additional ones, though of minor proportions, have been uncovered.

With regard to economic activities whose legality is at least ambivalent—if impartially tested, those engaged in them would not be found guilty of criminal activity—the most typical examples are the business partnerships between Chinese businessmen and the Thai politicomilitary elite. The Chinese merchants enter these partnerships to seek political protection; for the Thai elite, they are lucrative. The two parties have taken measures to maximize the benefits they derive from these partnerships. The Chinese have offered people in the various cliques of the military-bureaucratic elite membership in the business boards of their firms, to secure maximum political support and prevent hazards emanating from possible changes in the internal balance of political power. And the members of the politicomilitary elite are only too glad to be appointed to membership on as many boards as possible, to increase their profits—and indirectly, their political power.[100]

Another popular source for personal enrichment is membership on the boards of directors of those government enterprises controlled and managed by the various ministries.[101] Economic enterprises' either belonging to the Defense Ministry or being directly owned by diverse military units is a pure example of the nature and patterns of role expansion assumed by the Thai military establishment and hence differs from the type of activity pursued by the members of the elite as individuals or within the framework of small cliques. Further, this phenomenon possesses implications for the scope of permeability of the frontiers between the civilian and the military segments of the society. A review of these activities reveals the following:

1. In the last twenty years, a series of industrial enterprises and financial bodies have been set up within the framework of the Defense Ministry.[102]

2. Patronage is not confined to members of the standing army but also includes demobilized soldiers. The War Veterans Organization (WVO), founded in 1948, combines the roles of a holding company, a welfare organization, and a finance company for old soldiers. This body directly controls and manages such enterprises as the Wood Industries, the Sena Printing Company, and the Engineering Company. It also has investments in other economic enterprises.[103]

3. All the branches of the armed services of Thailand operate their own radio transmitters.[104] Legally, all these stations are experimental; however, for all practical purposes they operate on a commercial basis. The military owners of radio and television stations are partners in the Thai Television Company, which owns and operates commercial radio and television in Thailand.

This domination by the military of the means of mass communication is yet another manifestation of absence of relatively autonomous centers of mass communication capable of controlling and supervising the various political and economic authorities.[105] However, the control of the means of communication is by no means total, monolithic, and centralistic. On the contrary, what is peculiar is the quite unrestrained competition between the various government authorities and agencies over these communication media.

4. The intrusion of the armed forces into the sphere of civil action—a development brought about by the growing pressure of subversive activities along the border areas—also has economic implications. It is important to note that, unlike all the spheres of activity mentioned thus far, civic action through the Mobile Development Units evinces certain symptoms of entrepreneurial style and an innovating orientation directed at modernizing the agrarian sector.[106] The innovation and initiative that marked these activities lie in the authorities' efforts to free themselves from the one-directional bureaucratic and authoritarian approach in all matters pertaining to the relations between the center and the periphery and to create among the villagers sufficient will and motivation to adopt new principles of action in all matters linked with a certain degree of modernization in the life and economy of the village.

D. The Military and Its Ideological and Educational Activities

Observers of the Thai scene agree that the extensive complex of rivalries and conflicts among the military cliques and among the various strong men generally lack an ideological dimension.[107] It does not seem very likely that the armed forces or a section thereof will develop an ideology that could serve as a clear alternative to that accepted by substantial sections among the civilian elites.[108] Further, we should distinguish between an alternative ideology and a rationalization for justifying the seizure of power. Nevertheless, despite the great need to exercise maximum caution and to avoid attributing traits foreign to it to the Thai military elite, it appears that it would be an error to view this matter as being absolutely irrelevant to the present discussion. True, what is being discussed here is certainly not a completely thought out and clear-cut ideology or one given of a high level of articulation by the military leadership. In this respect, the Thai army has never approached the levels attained by the military elites of Burma, of Indonesia, or even of Pakistan. However, one can, even in the Thai case, note some ideological uniqueness—as demonstrated by the first period of Phibun's rule and to a certain extent also that of Sarit. Although the appointment of Phibun to the office of prime minister in 1938 does not mark a qualitative change in the basic characteristics either of the military regime set up in 1933 or of its power bases, yet the same principles underlying that regime took on pseudoideological legitimation. In the name of this pseudoideology, campaigns were mounted to arouse the people's patriotism (this included the organization of a pan-Thaist movement) and glorify military values. This went hand in hand with a fostering both of the attachment to Buddhism and of the cult of the personality of Phibun—reminiscent of the Fascist regimes prevalent in that period. Basically, it emphasized the preservation of the status quo of the autocratic political regime along with the cult of the leader and a recognition of the high prestige of the military man, on the one hand, and on the other, certain changes in life styles and in such normative attitudes as dressing patterns and etiquette. The second period of Phibun's rule, 1947-57, was only the palest reflection of his first. The international circumstances had completely changed, and with them the argumentation and the terminology that now studded the anti-Communist and pro-democratic slogans. However, the pseudoideological tone of the Thai military elite did not entirely disappear.

Some observers tend to view Sarit as having had ideological pretensions. They base this on the fact that his rule constituted a turning point in the country's political life. Sarit proclaimed the establishment of an absolutist regime without any of the trappings of formal democracy which all the military regimes previous to his had at least attempted to retain. Sarit and his aides explained the need for an absolutist regime by claiming that democracy was unsuited to Thai society in its stage of development. On one occasion, he maintained:

> It should be further admitted that Western democracy is not such a system of government as could be adopted and put into operation immediately by all countries regardless of the state of economic or political progress. As far as Thailand is concerned, it is high time we utilized the lessons we have learnt from the past practice of democracy in adapting our democratic system to suit local needs and conditions. . . . The garb of democracy was weighing down Thailand, whose ills were too serious to be cured by a palliative.[109]

These extreme and explicit attitudes have, undoubtedly, gone against the moods characteristic of even the most conservative civilian elites since the 1960s. It seems, therefore, that that period marked the emergence for the first time of a sort of contradiction between the military-bureaucratic clique and the civilian elites, and especially the intelligentsia. This divergence turned not so much around the de facto form of the prevalent administration as around the ideological sphere. It should, however, be reiterated that the attention we attempted to draw to the ideological uniqueness of the Thai army or to that of the personalities in it must not lead us astray in our efforts to determine the degree of that army's ideological articulation. Whatever the army's ideological activities, they were sporadic even at peak, never very sagacious—and came nowhere close to articulating a detailed and profound political program.

Finally, the activities of the armed forces in the field of education and of manpower training may be divided into two major parts. The first and more important is that set of activities aimed at training manpower and professional cadres for the armed forces. The second set of activities—of less importance from the educational (though not necessarily from the political) viewpoints—is linked with the formal and informal roles of army men in the civilian educational network.

The military's extensive control over the training of manpower permits, theoretically at least, the development and regulation of the social and politicoideological socialization of the Thai officer corps. Through this, their allegiance to the armed service, though not always to the actual commanders, can be secured.[110]

The military's involvement in civilian educational affairs was, in the relevant period, essentially in the form of control, formal at least, over the school network and over the universities. This control was exercised chiefly through making primary school teachers and holders of key positions in the universities subordinate to the minister of interior. For instance, in the 1960s the rector of the University of Chulalongkorn was the minister of interior and the country's strong man, General Praphas. General Phibun was also once the rector of this university. Moreover, the minister of defense in the 1960s served as the rector of Thammasat University, the university which became in the 1970s the focus of the opposition to the regime.

E. Summary and Conclusions

Since the 1932 coup, the military-bureaucratic establishment has become an integral part of the political landscape. Until the late 1960s and the beginning of the 1970s, it was very difficult to envision the emergence of a significant and lasting opposition which could seriously challenge the regime. Any challenge from the remote periphery, and to a certain extent from the politically powerless groups on the margins of the center, was offset by the political support provided to the ruling groups by the bureaucracy. In other words, in spite of the internal turmoil and rivalry between the different cliques, the political center has been very homogeneous. The internal differentiation there during the period involved has not reached the point beyond which the emergence of subcenters with wider prestige and reputation would be necessary. Operationally, the cabinet was still the backbone of political power and managed to apply rather successfully the somewhat fragile principles of reward allocation among the different cliques.

The scope and intensity of the ruling elite's exploitation of political power can be clearly and accurately understood in terms of a struggle over power and prestige by groups of patrons and clients located within the military-bureaucratic elite. The conflict has been by and large between nominated or self-appointed officials rather than between groups of elected politicians with a wider social backing in the periphery. The prospects of partnership and collaboration among the members of opposing cliques hinge, among other things, on the differences or similarities in career channels within the military and civilian bureaucracies and, in some cases, on a parliamentary career. An ill-defined separation of career channels thus tends to create an intricate crisscrossing of these channels, giving Thailand a political system characterized by conflict rooted in interests of a corporate rather than a class nature.[111] Conflict is largely focused on rewards derived from economic interest and control over sectors of the political and bureaucratic establishment. Rewards received in the form of bribery, gifts, and allowances further nourish the corporate interests of the chains of patrons and clients. The consolidation of these chains within certain political power positions eventually helped to establish an economic power base which in turn was exploited for further gains in the political sphere. Hence, since economic resources as such could not be easily converted into power resources, a major impediment to the achievement of political recognition by the Thai middle class, despite its possession of relatively abundant economic resources, was a lack of political power.

In contrast to the fairly high degree of institutionalization and modernization of the executive-administrative branch of the political system, the legislative branch was weak and unorganized. The egoistic and unrestrained employment of constitutions by the military oligarchy played a major role in undermining the organized and institutionalized basis of the legislature and the political organizations. Since the various constitutions did not succeed in promulgating universal rules of the political game, great tension has been generated between legal and informal rules. Nevertheless, it should not be forgotten that no regime up to the late sixties, even Sarit's, dared permanently to abolish the National Assembly. With all of its operational weaknesses and inability to impose sanctions, the National Assembly maintained an important potential for the legitimization of political processes in Thailand. The conditions under which the National Assembly could be converted into a more effective political instrument are difficult to determine. However, the qualitative and quantitative diversification of the politically conscious public and their rejection of apathetic compliance to the political decision-making process would be an important basic requisite. Such conditions became discernible in the early 1970s, especially after the overthrow of Thanom's regime.

In Thailand, as in other southeast Asian societies, the new politically conscious public has polarized between the periphery and the political oligarchy at the center. Intermediate political groups, such as political parties, trade unions, and other voluntary organizations, which in other circumstances might act as mediators, are here ideologically, organizationally, and financially too weak. One ramification of this polarization is an increase in the intensity and scope of political activities that finds expression in violence. This violence is restrained not only by external factors but—even more significantly—by the fact that Thailand is not a one-party state or a totalitarian regime. Thailand is more accurately defined either as a bureaucratic polity or as an authoritarian regime. The authoritarian regime is, by and large, inefficient because it lacks the professional political apparatus typical of one-party regimes.[112] Paradoxically, demands might be more easily articulated in a one-party regime, with its exclusive political channel, than in a bureaucratic polity such as Thailand, which substitutes a bureaucratic apparatus for clearly defined channels of articulating demands. In the period in question, the Thai bureaucratic machine has been able to absorb some pressures from the loyal part of the periphery. However, the bureaucratic channels of communication between some groups like the students, and the non-Thai periphery and the center, have become so tenuous that their capacity to deal with political tensions has become greatly reduced. The more traditional intermediate groups, such as the district officers and the Chinese merchants, who have usually mediated the relations between the center and the periphery, are no longer capable of dealing either with the new demands or the means used to achieve them by the periphery. It should be remembered, however, that all these reservations refer to very specific areas of Thailand and that the core of the Thai Buddhist periphery is still loyal to the political center.

In all matters having to do with a distribution of labor between the military elite and the civilian sector, a policy of symbiosis between the two sectors and permeable or, at most, fragmented boundaries existed. This symbiosis occured both on the personality and institutional levels. On the military elite level, it found expression in the occupancy by the army and police officers of high rungs in the focuses of military-political administrative and economic power. This phenomenon has been the primary source of personal enrichment and of the institutionalization of corruption that has spread into every stratus of the bureaucratic hierarchy. In the institutional sense, the military leadership personified the integration of most of the social, political, and economic elites of Thai society into a political core with great power and manipulative capability. This integration was one of the decisive factors in the high degree of stability of Thai society during the forty years discussed here. The unique position held by the armed forces in Thai society (a position attained by very few of the armed forces in countries with military regimes) has not served to foster a consciousness of reform and innovation.

The potentialities of the entrepreneurial traits of the military elite were brilliantly utilized in their entirety, mainly for personal ends. Though the army never rejected the self-image of a "modernizing agent," it took pains to impart to this image a most conservative and cautious character. This was demonstrated when the country's rulers publicly made the rare declarations aimed at formulating the basic premises of state policy. The rarity of these occasions indicates the relative irrelevance of ideological concepts and the absence of the kind of ambition in other military establishments which have striven for a respectable level of ideological articulation and sophistication. The symbiosis that marked the relations between the military and society in Thailand eventually left the initiative and the title "revolutionary" either to the country's most peripheral and marginal elements or to the intelligentsia, who had a much better access to the political center.

The intelligentsia have emerged as a serious challenge to the military, political, and economic elite complex. The challenge became real and eventually fatal in October 1973, when the students forced the ruling military elite to resign. There is no doubt that their sweeping victory surprised the students themselves. The students' willingness to fight the army and the army's reluctance to use all its force to crush the demonstration contributed.

We must note that the intelligentsia and the king—the two forces that opposed the regression from the level of competitive democracy that Thailand achieved in 1968—were part, although weak, of the national center. The change in the balance of power that has occurred in recent years *within* Thailand's political center has been one of the main reasons that Thanom and Praphas were unwilling to have a showdown with the students and the king—perhaps the most respected person in Thailand.[113]

The military elite tried for a long time to win over the intelligentsia by a large-scale distribution of benefits, ranging from cash to scholarships to advisory posts.[114] When these efforts and a limited use of force failed to neutralize the opposition, Thanom and Praphas preferred to withdraw and to go into exile. Another factor in the students' victory was the reluctance of some senior officers to continue the bloodshed.

If this analysis is valid, the collapse of the military rule does not contradict the thesis about the relative strength of the political center vis-à-vis its periphery. As in the past, only changes in the power balance *within* the center could effect the ouster of an incumbent elite. But this time the changes were not only personal but structural as well—namely, the transfer from military to civilian rule. At this stage, it would be hazardous to predict whether this change will continue or whether it will be remembered only as a passing episode.

NOTES

1. We shall not deal here with foreign affairs. Regarding Thailand's foreign relations, see, for example, Astri Suhrke, "Smaller Nation Diplomacy: Thailand's Current Dilemmas,"

Asian Survey, XI, no. 5 (May 1971), pp. 429-445; Clark D. Neher, "Thailand: Toward Fundamental Change," *Asian Survey*, XI, no. 2 (February 1971), pp. 137-138; Alan Bennet, "Thailand: The Ambiguous Domino," *Conflict Studies*, no. 1 (December 1969).

2. There were some abortive attempts to execute a coup before 1932, in 1912, and in 1917. For details, see Charles W. Weatley, "The Military Coup: An Exploratory Study of Overt Crisis in Political-Military Relations," (Ph.D. thesis, Columbia University, 1967), p. 290.

3. On the composition of the Promoters in terms of their military-professional branch affiliation, see Jin Vibhatakarasa, "The Military in Politics: A Study of Military Leadership in Thailand," (Ph.D. thesis, University of Oregon, 1966), p. 100.

4. For more details about the ideological differences among the various groups, see Walter F. Vella, "The Impact of the West on Government in Thailand," University of California Publications in Political Science, IV, no. 3, pp. 396-398.

5. Despite the coup, Pridi was not entirely removed from the political arena. Between 1933 and 1939, he served as minister of the interior, minister of foreign affairs, and minister of the treasury.

6. John Coast, *Some Aspects of Siamese Politics* (New York: Institute of Pacific Relations, 1953), p. 20.

7. Phibun was called in at the last minute to head the coup because of his unchallenged popularity in the armed forces. See Weatley, "Military Coup," pp. 314-315.

8. For an attempt to relate the coups of 1932 and 1947 to economic crises, see Vibhatakarasa, "Military in Politics," ch. 6. For the specific complaints by the officers against the government, see Kamol Somvichian, "The Thai Military in Politics: An Analytical Study" (Ph.D. thesis, University of London, 1969), pp. 123-125.

9. One of the main reasons for Phibun's invitation was that the officers were afraid that a Thai government under Phibun's leadership would be unwelcome to the Western powers. Regarding Khuang's personality, see Somvichian, "Thai Military," pp. 167-168; and Khuang Aphaiwong, *Kantorsu Kharng Kharhajao* [My Struggle] (Bangkok: Pramuansan Press, 1958).

10. Between 1948 and 1952, there were eight attempts to overthrow Phibun. For details, see *Thailand: Its People, Its Society, Its Culture*, ed. Wendell Blanchard (New Haven: Human Relations Areas Files Press, 1957), p. 125.

11. See Weatley, "Military Coup," pp. 322-323; see also Somvichian, "Thai Military," pp. 155-164.

12. For a description of these two personalities and their personal and group affiliations, see Somvichian, "Thai Military," pp. 182-187.

13. Fred W. Riggs, *Thailand: The Modernization of a Bureaucratic Polity* (Honolulu: East West Center Press, 1966), pp. 97-101, 105-109; N. J. Mosel, "Thai Administrative Behavior," in *Toward Comparative Study of Public Administration*, ed. W. J. Siffin (Bloomington: Indiana University Press, 1957), pp. 272-278.

14. Vella, *Impact of West*, pp. 368-370.

15. This change is understandable if it is true that Sarit's coup had the king's consent. See New York *Times*, 24 September 1957.

16. H. D. Evers and T. H. Silcock, "Elites and Selection," in *Thailand: Social and Economic Studies in Development*, ed. T. H. Silcock (Canberra: Australian University Press, 1966), p. 98; Donald E. Nuechterlein, "Thailand after Sarit," *Asian Survey*, IV, no. 5 (May 1964), p. 845; Donald Hindley, "Thailand: The Politics of Passivity," *Pacific Affairs*, XLI, no. 3 (Fall 1968), pp. 357-358.

17. Riggs, *Thailand*, p. 112.

18. An exceptional case is the constitution of January 1959 (Sarit's constitution). For

changes in the constitutions, see David A. Wilson, *Politics in Thailand* (Ithaca, N.Y.: Cornell University Press, 1962), ch. 5.

19. Ibid., pp. 158-159.

20. Regarding the composition of the cliques, the internal conflict, and changes that took place in the different cabinets between 1932 and 1963, see Riggs, *Thailand*, pp. 212-240. For an excellent description of the clique structure and its internal mechanisms, see J. C. Scott, *Comparative Political Corruption* (Englewood Cliffs, N.J.: Prentice-Hall, 1972), pp. 59-64.

21. Mosel, "Thai Administrative Behavior," p. 309.

22. The highest echelon, the "special class category," includes about 700 officials, and the "first class category," about 1,750. See Riggs, *Thailand*, pp. 328-329.

23. See, for example, William J. Siffin, *The Thai Bureaucracy: Institutional Changes and Development* (Honolulu: East-West Center Press, 1966); Malai Huvanandana and William J. Siffin, "Public Administration in Thailand," in *Public Administration in South and Southeast Asia*, ed. S. S. Hsueh (Brussels: International Institute of Administrative Sciences, 1962); Riggs, *Thailand*, ch. 4.

24. Between 1944 and 1958, the number of "ordinary officials" increased more than 2.5 times from 75,000 to 199,000. See *Statistical Yearbook of Thailand* (Central Statistical Office, Office of the National Economic Board, 1956-58), XXIII, p. 491. In 1965 their number reached 250,000. To this number should be added another 20,000 men who are known as nonstatus employees. See Siffin, *Thai Bureaucracy*, p. 151. Furthermore, there still was a fluid number of employers hired by the central government and the provinces. It should be noted that 40% of the "Ordinary Officials" were teachers and that 20% belonged to the police force. In the 1960s, the government employed about 25% of the nonagricultural labor force. See Daniel Wit, *Thailand: Another Vietnam?* (New York: Scribner's, 1968), pp. 128-129.

25. For a detailed bibliography, see Riggs, *Thailand*, p. 447, n. 160.

26. Compare the view of Riggs, *Thailand*, pp. 348-349, to that of Edgar C. Shor, "The Public Service," in *Problems of Politics and Administration in Thailand*, ed. J. L. Sutton (Bloomington: Indiana University, 1962). For a good summary of the control system of the patrons on the clients and its implication on the efficiency of the bureaucracy, see N. Jacobs, *Modernization without Development, Thailand as an Asian Case Study* (New York: Praeger, 1971), pp. 80-87; and Scott, *Comparative Political Corruption*, pp. 64-66.

27. Riggs, *Thailand*, pp. 362-363. We should mention the distinction between "decentralization" and "deconcentration." According to Jacobs, "Decentralized delegation of political and administrative authority connotes the right to regulate local affairs locally; channeled rights, privileges, and obligations flow in both directions between periphery and center. Deconcentration of authority connotes rights and privileges awarded patrimonially on grace to locals which enables locals to handle centrally conceived administrative problems on the local level. Thus, local government, in effect, is but an extension of central government" (*Modernization*, pp. 56-57).

28. For examples of petty corruption, see those cited in Scott, *Comparative Political Corruption*, pp. 61-72. In a comparative survey of seventy-four countries, Thailand was grouped with Burma and Pakistan into a category of countries "in which public administration was marked by considerable bureaucratic inefficiency but in which there was, nevertheless, a permanent body of administration." Corruption may have been common, and there may have been moderate instability of policy at higher levels of administration, but these phenomena did not operate to the point where they seriously interfered with government functioning. See Irma Adelman and Cynthia T. Morris, *Society, Politics and Economic Development* (Baltimore: Johns Hopkins, 1967), p. 78.

29. J.L.S. Girling, "Thailand's New Course," *Pacific Affairs,* XLII, no. 3 (Fall 1969), p. 355.

30. Thailand had, until 1970, five permanent and three provisional constitutions. In November 1971, the constitution of 1969 was abrogated by a new "coup." In 1973, after the overthrow of Thanom, a new constitution was in the making.

31. The democratic stage was supposed to have been realized either when half of the population had at least full primary education or no later than the year 1942. See Vella, *Impact of the West,* pp. 371-372; Wilson, *Politics,* pp. 202-203. Regarding foreign influence on the constitution (for example, that of Sun Yat-sen), see Riggs, *Thailand,* pp. 153-159.

32. The elections were held in November 1933, November 1937, November 1938, January 1946, August 1946, January 1948, March 1949, February 1952, February 1957, December 1957, March 1958, and February 1969. See Riggs, *Thailand,* pp. 154-155, for more information about the first eleven elections.

33. Vella, *Impact of the West,* p. 378.

34. The civilian faction of the 1932 Promoters, led by Pridi, established the Constitutional Front Party *(Naew Rathathammanum).* Another group of Pridi's followers from the Free Thai Movement founded the Cooperative Party *(Sahachip).* After the war the Free Thai became Pridi's private militia. Its dissolution became, in 1945-46, a political issue. An oppositional party emerged as well—the Progressive Party *(Kau-na),* headed by Kukrit Pramot. Its members were by and large intellectuals and sympathizers of the royal court but also included liberals and opponents of the authoritarian orientation of both Phibun and Pridi. For the political controversies during Pridi's premiership and the internal composition of the various factions, see Somvichian, *The Military,* pp. 130, 166-173.

35. Twenty-five parties registered for participation. The most important of these were: *Seri Manangkhasila,* the ruling party, whose secretary general was General Phao (for details, see Blanchard, *Thailand,* p. 129), the Democratic Party *(Prachatipat),* the chief opposition party since the 1940s. The Progressive Party, the main opposition party after World War II, joined with the Democratic Party (see ibid., pp. 131-132); the Unionist Party, which later changed its name to the National Socialist Party and was organized, or at least supported, by Sarit; and the Economist Party, the major leftist party. For a detailed discussion of the political party act of 1955, see Somvichian, "Thai Military," pp. 180-182. In 1956 a new and even more liberal election law was enacted. The electorate included about ten million voters. See Blanchard, *Thailand,* pp. 128-136, 141-142.

36. See, for example, Riggs, *Thailand,* pp. 167-170; Blanchard, *Thailand,* pp. 128-136, 143-144.

37. F. C. Darling, "Thailand: De-escalation and Uncertainty," *Asian Survey,* IX, no. 2 (February 1969), pp. 117-120; *Far Eastern Economic Review Year Book,* 1969, p. 317. On the changes in the position of the National Assembly and the senate after the election of 1969 until 1971, see Neher, "Thailand," p. 133. For more about political parties and election laws of 1968, see C. Ansuchote, *The 1969 General Elections in Thailand* (DeKalb: Northern Illinois University, Center for Southeast Asian Studies, 1970), pp. 4-15.

38. The UTPP received seventy-five seats out of two hundred nineteen (35%), the Independents, seventy-two seats (32%), and the Democratic Party, fifty-seven seats (25%). The last party had the upper hand in the Bangkok area, the UTPP, in the periphery excluding the northeast. For more details, see C. D. Neher, "Constitutionalism and Elections in Thailand," *Pacific Affairs,* XLII, no. 2 (Summer 1970), pp. 248-256; *Far Eastern Economic Review Year Book,* 1969, p. 317; Neher, "Thailand," pp. 131-132; Ansuchote, *1969 Elections,* pp. 18-39. For the political events in 1971 which resulted in the abrogation of the constitution and the silent coup of November 1971, see D. Morell, "Thailand: Military Checkmate," *Asian Survey,* XII, no. 2 (February 1972), pp. 157, 162-167.

39. These examinations strengthened the orthodox elements and prevented internal theological reforms. See Yoneo Ishii, "Church and State in Thailand," *Asian Survey*, VIII, no. 10 (October 1968), pp. 866. For more details on the bureaucratization of the Buddhist church and mechanisms of control, see Jacobs, *Modernization*, pp. 212-217.

40. Ishii, "Church and State," pp. 867-870. See also Jacobs, *Modernization*, p. 215.

41. For the historical, structural, and cultural factors responsible for the limited impact of Marxist ideology in Thailand, see David A. Wilson, "Thailand and Marxism," in *Marxism in Southeast Asia*, ed. F. N. Trager (Stanford, Calif.: Stanford University Press, 1959), pp. 58-101.

42. There are at least four Communist organizations: the Communist Party of Thailand (CPT); the Chinese Communist Party of Thailand (CCPT); the Communist Party of Vietnam (CPVN); the Chinese Communist Party of Malaya (CCPM). See Blanchard, *Thailand*, p. 135.

43. On the initial stages of the trade union movement in the twenties, see ibid., pp. 293-296; Wilson, "Thailand," p. 82.

44. Blanchard, *Thailand*, pp. 296-298; E. L. Fogg, "Labor Organization in Thailand," *Industrial and Labour Relations Review*, VI, no. 3 (April 1953), pp. 368-369.

45. Albert G. Pickerell, "The Press of Thailand: Conditions and Trends," *Journalism Quarterly* (Winter 1960), pp. 85-86; Riggs, *Thailand*, pp. 37-42. For an official survey of the Thai press, see Thailand Official Year Book 1964, pp. 409-415.

46. Joseph Fischer, *Universities in Southeast Asia* (Columbus: Ohio State University Press, 1964), p. 95. For types of internal organizations of students in the fifties, see F. W. Riggs, *Census and Notes on Clientele Groups in Thai Politics and Administration* (Bloomington: Indiana University, Institute of Training for Public Service, Department of Government, 1963), p. 13.

47. For a detailed description, see Somvichian, "Thai Military," pp. 193-195; see also Darling, "Thailand," p. 120.

48. For a concept of political power, see E. W. Lehman, "Toward a Macro-Sociology of Power," *American Sociological Review*, XXXIV, no. 4 (1969), pp. 453-464.

49. For example, the State Railways of Thailand, the National Lottery, Tobacco Monopoly, plywood company, Bank of Thailand. See Siffin, *Thai Bureaucracy*.

50. This generalization refers rather to what happens after the coup than to the coup itself.

51. Thus on the eve of the election of February 1957, the progovernment members of the National Assembly were granted an increase of 2,000 baht per month ($100) in their regular salary of 3,650 baht. It has been rumored that some other assembly members were offered as much as 6,000 baht ($1,000) in return for their support. See Blanchard, *Thailand*, p. 124; D. Insor, *Thailand, A Political, Social and Economic Analysis* (London: George Allen & Unwin, 1963), p. 72.

52. For a detailed description, see G. W. Skinner, *Leadership and Power in the Chinese Community of Thailand* (Ithaca, N.Y.: Cornell University Press, 1959), pp. 186-199; G. W. Skinner *Chinese Society in Thailand* (Ithaca, N.Y.: Cornell University Press, 1957), pp. 349, 359-360. See also Richard J. Coughlin, *Double Identity: The Chinese in Modern Thailand* (Hong Kong: Hong Kong University Press, 1960), pp. 127-143; Riggs, *Thailand*, pp. 254-304.

53. Riggs, *Census and Notes*, p. 13.

54. It should, however, be noted that among the least politicized institutions in Thailand are the high courts. On the legal system and courts, see Frank C. Darling, "The Evolution of Law in Thailand," *Review of Politics*, XXXII (April 1970), pp. 197-218.

55. In Thailand, there are four hundred forty-eight districts *(amphur)* and seventy-one provinces *(changwat)*.

56. H. P. Phillips and D. A. Wilson, "Certain Effects of Culture and Social Organization on Internal Security in Thailand" (The RAND Corporation, Memorandum R.M.-3786-ARPA, 1964), pp. 25-26; Boonsanong Punyodyana, "Social Structure, Social System, and Two Levels of Analysis: A Thai View," in *Loosely Structured Social Systems: Thailand in Comparative Perspective,* ed. Hans-Dieter Evers (New Haven: Yale University, Southeast Asia Studies, Cultural Report Series, no. 17, 1969). For an illustration, see H. K. Kaufman, *Banghuad: A Community Study in Thailand* (Ithaca, N.Y.: Cornell University Press, Monograph of Association for Asian Studies, 1960), pp. 70-75. See also Jacobs, *Modernization,* pp. 61-66.

57. The most prominent of these are as follows: (a) The Muslimized Malays on the Malaysian-Thailand border have religious, ethnic, and cultural differences that have prevented their integration with Thai society. (b) The Karens of Western Thailand, who are an integral part of the Karens inhabiting the eastern part of Burma. (c) In the remote north of the country, especially in the northwest, are the hill people (Montagnards), who include the Lisu, Yao, Meo, Lowa, and others. They have a distinctive language and a mainly animist religion. (d) The Khmers of the northeast represent an ever-growing nuisance to the central government. They have religious, cultural, and familial ties with Cambodia. (e) The Iassan-speaking peoples are neighbors of the Khmers and are the greatest problem for the administration. They inhabit the Laos-Thailand border, the most culturally deprived area of Thailand.

58. Of the nineteen sons of King Chulalongkorn who worked in the public service, eleven assumed high military posts. See Vibhatakarasa, "Military in Politics," p. 159.

59. Ibid., p. 164, table 22.

60. Ibid., p. 166.

61. Weatley, "Military Coup," p. 289.

62. Ibid., pp. 297, 302.

63. George L. Harris et al., *Area Handbook of Thailand,* (Washington, D.C.: The American University, 1963), pp. 497; Siffin, *Thai Bureaucracy,* p. 153; Wit, "Thailand," p. 136; Hindley, "Thailand," p. 358; Weatley, "Military Coup," p. 300.

64. Although the police force is considered to be civilian, the fact that it participated in several coups (as that of 1949) justifies its inclusion in this context within the framework of the armed forces. For estimates of the size of the police force, see Insor, *Thailand,* p. 69; Hindley, "Thailand," p. 358; Blanchard, *Thailand,* p. 196; Somvichian, "Thai Military," pp. 196-197, 215.

65. *Thailand Year Book,* p. 178. See also Blanchard, *Thailand,* p. 196.

66. Bruce M. Russett et al., *World Handbook of Political and Social Indicators* (New Haven: Yale University Press, 1964), pp. 71, 78.

67. *Thailand Year Book,* p. 174. On the recruitment of police, see Blanchard, *Thailand,* p. 196.

68. *Thailand Year Book,* p. 175; Harris, *Area Handbook,* p. 513.

69. This practice is workable under the Civil Service Act of 1928 (amended in 1954). Wilson, "Thailand," p. 23; Blanchard, *Thailand,* p. 196; Weatley, "Military Coup," pp. 302-303, 309; Somvichian, "Thai Military," pp. 120, 128, 221, 235.

70. For their structures, see *Thailand Year Book,* pp. 168-174; Harris, *Area Handbook,* pp. 506-510; see also Somvichian, "Thai Military," pp. 210-212.

71. Somvichian, "Thai Military," p. 165.

72. The first connections were actually established during World War II, when the Americans helped the Free Thai Movement. See Frank C. Darling, "American Policy in Thailand," *Western Political Quarterly,* XV (March 1962), p. 96.

73. Alex Campbell, "Thailand, Is There Something To Fall Back On?" *New Republic,*

26 March 1966, p. 18. In 1950, military aid reached a million dollars, in 1954 it was increased to $30 million, and in 1967-68 it reached $60 million (see Darling, "American Policy," pp. 99-106). In this last period, military aid surpassed the level of economic aid which was in 1966, $42.4 million; in 1967, $47.9 million; in 1968, $46.7 million. See F. C. Darling, "Thailand." For a general evaluation of the U.S. aid to Thailand and its impact on the economy, see George J. Viksnins, "United States Military Spending and the Economy of Thailand: 1967-1972," *Asian Survey*, XIII, no. 5 (May 1973), pp. 441-457.

74. F. Bell, "Thailand's Northeast: Regional Underdevelopment, 'Insurgency' and Official Response," *Pacific Affairs*, XLII, no. 1 (Spring 1969), p. 49.

75. Hubert Freyn, "False Alarm?" *Far Eastern Economic Review*, LIII, no. 3 (July 1966), pp. 101-102; Wit, *Thailand*, p. 159; Bennett, "Thailand," p. 10. For a report on guerrilla warfare in 1971, see Morell, "Thailand, Military Checkmate," and "Thailand," *Asian Survey*, XIII, no. 2, pp. 170-171.

76. Wilson, *Politics*, p. 262. See also Neher, "Constitutionalism," p. 240.

77. Wilson, *Politics*, p. 269.

78. Between 1947 and 1950, there were four coups: between 1951 and 1954, two coups: between 1955 and 1958, one or two coups (it depends on whether one takes into consideration the affair of 1958): between 1959 and 1970, no coups, and in 1971, one coup.

79. According to Vibhatakarasa, the officer supervision ratio in Thailand is one of the highest in the world. After 1945, there were five field marshals and seventy-five full generals. In 1957 there were seven field marshals and seventy-six full generals ("Military in Politics," pp. 136, 229).

80. Ibid., tables 19, 40. See also Morell, "Thailand," p. 176.

81. Vibhatakarasa, "Military in Politics," table 20. For more and sometimes different figures and estimates concerning the military budget, see Vella, *Impact of the West*, p. 380; Blanchard, *Thailand*, p. 122; Wilson, *Politics*, p. 176; Coast, *Some Aspects*, p. 15. The Institute for Strategic Studies gives the 1964 military budget as 3.5% of the GNP (about 15% of the total expenditure). Another source informs us that in 1959 it reached 3% of the GNP (see Russell et al., *World Handbook*, p. 79). For the years 1964 and 1959, see A. A. Jordan, *Foreign Aid and the Defense of Southeast Asia* (New York: Praeger, 1962), p. 72. See also *Thailand Year Book*, p. 168, and Bennett, "Thailand," p. 5.

82. Riggs, *Thailand*, pp. 313-319. See also Wilson, *Politics*, p. 155; Wit, *Thailand*, pp. 116-117.

83. Civil service may here include police officers. One can find higher figures of military participation in Vibhatakarasa, "Military in Politics," table 10, pp. 108-111.

84. Riggs, *Thailand*, p. 316; Somvichian, "Thai Military," pp. 257-258.

85. Neher, "Constitutionalism," p. 163. In 1970, the number of officers was reduced to twelve of twenty-nine cabinet members.

86. In 1952, twenty district governors were recruited from high-ranking police officers (Blanchard, *Thailand*, pp. 144-145). In the late sixties, four generals were appointed district governors. Siffin notes that, in 1958, for example, when there were about three hundred special managerial posts in the civil service, fewer than twenty of them were held by military officers (*Thai Bureaucracy*, p. 157). According to Vibhatakarasa, twenty-nine officers held high-ranking administrative posts ("Military in Politics," p. 228). The following are posts held by military officers in the period concerned: the under secretary of state for economic affairs; the under secretary of state for the interior; director general of the Tourist Organization; director general of the State Highways Department; chairman of the board of directors of the Dairy Industry; traffic manager of the State Railways Organization. See Harris, *Area Handbook*, p. 502; Hindley, "Thailand," p. 357. See also F. von der Mehden,

"Politics and Military in Burma" in J. P. Lovel et al., *The Military and Politics in Five Developing Nations* (Washington, D.C.: Center for Research in Social Systems, 1970), p. 325.

87. This practice of nominating officers to the National Assembly began in 1932, when sixteen were nominated to the seventy-member House of Representatives. In 1947, during Pridi's administration, of a total of sixty-five senate members, 28-45% were officers and in the House of Representatives, out of one hundred sixty-five members only eighteen (or 10%) were officers. In 1952, the number of officers among the nominated of the assembly reached the 83% mark (100 out of 120), but they constituted only 13% of the elected members (16 out of 122; see Weatley, "Military Coup," table 11). In 1962, during Sarit's rule, military officers made up as much as two-thirds (159 or 235) of the membership of the constituent assembly. In 1962 the Senate, with one hundred sixty-four members, included one hundred twenty-eight military and police officers. On the other hand, for the first time since 1932 there were no military officers in the lower house. However, of its two hundred nineteen members, twenty-seven were officials of the government (see Neher, "Constitutionalism," pp. 241-256).

88. It is difficult to see the previous attempts, in 1932-35 and 1947-51, as serious efforts to establish a political party. One may consider them more as manipulation of parliament members.

89. Blanchard, *Thailand*, pp. 130-132; Riggs, *Thailand*, pp. 169-170; Freyn, "False Alarm?" p. 11.

90. For more details on the secretaries of the Nationalist Socialist Party and its dissolution by Sarit, see Darling, "American Policy," p. 174.

91. Neher, "Constitutionalism," p. 245; *Far Eastern Economic Review*, 17 June 1968, p. 644; J.L.S. Girling, "Thailand's New Course," *Pacific Affairs*, XLII, no. 3 (Fall 1969), p. 354, n. 23.

92. *Thailand Year Book*, p. 169.

93. See Bell, "Thailand's Northeast," pp. 53-54.

94. Campbell, "Thailand," p. 18. On salaries in the fifties and sixties, see Weatley, "Military Coup," p. 301, and Vibhatakarasa, "Military in Politics," pp. 65-66; Somvichian, "Thai Military," p. 244.

95. Blanchard, *Thailand*, p. 193. See also Coast, *Some Aspects*, p. 39; Insor, *Thailand*, p. 11; Evers and Silcock, "Elites and Selection," p. 95.

96. Insor, *Thailand*, p. 70.

97. Weatley, "Military Coup," p. 318; Coast, *Some Aspects*, p. 51.

98. Bangkok *Post*, 28 May 1964; the New York *Times*, 6 April 1964; D. A. Wilson, "Thailand—Scandal and Progress," *Asian Survey*, V, no. 2 (February 1965), pp. 108-116.

99. Darling, "American Policy," p. 102. Phao's businesses included banks, hotels, night clubs, construction companies, and insurance syndicates. Sarit's business empire covered banks, the match monopoly, construction contracting companies, shipping companies, and insurance.

100. The scope of these partnerships was most impressive. Between 1952 and 1957, there were forty-two companies with three or more cabinet politicians out of a total of one hundred seven firms. The remaining sixty-five companies included twenty-five with two politician members and forty with only one such member. See Riggs, *Thailand*, p. 255. See also Somvichian, "Thai Military," pp. 244-245.

101. For a list of relevant enterprises, see Riggs, *Thailand*, pp. 304-310; Evers and Silcock, "Elites and Selection," pp. 95-97; Blanchard, *Thailand*, pp. 124, 130. Most of the directors of these boards were officers of the armed forces. Police officers were a minority because, as government enterprises, the boards did not need police direction.

102. For details, see Riggs, *Thailand,* p. 307; Wilson, *Politics,* p. 184; Harris, *Area Handbook,* pp. 504-505; Vibhatakarasa, "Military in Politics," pp. 69-70. See also Robert J. Muscat, *Development Strategy in Thailand* (New York and London: Praeger, 1966), p. 296; Somvichian, "Thai Military," p. 240.

103. For other monopoly rights of the WVO, see Silcock, "Summary Assessment," p. 309.

104. See Riggs, *Thailand,* pp. 151-152; Blanchard, *Thailand,* pp. 219-221.

105. Some of the major newspapers were owned by military officers as well. See Riggs, *Census and Notes,* p. 37.

106. The major efforts of the MDU were in the initiation of short-range projects, mostly lasting a few days, undertaken in the villages and executed, wherever possible, with the cooperation of the villagers themselves. In this context, note the activities of the Border Patrol Police. See Hugh Hanning, *The Peaceful Uses of Military Forces* (New York: Praeger, 1967), p. 182; Edward Bernard Glick, *Peaceful Conflict* (Harrisburg, Pa.: Stackpole Books, 1967), pp. 167-168.

107. David A. Wilson, "The Military in Thai Politics," in *The Role of the Military in Underdeveloped Countries,* ed. J. J. Johnson (Princeton: Princeton University Press, 1962), pp. 267, 270, 275; Mosel, "Thai Administrative," p. 23.

108. The "denial" of ideological dimension does not mean that the officer corps does not encourage exclusive collective values. On the contrary, the military sees itself as the symbol of national honor, defender of national integrity, and executor of national interests. In this respect, it considers itself as first among equals; thus the concept of military subordination to the civil authority is unacceptable. See Wilson, *Politics in Thailand,* p. 187; Somvichian, "Thai Military," pp. 229-230.

109. Cited in Darling, "American Policy," p. 172. See the statement by Thanat Khoman, ibid., pp. 176-177. See also another address delivered by Thanat at the American Association of Thailand, 8 March 1961, in *Foreign Affairs Bulletin,* I, no. 3 (December 1961-January 1962).

110. See the discussion of the politicization of military cadets and the comparison of their attitudes with those of political science students in Vibhatakarasa, "Military in Politics," pp. 46-48, 54-59. See also Wilson, "Military in Thai Politics," pp. 186-189, for a discussion of the components of military education and its impact on the military's role in politics.

111. See S. E. Finer, *The Man on Horseback: The Role of the Military in Politics* (London and Dunmow: Pall Mall Press, 1962), p. 24.

112. On the distinction between a bureaucratic state and one-party state, see Riggs, *Thailand,* p. 379.

113. The king's negative attitude toward the military regime was shown by the fact that he did not officially pardon the coup group for its action of November 17, in contrast to similar occasions in the past. See Morell, "Thailand," p. 168.

114. Ibid., p. 166.

Chapter 4

PATRONAGE AND SOCIOPOLITICAL HIERARCHY IN

THAILAND'S SOCIAL STRUCTURE

A. INTRODUCTION

The consolidation of the military-bureaucratic elite at the apex of Thailand's political social and economic system has been accompanied by a deep, intensive penetration by the military elite into different civilian institutional spheres. This phenomenon involves more than political developments and power politics. It has certainly been influenced by and had its own impact on the social stratification of present Thai society. However, Thai social stratification is not of interest only within the narrow context of the military elite's position and status in Thailand. The analysis of Thailand's social stratification may well clarify some of the issues raised in Chapter 2 about stratification and modernization. Thailand may demonstrate the degree and scope of synthesis between traditional and modern elements in social stratification in transitional or traditional societies.

In the case of Thailand, we shall consider two specific issues: (1) the confrontation between universalistic achievement and individualistic principles of stratification, on the one hand, and particularistic ascribed and hierarchical principles, on the other; (2) the extent of the impact of the compound of different elements of stratification on different sectors of the society.

The literature of the last two decades on the structure of stratification contains a profusion of evaluations.

For instance, Hanks asserts that "efforts to depict social classes in Thai society founder because of misconstruing the nature of this social order which resembles a military organization more than an occidental class type society."[1] He concludes that Thailand has no stratification whatsoever—only social differentiation.

"Thai society differentiates positions and gives them value; it does not restrict movement, as stratification implies, but rather establishes the rules of mobility."[2]

Evers, on the other hand, thinks that a "class system is just in the process of evolving and rapid social change makes it difficult to construct a static model of Thai society."[3] Evers presents evidence that the fluid and loose nature of the stratification structure is steadily being replaced by a class system, one of the side effects of which is a decline (temporary at least) in the rates of social mobility.[4]

The differences of opinion and the difficulties seem to spring chiefly from the (supposed) contradiction between the uninstitutionalized structure of such basic social frameworks as the family and the village communities, on the one hand, and the ritual attitude toward the hierarchical structure and the master-client relationships, on the other.[5] The scholar becomes even more confused when—aside from methodological and theoretical difficulties about the significance of the concepts of class and status group—he finds a categorization employing explicit names and labels of social groups.

Thus, for instance, we read about a predictable distinction between the urban upper class and rural villagers.[6] Furthermore, although most scholars argue that it is difficult to discern clear-cut strata beyond this, they also advise us to distinguish among four economic groups: (a) free laborers, primarily urban; (b) farmers and fishermen; (c) the governing group; (d) the commercial class.[7]

This rough distribution along lines of prestige, political power, and economic pursuits alters when the discussion revolves around urban society (more specifically, Bangkok's). Then we are advised to accept a differentiation of strata far more subtle and complex.

Wilson, for instance, makes a distinction among old elite; new elite; upper middle class; lower middle class; and lower class.[8]

This differentiation is accompanied by a process of exclusiveness and internal cohesion of the new elite. In this sense, the three basic traits attributed by all the scholars to the social structure of Thailand (apart from the Chinese sector) that distinguish it from most other Asian societies are steadily changing. These traits are: (1) the absence of powerful enduring family lineages (except perhaps in the royal aristocracy); (2) the difficulty of accumulating transferable wealth; and (3) the essentially nonhereditary basis of status.[9]

These classifications and diagnoses do give a true picture of certain aspects of the stratification structure of Thailand. They overlook, however, the problems that arise from the simultaneous existences of a hierarchy, thoroughly particularistic in character, on the politicoadministrative level, on the one hand, and a reasonable degree of social mobility governed by universalistic principles, on the other. This combination of characteristics comes from deeply rooted politicosocial traditions and has many implications for the nature and ability of

Thailand's Social Structure

Thailand's sociopolitical regime to cope with the problems posed by its desire to alter and renovate, though at a moderate pace, the fabric of Thai society. We shall not elaborate on this last topic, as it lies outside the confines of this chapter. We shall merely point out that the relative calm of the Thai countryside and the political (though not always the personal) stability of the limited circle of rulers chosen from among the politicoadministrative leadership may be due, among other things, to the special nature of the country's structure and stratification.

B. THE STRUCTURE OF STRATIFICATION IN THE PERIOD OF ABSOLUTE MONARCHY

From the second half of the fifteenth century down to the start of the twentieth and the end of Chulalongkorn's reign, Thailand's stratification structure was characterized by four basic groups: (1) hereditary nobles; (2) government officials—many of them hereditary nobles; (3) freemen; and (4) slaves (two types).

This structure was hierarchical (de facto) and also provided legal-normative sanction embodied in the system of *Sakdi-na*. According to this, "every position was given a numerical value and thus indicated clearly one's position in the society at the particular time."[10]

These positions could not be handed on. Attaining one depended considerably on the traits and capabilities of the individual. There were no formal and normative obstacles of an ascriptive nature to those aspiring to climb from one rank to another. Yet the very existence of a class of hereditary nobles implied an ascriptive element. One's status in this class was determined by the degree of blood ties to the king. However, even such ties did not promise the hereditary nobles continuous possession of their class position, as the king could order such a noble stripped of his rank. Furthermore, a nobleman could not bequeath the titles of nobility which he had carried in his own life. There was rule of declining descent, "according to which an inherited rank was reduced by one degree in each succeeding generation until after five generations, heirs were reduced to the status of a commoner."[11]

So long as the noble held his title, his prospects for acquiring better positions were in general far better than those of one not related to the royal family. Yet the factor that above all determined status in this hierarchical structure was the nature of the services rendered by the individual to the state and, more particularly, to his superior. A noble's retention of his title,[12] his status, and his political and economic power depended on his carrying out his duties and obligations. Thus, the bureaucratic elite of that period may be defined as an "aristocracy of merit." These arrangements permitted a notable degree of personal mobility in the bureaucratic ladder—both upward and downward.

If, therefore, ascriptive elements were not exclusive even in the period of absolute monarchy, particularistic elements constituted an integral part both of the bureaucratic structure and of the other social frameworks (village, family, etc.). The particularistic dimension was apparent in the fostering of the ritual elements in the master-subject relationship with their symbolic ramifications in reciprocal honor patterns, communication patterns, etc. Master-client relationships were a permanent and stable element in the entire complex of social ties, despite the *personal impermanency* of such ties.[13] The combination of the ritualization of the master-client relationship and the personal impermanency of these relations explains, in part at least, the peculiar blend of near-anarchic individualism and the rather rigid hierarchical status system. The permanent and stable elements in Thai culture—particularly in its principles of stratification—will be found in this configuration of traits which is still a very marked feature of the society, even though the inner substance of this configuration has changed somewhat. It changed markedly after the military coup of 1932, when the center of power shifted from the royal house to the bureaucratic-military oligarchy.

This relatively new oligarchy is the source, almost exclusively, from which the new elite of Thailand is recruited. It sets the pattern for her new pyramid of social prestige. The implications of this for the country's social differentiation and its stratification structure will be considered shortly. Before proceeding, however, we shall discuss occupational and economic differentiation in modern Thailand.

C. OCCUPATIONAL DISTRIBUTION AND SALARY DIFFERENCES

Since there are no accurate data for the time before World War II, we shall confine our discussion to the period after 1947. Indirect evidence indicates that, at least for the majority of Thais, there have been no significant changes (except in the urban sector) in occupational distribution between the 1930s and the beginning of the 1960s. The characteristic traits of the agrarian societies of southeast Asia are reflected by the labor force in Thailand.

In 1947, 7,683,966 persons were engaged in agriculture (including fishing and forestry). This was 85% of the total labor force of fourteen years of age and over. Commerce accounted for the second largest number of people employed, a mere 8% of the labor force, or 706,974 persons. Next in line were the services—physicians, attorneys, high-ranking government officials, barbers and waiters—3% of the total labor force, or 273,688 persons. These were followed by manufacturing (2.2%) and construction (1%).[14] It is particularly important that the decisive majority of the employed are self-employed or family workers.

The vast majorities of farmers possessed holdings of their own[15] and of the otherwise employed possessed businesses of their own—which accounts for the immobile and essentially rigid nature of the Thai labor force in this period. This has far-reaching political implications for the society. For instance, the country's lack of acute agrarian problems has made the rural periphery relatively passive. In general, except for the northeast and southeast, Thailand's rural areas, unlike others in southeast Asia, do not constitute centers of active resentment against the authorities.

Data for 1960 show the farm population as 82.2% (11,334,382 persons) of Thailand's total labor force. This change seems to be negligible. However, occupational distribution by age reveals that, "while 82% of employed males over 60 years of age are farmers, only 72% of those in the 20-24 age range are engaged in this activity."[16] Nor has the proportion of hired labor in agriculture undergone any notable change. The figure was 319,000 (or 2.7%) out of a total of 11 million.[17] Commerce remained the second largest source of occupation: 779,904 persons, or 5.7% of the total labor force. Following these were the services which engaged 655,271, or 4.8%, and manufacturing, which accounted for 471,027, or 3.4%.[18]

A comparison of the data for 1947 and 1960 reveals that there was a drop from 8% to 5.7% in the proportion of those engaged in commerce. In contrast, those in the services rose from 3% to 4.8%. The proportion engaged in manufacturing also rose by 2.2%, to 3.4%. Though these changes reflect processes of industrialization and urbanization, they also mirror an increase in the number of persons employed in the government bureaucracy.[19] About 400,000 persons were employed by the government in 1960. However, Thailand in the 1960s remained one of the world's most agrarian countries, ranking eighth in a list of ninety-eight.[20] In contrast, of seventy-seven countries giving the proportion of the total labor force employed in nonfarm labor, Thailand ranks sixty-ninth.[21]

Ethnic and Occupational Distribution

It is impossible to discuss occupational distribution in Thailand without referring to the ethnic dimension. The prospects created by the geographic and occupational immobility of the Thai peasant despite the large demand for nonfarm work that followed urbanization were intensively exploited by Chinese immigrants. The Chinese began flowing in great waves to Thailand at the end of the nineteenth century. Indeed, before World War II, the Chinese constituted between 70% and 90% of the nonfarm labor force. At that time, Thais were employed chiefly in agriculture and government service. The government's efforts to alter these occupational patterns through laws aimed at the Chinese wrought no substantial changes.

These laws circumscribed Chinese immigration. They also directly restricted Chinese labor, either by requiring that a given proportion of Thai citizens be employed in various occupations and industries or by excluding aliens entirely from certain occupations, such as food vending, salt making, and tobacco growing.[22]

The Thais failed to utilize these opportunities, because of the *absence* of disintegrative processes in the Thai village and because the Thais were not motivated to enter occupations they perceived as possessing low prestige value.[23] Further, the possibilities the Chinese had to circumvent discriminatory laws by opting for Thai citizenship helped to neutralize those laws. The changes in the ethnic composition of the labor force in Thailand have been due more to indirect economic and political processes than to formal laws that long operated in a vacuum. The most comprehensive and systematic study of occupational distribution along ethnic lines shows that, at least for the 1950s, the schematic portrayals pointing to an extreme occupational polarization of the Thais and the Chinese do not conform to reality. A study carried out in one of the districts of Bangkok, where the Chinese constitute a majority, yielded a number of results.[24] In this district, 6.2% of the Thai population and 2.7% of the Chinese population held jobs of high status in terms of prestige, income, and qualifications. Jobs of mid-high status were held by 51.3% of the Thais and 46.5% of the Chinese. Jobs of mid-low status were distributed among 12.9% of the Thais and 27.5% of the Chinese. The poorly esteemed occupations accounted for 29.6% of the Thais and 23.3% of the Chinese. Thus Chinese and Thais are found in all four occupational status categories. However, the two groups are not always represented in proportion to their respective numbers in the area's population. Whereas the Chinese constitute 55% of the area's total population, they hold only about 34.5% of the high-status jobs. On the other hand, they hold about 52% of the mid-high status jobs—a figure that comes very close to their proportion of the area's population. The Chinese hold about 72% of the mid-low status jobs and roughly 48% of the lowest status jobs.[25] Hence, the Chinese are rather well represented in the mid-high and low status jobs, underrepresented in the highest status jobs, and overrepresented in the mid-low status jobs.

The overrepresentation or underrepresentation of Chinese in each of the four occupational status categories does not contradict the fact that there are certain occupations from which they are almost absent and some in which they preponderate overwhelmingly. For instance, Skinner reports that the Thais constitute a clear majority in the following occupations: high-ranking office staff, high-status industrial staff, lesser and semiprofessional staff, government clerks, farmers, fishermen, and low-status domestic service. In contrast, the Chinese are a considerable majority in the following occupations: business clerks, tailors and dressmakers, repairmen-mechanics, unskilled workers, business owners, and managers.[26] However, there is clearly no sharp differentiation between Thais and Chinese. They overlap at many points of the occupational status structure. The correlation between ethnic origin and occupational categories (not necessarily specific professions) is today smaller than ever.

Differential Levels of Income

A scrutiny of the country's occupational structure shows that the wage and salary earners are only a small fraction of the population. Russett puts them at 11% of the country's total labor force. In this sense, Thailand is at a very low level of development. In a comparative study made of the relative weight of the wage- and salary-earning sector in 79 countries, Thailand was placed as low as seventy-sixth.[27] One manifestation of this economic structure is the low average income. According to data for 1954, the average weekly pay of a wage earner was 143 bahts, or about $7.[28] The average weekly salary of men was 153 bahts, of women, 106 bahts.[29] These figures are general for the entire country and ignore distinctions of occupation and differences between the country's various geographical regions. The following data provide a somewhat clearer picture: Managers and senior officials earned 303 bahts a week, whereas salesmen averaged 96 bahts a week.[30] The average weekly earnings of men in the urban areas was 167 bahts; of women, 114 bahts. In the villages, the average weekly income of men was 126 bahts; of women, 87 bahts. The differences in wage levels between the various occupational categories is even greater when the salaries of managers and senior officials in the Bangkok area are compared with the income of the country's farmers. Figures pertaining to 1954 show that the former earned 420 bahts a week, whereas male farmers averaged no more than 97 bahts a week.

There are also rather sharp differences in salaries paid to those in government services. "According to the general salary and classification plan adopted in 1954, and subsequently modified, a scale of monthly pay grades prevails, ranging from a starting scale of 450 for fourth-class officials to 8,000 bahts as the maximum for special class officials."[31] In this connection, let us note that a government employee with a B.A. earned, in the early 1960s, a starting salary generally lower than the average earned by a skilled worker.[32] This low level of civil servant salaries, especially at the lower echelons, may well account for the widespread corruption found among government employees.

The salaries of teachers provide another example of the low wages paid to government employees. A teacher who had completed two years of training in a teachers' college received $270 a year. A graduate of the College of Education received $650 a year, whereas a professor on the highest level earned $1,350-$2,150 a year. There are average wage differentials between wage earners who possess no more than four years of formal primary education and those with university degrees. In Bangkok the ratio is 1 : 5 (1,105 bahts a month against 5,582 bahts a month) and in the entire country the ratio is 1 to 3.4.

Data for 1962-63 give us the proportion of families found at every income level.

> Almost one half (48.4%) of all families in Thailand received less than 3,000 bahts in cash income for the year. 21% received between 3,000 and 6,000 bahts, 20% between 6,000 and 12,000 bahts, 11% between 12,000 and 18,000 bahts or more. This distribution reflected primarily the effect of low village earnings. In towns, about 18% of all families reported incomes below 3,000 bahts and in Bangkok-Thonburi, only 5% were below this level.[33]

It is not easy to compare average salaries (and incomes for 1954 with those for 1962-63, since the latter relate to average *family* salary and income, whereas the former refer to average *individual* salary and income. The average *monthly* family income in 1962-63 was 620 bahts, or 1,360 bahts a year per capita. Another estimate gives the average *family* income as 723 bahts a month and 1,500 bahts a year per *person*. [34]

A starting salary in the civil service is 450 bahts per month; a high salary, 8,000 bahts a month. The ratio is 1 : 17. In privately owned companies, a starting salary is 812 bahts per month; a peak salary, 28,000 bahts a month. The differential is about 1 : 35.[35]

The internal salary differentials in each sector (particularly the discrepancy between the two) explain at least some of the conditions that have spawned large-scale corruption in Thai public administration.[36] In 1966, this situation led to certain adjustments in the salary levels of government employees. The starting salary was raised to 520 bahts,[37] but it is doubtful that this reform will change much. Additional sources of income which had served previously will probably go on serving in the future. This is especially true of semiofficial income sources. Typical of these are particiaption in various government and public committees, various bonuses, and most important of all, private businesses.[38] The unequal rates of income are, of course, relative. It is particularly difficult to compare the differential rates of countries with a high GNP with those of countries with a low GNP. According to one instructive investigation on the subject, the inequality score in Thailand is rather high among countries with a low GNP.[39]

How do these income and other dimensions, some objective and some subjective, find expression in the formation of the authentic class structure in Thailand?

D. THE PRESTIGE HIERARCHY

Scholars of Thai society agree on the existence of a prestige hierarchy there. However, the great majority of their evaluations are based, not on a survey of the subjective attitudes of Thai citizens, but on the impressionistic observations of the scholars themselves. Nonetheless, it is reasonable to assume that these evaluations are in principle correct and reliable. The prestige hierarchy most accepted by the scholars is made up of the following status groups:

1. *The royal family and the holders of royal titles* (a hereditary nobility).

2. *The "ruling class,"* itself composed of a number of tiers, the uppermost of which includes—above all—army men. (These have, in recent years, been joined by a number of civilians.)[40] This entire group embraces no more than 1% or 2% of the total population. The lower tiers include part of the traditional bureaucracy and a number of economic entrepreneurs, most of them Chinese.[41]

3. *The middle class.* This class comprises mainly the middle ranks of the army and the civil service, as well as the liberal professions. All these are Thais. The Chinese who belong to this class are the "middle" traders. The lowest stratum of the Chinese middle class is made up of lower-echelon civil servants and skilled workers. The overwhelming majority of Thais in this stratum are, of course, those in the civil service. This group, not all of whose gradations are part of the middle class, has steadily expanded since World War I. In 1965, the civil servants amounted to 250,000 persons. (In addition, some 200,000 persons worked in the government as nonstatus employees; all of them belonged to a lower stratum.)[42]

It is important that, in terms of prestige, the civil servants belong to a status group which is clearly distinct from the higher strata of politician-bureaucrats making up the ruling circles. The country's political power and policy making are concentrated in the ruling class. This fact sets its members apart from the hereditary aristocracy, whose political power is extremely limited. The distinction between civil servants and those not in government employ is also clear-cut and unequivocal—a circumstance due to the civil servants' monopoly, in one degree or another, of the services required by the public. This monopoly is the source of the prestige enjoyed by the government bureaucracy. The distinctiveness of the civilian bureaucracy is also notable when it is compared with other groups, such as those operating in the commercial sphere. The feature that most distinguishes it from these other groups is its ethnic character.

4. *The mass of peasants,* living in 40,000 villages, and the *peddlers, artisans, and unskilled laborers* of Bangkok and other smaller towns. Most of those in this category are Thai, though not a few of Bangkok's Chinese belong to it.

Where does the clergy fit into this setting? In general, the hierarchy of the clergy is somewhat separate from the civilian hierarchy. The priest per se enjoys a very high degree of prestige which in theory is surpassed only by that of the king and princes. The king and the priest represent "the symbolic elites" of Thai society. They personify the best in the Thai-Buddhist tradition. In practice, however, both the status of the individual priest and even the sociopolitical power of the clergy conform only partially to this theory.

This division of Thai society into prestige groups, like every schematic division of social gradations, strata, and status groups, is defective. It does not distinguish the more subtle shades and various links connecting the larger categories, as well as the various status groups found within the categories. Siffin provides such links. In addition to describing the differential traits of the various groups, he also deals with the situations in which the various groups meet in institutionalized and noninstitutionalized contexts. An interesting instance are the contexts in which the civilian bureaucracy meets with the clergy. "The line between the religious and the bureaucratic way of life is clear enough. But the separation is not total. Each male official is entitled to one leave-with-pay period of up to 120 days to allow him to serve in the priesthood. The upper levels of the Buddhist religion are themselves bureaucratized to some extent," being affiliated in some way to the Department of Religious Affairs within the Ministry of Education.[43]

Another example of intergroup mingling is the cooperation between the political-bureaucratic elite and the economic elite from among the Chinese minority. Evers writes that "high military rank is often given to high-ranking civil servants."[44] The fine distinction between the civilian bureaucracy and the army, at least on the symbolic level, is thus blurred. In this manner, a common base—though not of equal rights and privileges—is created between the two bureaucracies for exercising a monopolistic control over political power.

The salience and distinctiveness of these status groups, especially of the bureaucracy, may be attributed to, among other things, the fact that until recently their differential prestige emanated from the large degree of internal congruence between the various components of their status.[45] The ruling class monopolized the political sphere, enjoyed varied economic benefits (from both legal and illegal sources),[46] and had secondary and often advanced military or civilian education.[47] The achievements of lower-status groups in each of these areas were more modest.

However, even this relatively simple structure has always possessed deviations which have spoiled the principles of internal equilibrium. The first of these anomalies is the royal family. Though it was shorn of its political power in the coup of 1932, its economic position, its ascriptive origin, its level of education, and its style of life have allowed it to retain much of its earlier prestige. Another is the Chinese economic elite, whose influence and economic power are far greater than the political weight it exerts.[48] Still another is the position of the top ranks of the Buddhist clergy.

These deviations to some extent refute the claim that the prestige structure of Thai society is absolutely uniform. They suggest the existence of a number of offshoots—the Chinese merchants, the aristocracy, and the clergy—from the main hierarchical stem. Other offshoots may spring from the intellectual elite outside the bureaucratic establishment and from the nucleus represented by the Thai economic entrepreneurs. Thus far, the public esteem enjoyed by these potential offshoot groups is rather low and their degree of frustration high.[49] There is much truth in Mosel's statement that "we do not find a pluralism of elites based on different values (such as wealth, knowledge, prestige, etc.). A person's standing on such non-political values tends to correspond rather closely to his standing in the political dimension."[50]

Thus far we have given a general description of the most important gradations of the prestige hierarchy. Let us go on to a more detailed analysis of some of these strata.

If it is at all possible to locate and identify a middle class in Thai society, that class is to be found, first and foremost, in and perhaps confined exclusively to Bangkok. Using conventional and inaccurate concepts, we may distinguish two subgroups: (1) an upper middle class, comprising largely middle-echelon army men, clerks, a handful of merchants, and technicians and professionals; and (2) a lower middle class chiefly composed of skilled workers and low-ranking clerks.

Ethnically, the middle class is the most diversified of all. Though there are Chinese in all the social strata of Bangkok's population, they are found in highest proportions in the two sections of the middle class.[51] However, the government bureaucracy and the officer corps are manned almost entirely by Thais. Commerce, especially wholesale trade, is virtually monopolized by the Chinese. This is true, however, only if we ignore their partly concealed partnership with top Thai leaders. In addition to feeling rather negative about engaging in commerce, those Thais who try advance their positions in commerce come up against the Chinese monopoly. Another serious obstacle to any notable entrepreneurial endeavors by the Thais is that presented by the traditional monopoly exercised by the government administration, which finds expression in the complete or partial control of many economic enterprises. At this stage, the Thais are satisfied to pursue petty trade and peddling, and numerous clerks join them after their work day (the *seng-li* system).[52]

The way in which a considerable proportion of the Chinese minority has arrived at its present standing and the manner in which they employed resources of various kinds to secure their achievements have been investigated extensively and systematically by a number of observers of Thai society.[53] We shall only make a few comments relevant to our discussion. In the literature on the Chinese in Thailand, there are diverse evaluations of the degree with which this minority group has assimilated into Thai society and of the extent to which its distinctive traits as a status group have become blurred. The diversity is apparently chiefly the result of the fact that scholars have referred to different periods. As Skinner has attested, the assimilation of the Chinese began immediately after their immigration to the country in the fourteenth century. The overwhelming majority of their descendants were completely assimilated into Thai society. However, this assimilation was halted decisively from the early part of this century down to the 1950s.[54] As a consequence, much of the peculiar position of the Chinese as a discrete status group in the economic, political, ethnic, and linguistic planes crystallized at an accelerated pace, especially during that period. (Since the 1950s, numerous indications testify to a certain weakening of the separateness of the Chinese community. Observers are, however, divided on the precise significance and on the extent to which they will persist.) Many factors—demographic, economic, religious, and political—helped the Chinese assimilate until the early twentieth century. When these factors, especially the political and economic ones, changed, the assimilation stopped.[55] Politically, the decisive cause of this halt was the rise of Thai nationalism that began in the late nineteenth century and reached maturity after the 1932 coup. The zeal for political independence and for the total Thaification of key political and bureaucratic positions began making itself felt in the economic sphere as well, in sanctions imposed on the Chinese. Ultimately, the Thai elite preferred a business partnership with the Chinese (to combine their own political power with economic benefits) to a futile struggle with the economic power of the Chinese sector. Of course, this was attractive to the Chinese as well, as it enabled them to evade economic sanctions.[56]

Historically, the road which led the Chinese to their present economic position was taken when they shifted from skilled and unskilled manual labor (building roads and ditches) to wholesale and retail trade. When the Thai peasants were satisfied with increasing their yields (in rice) and the Thai upper class were entrenching themselves more securely in the pivotal bureaucratic and political posts, the Chinese steadily monopolized every phase in the two-way commercial traffic between the producers on the periphery and the markets of the world.[57] In time, they also came to control a substantial proportion of the industries that developed in Thailand, such as tin and rubber.[58]

A drastic curtailment, partly de jure and partly de facto, of the channels of social mobility previously available to the Chinese minority contributed more than anything else toward strengthening their separatist tendencies during the first half of the twentieth century. This ecological, occupational, and social separatism led to the evolution of criteria, peculiar to this Chinese minority, for evaluating the importance of the various components of social status. Thus, for example, the component lending greatest status was the wealth a person accumulated chiefly from commercial enterprise. The importance of this yardstick is manifested in many standards of behavior to which the Chinese elite of wealth in Thailand adhere strictly.[59] The accumulation of wealth and economic power is not, of course, a rare phenomenon among members of the Thai political elite. However, they consolidate their economic power by imposing a tax on rich Chinese, and in return grant these Chinese political patronage and services. Being a minority in Thai society, the Chinese are almost totally excluded from participating in political power on the national level. Hence, the Chinese elite's political power is confined to the Chinese community —specifically, leadership and power positions in Chinese organizations. And as Skinner writes: "Positions of authority in Chinese organizations of all kinds are in general highly prized and the institutionalized expressions and rituals of modesty with regard to assuming office can only be interpreted as reverse symbolization."[60]

The wealthy Chinese in Bangkok generally hold the key positions in the many organizations and associations developed by the Chinese community. The fusion of economic wealth and leadership-administrative power greatly enhances prestige—which, in Skinner's opinion, constitutes a status dimension of its own. It is, however, not easy to assess the specific content of this dimension, as it is apparently made up entirely of a combination of extremely diffuse and particularistic symbols. In this connection,

> few public steps of real importance to a Chinese in Bangkok are taken without recourse to the highest prestige symbols available. It would almost appear that the value of a person is largely measured by the prestige of those who officiate at his wedding, lend their presence to the formal opening of his shop, attend his mother's funeral, or sign his obituary notice.[61]

Other factors that contribute to an individual's prestige among the Chinese are instrumental capabilities (manual labor) and religious values, both of great import among the lower classes. The independent prestige hierarchy of the Chinese community in Bangkok, as evolved during the first half of the twentieth century, has been structured, above all, on the varied spectrum of its internal associations. It is because of the diverse functions of these associations that the Chinese community's segregation from Thai society has been intensified and deepened.[62]

The Chinese insulation is today much less complete. Many breaches may be discerned in the social wall that surrounded them after this century began.

Among the most important reasons accounting for this new development are the following:

1. The flow of Thais from the rural areas into Bangkok and other towns has led to competition between them and the Chinese over occupations which had previously been a preserve of the latter.

2. The process of mobility in Thai society itself has given rise to a middle class that evinces a (still somewhat limited) interest in careers other than in the governmental civilian and military bureaucracies. This class also aspire to strengthen their positions in the various technical and professional fields as well as in commerce and finance.

3. A strong stimulus to the removal of the ethnic nature of certain occupations has been the network of ties woven by the politicomilitary leadership with the Chinese economic elite. This was made possible primarily by changes in the ranks of Chinese leadership. A considerable proportion of this leadership has evinced a growing inclination to cooperate with the new Thai elite which came to power after World War II—more specifically, after the dismissal of Phibun Songkhram.

These trends created potential meeting points between the two sectors and somewhat softened the polarity of the urban society in Bangkok. However, it is not easy to predict whether the near future will see a proportional and representative dispersal of the Chinese minority into the various peculiarly Thai occupational categories.

Further, in Thailand to date, there has not evolved a distinct and clear-cut status group whose mixed ethnic identity would allow it to serve as intermediate to the Thai majority and the Chinese minority. Skinner states that, in the 1950s, it was possible to distinguish

> thousands of intermediate individuals who identify as Chinese in some social situations and as Thai in others, who have both a Chinese and a Thai name, either of which is used according to suitability and can speak Thai and Chinese with equal fluency. But such individuals are not developing relationships among themselves that are more frequent and enduring than the social interaction which they have with those who are unequivocally members of Chinese or of Thai society.[63]

E. PATTERNS OF SOCIAL MOBILITY

In all things concerning social mobility, both scholars and laymen have viewed Thai society as being optimally open and marked by much upward mobility. This opinion is nurtured chiefly by the potential implications for social mobility of the style of life and of the Buddhist religious norms that govern social attitudes. For instance, the dedication to an individualistic style of life and the prominence of religious merit over ascriptive criteria are regarded as unequivocally encouraging the individual to try to change his status. Furthermore, religious merit no doubt supports the universalistic principles employed in playing various roles.[64] This situation, to those who have Buddhist norms in mind, is an old and institutionalized phenomenon which found expression as early as the period of absolute monarchy in the rule of declining descent.

However, this view falls considerably short of the real situation, which is more complex than the conclusions that can be drawn from an academic scrutiny of those normative principles with implications for social mobility. The gap between reality and the normative system is, apparently, not small. This contradiction is not easy to resolve, since only partial evidence is available.[65] The best obtainable data pertain to the highest tier of the bureaucracy and the intelligentsia. The two groups are not only largely identical but also overlap. According to Siffin, this tier is continuously increasing in numbers.[66]

In the 1960s, an estimated 25,000 to 30,000 persons had had higher education. In addition to the growth of the number of persons possessing higher education, there has been an increase in the proportion of degree holders from overseas universities. These now constitute the elite among Thailand's university graduates, with the very substantial advantage of having access to the senior posts in the government administration.[67] In this connection, an interesting question arises: To what extent does the supply of manpower from institutions of higher learning square with the absorptive capacity of the market—particularly that of the administration? It may safely be asserted that, for the period of this study, Thailand does not belong to that wide category of developing countries where education outstrips absorption, much to the detriment of social stability. Thus far, Thailand has largely succeeded in preventing the creation of too large a gap between the reservoir of manpower with advanced education and the supply of government and other jobs.[68] Observers consider this to be the paramount factor in the relatively high stability of Thai society compared with the other countries of southeast Asia.[69] In the absence of a colonial regime, Thailand's sovereign government was able to meet the needs of the educated public by expanding the administration, the army, and the police. This trend was supported by the practice which limited the accessibility of senior posts to graduates of universities and military academies. In this sense, the Thai regime answered, at least partially, the need both for expanding state services in defense, education, health, and welfare, and for providing jobs to persons with advanced education. However, this task was growing increasingly difficult in the 1960s. The competition for senior posts is becoming increasingly severe, with two consequences. The value of higher education has become somewhat deflated, and those who have it need to rest content with lower-ranking jobs or with careers outside the government bureaucracy and therefore of lower prestige.[70] Second, a trend has begun toward oligarchy and exclusiveness at the top tier of the civilian and military bureaucracy. Evers suggests that the consolidation of the bureaucratic elite has been determined by three interrelated processes: (1) differential fertility between social strata (the reproduction rate of the bureaucratic elite is still high enough to permit recruitment of new members from its own class); (2) differential acculturation and monopolization of status symbols; and (3) bureaucratic control of wealth.[71]

We are concerned with only the last two. Those persons who have gone furthest in terms of Westernization possess the advantage in competing for positions of leadership. Hence the great advantage of the graduates of overseas institutions—who enjoy, in addition, special legal privileges and prospects of promotion irrespective of seniority considerations.[72] Patronage is feasible because the top bureaucratic positions monopolize not only the status symbols but the sources of political and economic power. Achievements in the economic sphere have been made by cooperating with the Chinese economic elite, among other things. Thus it would be far-fetched to conclude that higher education (even overseas) represents the sole avenue to political and economic power. The conversion of an individual's status in the administration (achieved through his education) into political and economic power at the supreme levels must confront the severest competition by the top-ranking men in the army, where mobility hinges only partly on educational attainments.[73] Ultimately, the creation and increase of the sources of political power are not confined to the civilian bureaucracy but are nurtured in the army—more specifically, in certain cliques in the army.

The internal consolidation of the top bureaucratic-political ties is not of much value to us in determining the rate and scope of mobility in the lower strata of the Thai population. The quantitative data on this question are very limited and what little is available relates chiefly to the Chinese community. We have, however, presented indirect evidence on the scope of mobility in the lower strata when discussing changes in occupational status in the past generation.[74]

Images of Role and Status

Additional indirect evidence of the patterns of mobility may be gleaned from the information available on the manner in which Thais perceive role and status and on everything concerning the personal and collective attitudes toward mobility in general and the specific channels of mobility in particular. A great consensus exists in Thai society on the vital importance and naturalness of a rigorous and meticulous hierarchy of roles and status. However, together with this, Thais stress the *temporariness* of status and the axiomatic prospect of positive and negative *changes* in a person's standing. The two concepts, especially the second, are nourished by the basic normative principles of the Buddhist religion. For example, the very doctrine of reincarnation, where one's form in one's next metamorphosis depends on one's accumulation of individual merit, excludes any possibility of a belief in an equality of status for all men. Furthermore, this reinforces identification with social interactions guided by hierarchical principles. However, the conception of merit also sanctifies that of the *impermanence* of an individual's position on this or that rung of the hierarchical ladder. The time required for such status changes may indeed be in the distant future and involve possible alterations of status in one's next metamorphosis. Nevertheless, the principle of change and the negation of permanence have an impact both on daily life and on the ideological arguments about everything concerning stratification patterns and attitudes toward personal mobility.[75]

The hierarchical interrelationships are extremely varied. Underlying them is the principle of relative monopoly over the resources of political power and economic wealth, education, an esteemed position in the government bureaucracy, and the like, from all of which it is possible to derive material benefits and to share them with inferiors. Further evidence of hierarchical relations may be found in the fact that, in certain situations when no basis exists for hierarchical differentiation, one is provided by existing differences of age, be these differences as small as that between twins.[76]

The combination of particularistic criteria (the acceptance of the principle of patronage in the patron-client relations) with personal achievement criteria (identification with the principle of merit which is entirely connected with the action and inaction of the individual) constitutes the most dominant feature of status and role in Thai society. As this largely nurtures the behavior of politicians and the public at large, it has many implications for the nature of the country's political culture. This generalization is valid for both the rural and urban periphery. However, the absence of ascriptive structural principles does not automatically mean that Thais—at least those in the villages—are, despite the relative paucity of barriers, highly motivated to get ahead socially.[77]

The particularistic character of the perceptions of status and of hierarchical relations is most strongly manifest in the predominant nature of the power dimension as a component of an individual's status. Let us note again that the resources of power are the virtual monopoly of the military leadership and of parallel rungs in the civilian bureaucracy. The educational attainments that serve as a prerequisite for acceptance into senior roles in the government bureaucracy were viewed, at least in the past, not as an end in themselves but rather as a lever of mobility in that bureaucracy. The small academic community is held in esteem. Academic degrees, especially those gained abroad, are deemed very valuable assets. Yet opinion is unanimous that educational achievements combined with some affiliation to a bureaucratic-political power position are preferable and more esteemed than merely academic standing. The intense urge to obtain and retain government jobs is due, among other reasons, to the socioeconomic security that such jobs provide—a security generally preferred to the risky prospects held out by the private sector. This trend has persisted without letup since the period of absolute monarchy.[78] However, the economic and social security conferred by membership in the civil service is not a certainty for high-ranking officials. In these ranks, which are political, it is usual for officials to belong to cliques or to circles composed of patrons and clients. As an individual's status and the benefits he is able to derive from it depend in great measure on the position of the patron, joining such a group represents a certain risk. Thus the composition of these groups is extremely fluid. Clients do not hesitate to switch their allegiance when their patrons are unable or do not wish to share their resources. Power is thus viewed as possessing moral implications because of its link with the manipulation—often formally illegal but not illegitimate in terms of accepted practice—of manpower and material resources. One way or another, the monopoly over this or that type of power complements the validity both of the concept of "merit" as a potent yardstick in explaining social mobility and particularly of those phenomena which refute or contradict the principle of merit.[79]

What has thus far been said refers, of course, to Thai society. The manner in which the Chinese population view role and status is very different, for both objective and subjective reasons. The characteristic images of status and mobility expectations of the Chinese in Thailand are focused chiefly on economic activity as *private entrepreneurs.* Only a small proportion of the young Chinese strive for higher education—which leads almost exclusively to mobility within the civil service. As a substitute for direct political power which, as a tolerated minority, the Chinese cannot acquire by the accepted modes of moving up the social ladder, they attempt to acquire indirect influence and bargaining power through cooperating with Thai senior officers and officials in legal and illegal business enterprises.[80]

Although conventional criteria of social status are widespread and accepted in Thai society (especially urban society), the strikingly dominant nature of the hierarchical interrelationships and the institutionalization of master-client relations lend, by means of the power component, an extremely particularistic character to the other components of status, such as education and control over economic resources. These last two are not pursued as ends in themselves with the same drive as is power. The ideal is their conversion into improved positions on the hierarchical ladder of political patrons and their clients.

F. DEGREE OF INTERNAL COHESION OF THE SOCIAL STRATA

To what extent do the salience of the particularistic dimension and the importance of patron-client relationships have an impact on the degree of sociopolitical cohesion of the various status groups in Thai society? In general, the partial and fragmented hierarchization created by patron-client relationships, particularly in the centers of political and administrative power, is contractual in character, involving not groups but individuals. Hence we may expect to see a relatively small degree of vertical social cohesion. In other words, economic and political interests as well as the execution of religious precepts are more clearly marked with the individualistic than with the familial or group stamp. This is true more of the Thai society than of the Chinese. An indirect proof of the individualistic character of relationships may be found in the rather small number of functional and formal associations and their marginal status as pressure groups. For acquiring benefits, the Thais still prefer to depend on personal contacts rather than on formal pressure groups—especially since the political climate makes the latter route unfeasible. The little participation in the various formal and voluntary associations mitigates to a great extent the trend toward regimentation that is fed by the complex of relationships between patrons and clients in the hierarchical structure of the bureaucracy.[81] The trend toward regimentation is further weakened by the fact that not a single one of the informal and formal social organizations presents any comprehensive and extensive demands to the individual. This is true of the nuclear and of the extended family as well as of the village and of the central administration. The rural areas have no cohesive age groups, rural committees, or councils, and in the towns not many occupational organizations and no neighborhood groupings may be found.[82]

In this social context, the only group that possesses social cohesion is the hereditary aristocracy. And this group is by definition a tightly closed entity. However, here the rule of declining descent serves as an effective brake on the total institutionalization of this trend. A status consciousness similar to that found among the hereditary aristocracy, but on different grounds, may be found among the military-political elite. This small group, born in the 1932 coup, embraces (together with various satellite groupings) no more than a few hundred families. Forty years of involvement in the country's political life has produced, despite internal struggles and disputes, a sense of exclusiveness and group identity that is not at all negligible. However, both de facto and de jure, this group is more open than the hereditary aristocracy.

These two groups are the only ones in Thai society that possess a status consciousness.[83] The Chinese sector is excluded from this generalization. The period of segregation and of antiassimilationism among the Chinese has to some extent receded. Despite differences in culture and mentality and varying economic and social interests, the Thai and the Chinese have been coming notably closer to each other in recent years.[84] Nevertheless, one cannot speak of the disappearance in the foreseeable future of the separate ethnic identity of the Chinese community.

Other groups of Thai society are not generally analyzed by scholars through the concepts commonly employed for Western urban society, as it is assumed that distribution according to such criteria as working class, middle class, lower middle class, and upper middle class are not applicable to Thai society. The skepticism about these concepts is understandable. They are not just unsuited to the differentiation of Thailand's urban society; it is doubtful that they could be of much use even for understanding Western societies of the 1960s and 1970s. One must not forget, in this connection, that the Thai urban sector is at present in too early an evolutionary phase of the crystallization of a stratified structure to permit analysis through concepts borrowed from Western societies. Moreover, Thai society itself has, since the 1960s, developed beyond the stratification models accepted since the start of this century. At any rate, clear-cut distinctions between status groups and associations of people of identical socioeconomic indicators pursuing specific aims are still very rare in Thai society.[85] It is important, however, that there already exist potential meeting points for such associations in the form of social organizations, political groups, and informal forums. However, the great potential inherent in these points of convergence are little utilized. This generalization does not, of course, take in the hereditary aristocracy and the military-political-administrative elite. The pattern of stratification, at least for Thai urban society, may thus be summed up, more or less, as follows:

> The term "class" must be understood not in the sense of restrictive and exclusive classes, but rather in the sense of a group of discrete individuals who by virtue of various implied and arbitrary criteria have a common prestige status.[86]

Stratification in the Rural Periphery

If, on the national level, the peasantry is found on the lowest rung of the social ladder, on the rural level itself, the degree of social differentiation is very small. Strictly speaking, it is not always easy to define the scope of the differentiation, as the very term "village," denoting a social set of relationships, is extremely fluid in at least a number of the country's areas, such as the north. Thus, for instance, one of the observers of the Thai scene writes that "a village is made up of individual land-owning households, it is not a case of the community allocating its corporate resources among its members."[87]

This hints at the most decisive fact about the agrarian structure of Thailand—the almost total absence of a stratum of rural landlord gentry. Blanchard adds that "rural society is characterized by the absence of a hierarchical class structure and by a relative lack of elaboration, complexity and institutionalization in the social forces."[88]

However, a traditional differentiation did exist in the Thai countryside. It was based on age and sex differences, outstanding ability in astrology and music, and above all on the performance of meritorious deeds in the religious-social sphere.

Distinction there was very important as a status component and of as much value in the rural context as economic assets or political power.[89] The willingness to perform meritorious deeds was also a mechanism of equality.

Charity and generosity, particularly on the material plane, which the more successful among the peasants are expected to display, also reduce the relatively small status differences between the peasants.[90] There are, of course, other factors that account for the relatively small differences in the size of peasant holdings.[91] One of these is that most of the areas of the country are favored with a surplus of land. Another is that no restrictions have been imposed on the buying and selling of lands. As Blanchard writes, "We see here a peasantry treating land as a commodity, not as a traditional heritage, nor as a symbol of membership and status in a local community."[92]

The absence of owners of large tracts reduces to a minimum both the proportion of hired labor and the prospects of farm tenancy. In these conditions, it is not surprising that farmer associations like those widespread in Burma, Indonesia, and other countries of southeast Asia cannot be found in the Thai countryside.[93]

This agrarian structure confines the rural formal and informal social elites to a very small group. It includes the priests of the local temple,[94] the village headman,[95] and the relatively well-to-do peasants. These last are increasing in number, especially in areas adjacent to Bangkok. In recent years, speculation in land has become rife. Town dwellers are evincing a growing interest in land as means of production, chiefly of exportable rice. This has led, in certain areas, to a growth in the number of landless villagers and to the enrichment of some peasants.[96]

Another group to be added to this small rural elite is that residing in provincial towns. This elite is composed chiefly of government officials, merchants and teachers. Totally absent from the rural scene are the hereditary aristocracy and the circles of the new elite whose power is derived from the politico-military leadership. These mostly prefer to live in Bangkok, the capital.

It appears that, essentially, the controversy over the face of stratification in Thailand is largely sterile. There is in fact no contradiction between so-called loose structure in certain spheres that encourages horizontal and vertical mobility, and the not inconsiderable degree of hierarchical interrelationships, particularly on the politicobureaucratic level. At any event, the interesting and rather rare synthesis between hierarchization and individualism, on the one hand, and particularistic and achievement orientations, on the other, seems to operate smoothly in Thai society. This fact has ramifications for, for example, the country's political culture and the problems with which the country's leaders must grapple. This synthesis of factors largely accounts for the fact that the military-political elite has not thus far found it necessary to cope with status groups or social strata, besides the students, possessed of a collective consciousness. This leadership has thus been able to play the political game by making bargains with individuals or small groups. As these individuals struggle first and foremost for improved positions or for greater economic benefits, the rules of the game that have evolved within the complex of hierarchical interrelationships among those holding the reins of political and administrative power have contributed substantially toward the "solution" of political and economic problems in limited circles of patrons and clients.

NOTES

1. L. M. Hanks, Jr., "Merit and Power in the Thai Social Order," *American Anthropologist*, LIV, no. 6 (December 1962), p. 1252.

2. Ibid., p. 1259, n. 7.

3. Hans-Dieter Evers, "The Formation of a Social Class Structure," *Journal of Southeast Asian History*, VII, no. 2 (September 1966), pp. 103-104. Tominaga and his colleagues take a more extreme approach. See K. Tominaga et al., "The Modernization and Industrialization of Thai Society," *East Asian Cultural Studies*, VIII (1-4 March 1969), p. 3. For a similar view, see N. Jacobs, *Modernization without Development: Thailand as an Asian Case Study* (New York: Praeger, 1971), pp. 199-202.

4. Most scholars—for example, Wilson, Shor, Mosel, and Skinner—occupy some point between these two approaches. The majority incline toward Ever's position. At any rate, all admit the problems that arise from any discussion of Thai stratification structure in the classical terms of class structure. See David A. Wilson, *Politics in Thailand* (Ithaca, N.Y.: Cornell University Press, 1962), pp. 45-50; Edgard L. Shor, "The Public Service," in *Problems of Politics and Administration in Thailand*, ed. J. L. Sutton (Bloomington: Indiana University Press, 1962); N. J. Mosel, "Thai Administrative Behavior," in *Toward Comparative Study of Public Administration*, ed. William J. Siffin (Bloomington: Indiana University Press, 1957), p. 304; William G. Skinner, *Chinese Society in Thailand* (Ithaca, N.Y.: Cornell University Press, 1951), pp. 304-350.

5. It is important that Embree, the first to refer to Thailand's social structure as loosely integrated, emphasized the cultural symbolic aspect rather than the structural; "loosely integrated here signifying a culture in which considerable variation of individual behavior is sanctioned." The examples he presents show that this is the case. Thus he notes "almost determined lack of regularity, discipline and regimentation, lack for administrative regularity, and no individual time sense" (John F. Embree, "Thailand–A Loosely Structured Social System," *American Anthropologist*, LII, no. 2 [April-June 1950], pp. 182-183). For a comprehensive discussion of Embree's paper, see *Loosely Structured Social Systems: Thailand in Comparative Perspective*, ed. Hans-Dieter Evers, Cultural Report Series, no. 17, Yale University, Southeast Asia Studies, 1969.

6. Mosel, "Thai Administrative Behavior," p. 304.

7. Wilson, *Politics*, p. 58; and Wilson, "Thailand and Marxism," in *Marxism in Southeast Asia*, ed. F. N. Trager (Stanford: Stanford University Press, 1959), pp. 64-65.

8. Wilson, *Politics*, p. 53. For a similar description including crude estimates of quantitative distribution of these groups, see George L. Harris et al., *Area Handbook for Thailand* (Washington, D.C.: The American University, 1963), pp. 101-103.

9. Mosel, "Thai Administrative Behavior," p. 304.

10. Eliezer B. Ayal, "Value Systems and Economic Development in Japan and Thailand," *Journal of Social Issues*, XIX, no. 1 (January 1963), p. 48.

11. Harris et al., *Area Handbook*, p. 97. See also Embree, "Thailand," pp. 188-189; Mary R. Hass, "The Declining Descend Rule for Rank in Thailand: A Correction," *American Anthropologist*, LIII, no. 4, part 1 (October-December 1951), pp. 585-586; Evers, *Loosely Structured Systems*, pp. 121-122. However, by inter-marriage status could be maintained. See also Tominaga et al., "Modernization," p. 7.

12. The ranks with which we are concerned here were those conferred by the king in exchange for services rendered to him. This system was abolished after the 1932 coup. One must distinguish between these ranks and those conferred on the members of the extended royal family.

13. See Harris et al., *Area Handbook*, p. 96; Jacobs, *Modernization*, pp. 80-87, 190-191, 201.

14. *Thailand: Its People, Its Society, Its Culture*, ed. Wendel Blanchard (New Haven: Human Relations Area Files Press, 1957), p. 271, table 13.

15. According to Blanchard, the farm wage laborers accounted for some 6% of the total agricultural labor force. However, this percentage appears to be too high; the actual figure is unlikely to exceed 3% (Blanchard, *Thailand*, p. 276; see also Tominaga et al., "Modernization," pp. 15-16).

16. J. C. Caldwell, "The Demographic Structure," in *Thailand: Social and Economic Studies in Development*, ed. T. H. Silcock (Canberra: Australian National University, 1966), p. 50.

17. Harris et al., *Area Handbook*, p. 232. For figures which indicate the stability of the population engaged in agriculture since 1929, see Tominaga et al., "Modernization," p. 15.

18. Harris et al., *Area Handbook*, p. 230, table 3.

19. Ibid., p. 233; and Richard J. Coughlin, *Double Identity: The Chinese in Modern Thailand* (Hong Kong: Hong Kong University Press, 1960), p. 127.

20. Russett et al., *World Handbook*, table 50.

21. Ibid., table 52.

22. Blanchard, *Thailand*, p. 275; Harris et al., *Area Handbook*, pp. 235-236; and Coughlin, *Double Identity*, pp. 127-143.

23. Coughlin, *Double Identity*, pp. 121-124.

24. Skinner, *Chinese Society*, p. 300, table 21; see also Tominaga et al., "Modernization," pp. 35-36.

25. Skinner, *Chinese Society*.

26. Ibid., p. 304, table 23.

27. Russett, op. cit., table 3.

28. 1 baht = 5 cents U.S.

29. Thailand Central Statistical Office, *Economic and Demographic Survey* (Bangkok: Government of Thailand, 1954; mimeo). 1st Series, Municipality of Bangkok, tables 18-1, 18-2, 18-3.

30. Ibid., p. 412, table 18-1.

31. Fred W. Riggs, *Thailand: The Modernization of a Bureaucratic Polity* (Honolulu: East-West Center Press, 1966), p. 246.

32. Shor, "Public Service," pp. 31-32.

33. Thailand Central Statistical Office *Household Expenditure 1962-63* (Bangkok: Government of Thailand, 1964), p. 81; see also p. 82 for similar figures derived from a sample of five hundred families in Rangoon, see Tominaga et al., "Modernization," p. 19.

34. *Household Expenditure*, pp. 81-82.

35. Silcock, "Promotion of Industry and the Planning Process," in Silcock, *Thailand*, pp. 264-267, tables 11-1, 11-2.

36. For more information on average monthly income in various firms in Bangkok, see

Thailand Department of Labor, *Year Book of Labor Statistics* (Bangkok: Government of Thailand, 1965).

37. *Far Eastern Economic Review 1966 Year Book* (Hong Kong: Far Eastern Economic Review, 1967), p. 330.

38. Evers and Silcock, "Elites and Selection," in Silcock, *Thailand*, pp. 91-97.

39. Phillips Cutright, "Inequality: A Cross-National Analysis," *American Sociological Review*, XXXII, no. 4 (August 1967), p. 477.

40. Mosel, "Thai Administrative Behavior," p. 306.

41. For internal distribution in one of the quarters of Bangkok, see Skinner, *Chinese Society*, p. 361, table 21.

42. William J. Siffin, *The Thai Bureaucracy: Institutional Change and Development* (Honolulu: East-West Center Press, 1966), pp. 151-152. All teachers—including faculty members of universities—are included in the category of officials. Although the middle class is in the process of development, its scope is still very limited.

43. Ibid., p. 158.

44. Evers, "The Formation of a Social Class Structure: Urbanization, Bureaucratization and Social Mobility in Thailand," *American Sociological Review*, XXXI, no. 4 (August 1966), p. 483.

45. For status consistency and its relevance to the analysis of the problem considered here, see "Status Crystallization: A Non-Vertical Dimension of Social Status," Gerhard E. Lenski, *American Sociological Review*, XIX, no. 4 (August 1954), pp. 405-412. I. W. Goffman, "Status Consistency and Preference for Change in Power Distribution," *American Sociological Review*, XXII, no. 3 (June 1957), pp. 275-281. G. E. Lenski, *Power and Privilege* (New York: McGraw-Hill, 1966), chs. 8, 9; Johan Galtung, "Rank and Social Integration: A Multidimensional Approach," *Sociological Theories in Progress*, eds. J. Berger, M. Zelditch, Jr., and B. Anderson (Boston: Houghton Mifflin, 1966), pp. 145-199.

46. Mosel, "Thai Administrative Behavior," pp. 306-307. Scott distinguishes between two types of bureaucrats who translate power into wealth. "Bureaucratic capitalists" are "those who take direct advantage of legal monopolies, state subsidies or quotas, and government contracts to amass private fortunes." The "bureaucratic extortionists" are those who "may simply exploit commercial elite by systematically extorting benefits from it and selling protection." See J. C. Scott, *Comparative Political Corruption* (Englewood Cliffs, N.J.: Prentice-Hall, 1972), p. 69.

47. Wilson, *Politics*, pp. 60-61; Blanchard, *Thailand*, p. 408.

48. Skinner, *Chinese Society*, p. 306.

49. See Wilson, *Politics*, p. 65; F. W. Riggs, *The Ecology of Public Administration* (New Delhi: Asia Publishing House, 1961), p. 123.

50. Mosel, "Thai Administrative Behavior," p. 306.

51. See Blanchard, *Thailand*, p. 410; Harris et al., *Area Handbook*, p. 101.

52. Mosel, "Thai Administrative Behavior," pp. 305-306.

53. For example, Skinner, *Chinese Society*.

54. W. G. Skinner, "Chinese Assimilation and Thai Politics," *Journal of Asian Studies*, XVI, no. 2 (February 1957), pp. 237-238.

55. Ibid., pp. 238-239.

56. See Coughlin, *Double Identity*, pp. 127-143.

57. Wilson, *Politics*, pp. 116-120.

58. Skinner, *Chinese Society*, pp. 351-353.

59. G. W. Skinner, *Leadership and Power in the Chinese Community of Thailand* (Ithaca, N.Y.: Cornell University Press, 1959), p. 80.

60. See also Coughlin, "The Chinese in Bangkok," *American Sociological Review*, XX, no. 3 (June 1955), pp. 314-315.

61. Skinner, "Leadership," p. 80.
62. See Blanchard, *Thailand*, pp. 217-218; and Harris et al., *Area Handbook*, pp. 105-106.
63. Skinner, *Chinese Society*, p. 299.
64. Hanks, "Merit and Power," p. 252; Evers, "Formation," p. 47; A. Thomas Kirsch, "Loose Structure: Theory or Description," pp. 52-53; and J. A. Niels Mulder, "Origin, Development and Use of the Concept of 'Loose Structure' in the Literature about Thailand: An Evaluation," pp. 19-20, both in Evers, *Loosely Structured Systems*.
65. For arguments against Thailand as a mobile society, see Evers and Silcock, "Elites and Selection," pp. 87-88. In a comparative study based on quantitative indicators, Thailand was placed in category 2 (out of 3 categories), whose characteristics were defined as "fairly limited social mobility as indicated by school enrollment ratios of less than 40% but more than 25% and by the fact that middle-class occupations formed only 5-10% of the active male population." See Irma Adelman and Cynthia T. Morris, *Society, Politics, and Economic Development: A Quantitative Approach* (Baltimore: Johns Hopkins University Press, 1967), p. 35. Tominaga states that intergenerational occupational mobility cannot be considered small; however, the distance of occupational mobility is short. "We conclude that opportunities for mobility are very scarce from whatever angle one cares to investigate and that accordingly Bangkok is a closed society" (Tominaga et al., "Modernization," part II, p. 9).
66. Siffin, *Thai Bureaucracy*, pp. 244-245.
67. Evers and Silcock, "Elites and Selection," pp. 90-91.
68. Part of the oppositional elite is indeed recruited from the more educated who, for various reasons, are dissatisfied with their own mobility. About the rigid selectivity of the universities, see Joseph Fischer, *Universities in Southeast Asia* (Columbus: Ohio State University Press, 1964), p. 95. One should also mention in this context the possibilities for mobility offered to village boys within the comprehensive Buddhist educational system. The talented boys may enter Buddhist universities and even study secular sciences. See S. J. Tambiah, "The Persistence and Transformation of Tradition in Southeast Asia, with Special Reference to Thailand," *Daedalus* (Winter 1973), pp. 74-76.
69. Wilson, *Politics*, pp. 61-64.
70. Mosel, "Thai Administrative Behavior," pp. 305-306. One should consider this trend as a component of the background to the growing militancy of the students since the beginning of the 1970s.
71. Evers, "Formation," p. 488.
72. Evers and Silcock, "Elites and Selection," pp. 85-87; Harris et al., *Area Handbook*, p. 97; Hanks, "Merit and Power," pp. 1250-1251.
73. One can certainly find reverse processes—the conversion of economic power into political-administrative power. This, however, mainly involves Thais and not Chinese. See Evers and Silcock, "Elites and Selection," pp. 94-95.
74. About geographical mobility, see Wilson, *Politics*, pp. 48-49; and Harris et al., *Area Handbook*, pp. 46-47.
75. Evers, "Models of Social Systems: Loosely and Tightly Structured," in Evers, *Loosely Structured Systems*, p. 124.
76. Hanks, "Merit and Power," pp. 1247-1249. The traditional-religious interpretation of the individual status and his achievements also has a significant social aspect. See Blanchard, *Thailand*, pp. 45-48, 51-52.
77. Evers, "Formation," p. 482.
78. Boonsanong Punyodyana, "Social Structure, Social System, and Two Levels of Analysis," in Evers, *Loosely Structured Systems*, pp. 99-102. See also Evers, ibid., p. 124;

Fischer, *Universities,* pp. 95-96; Skinner, *Chinese Society,* p. 305; Coughlin, *Double Identity,* pp. 124-129; Tominaga et al., "Modernization."

79. Hanks, "Merit and Power," pp. 1254-1255.

80. Riggs, *Thailand,* pp. 250-254; Coughlin, *Double Identity,* p. 124.

81. About formal associations, see Blanchard, *Thailand,* pp. 300-301.

82. H. P. Phillips, "Relationships between Personality and Social Structure in a Siamese Peasant Community," *Human Organization,* XXII, no. 2 (1963), p. 106.

83. For class consciousness among farmers, see Punyodyana, "Social Structure," pp. 89-93.

84. Compare Coughlin, "The Chinese in Bangkok," p. 312, and Skinner, *Chinese Society,* pp. 310-322. See also Riggs, *Ecology,* pp. 21-22.

85. Mosel, "Thai Administrative Behavior," p. 309; Wilson, *Politics,* pp. 53-54.

86. Phillips, cited in Wilson, *Politics,* p. 53.

87. G. Wijeyewardene, "Some Aspects of Rural Life in Thailand," in Silcock, *Thailand,* pp. 69-71; see also Steven Piker, " 'Loose Structure' and the Analysis of Thai Social Organization," in Evers, *Loosely Structured Systems,* pp. 62-65.

88. Blanchard, *Thailand,* p. 399.

89. Harris et al., *Area Handbook,* pp. 111-113; H. K. Kaufman, *Bangkhuad: A Community Study in Thailand* (Ithaca, N.Y.: Monograph of the Association for Asian Studies, Cornell University Press, 1960), pp. 31-36.

90. M. Moerman, "Ban Ping's Temple: The Center of a 'Loosely Structured' Society," in *Anthropological Studies in Theravada Buddhism,* ed. M. Nash (New Haven: Yale University Press, 1966), p. 153.

91. The average size of peasant holdings varies from 6.2 *rai* to 40.0 *rai* in the different provinces. See Wijeyewardene, "Some Aspects," tables 3-6 and 3-7. See also Blanchard, *Thailand,* pp. 305-306.

92. Blanchard, *Thailand,* p. 75.

93. E. L. Fogg, "Labor Organizations in Thailand," *Industrial and Labor Relations Review,* VI, no. 3 (April 1953), pp. 368-377.

94. Blanchard, *Thailand,* p. 403; Moerman, "Ban Ping's Temple," pp. 155-157. It has been the custom in the villages to move alternately from the status of a monk to "normal" status. Half the peasants have stayed some time in their lives in a Buddhist monastery. See Mosel, "Thai Administrative Behavior," p. 304. The status of the Buddhist monk is not the same in all the provinces of Thailand; it is much lower in the northern provinces (see Moerman, "Ban Ping's Temple," pp. 143-147).

95. Formally, the headman is elected by the village members. As a matter of fact, he is nominated by his predecessor and the representatives of the local governor. The headman represents the lowest echelon in the administrative hierarchy. His monthly salary is about $3.00.

96. S. Piker, "Sources of Stability and Instability in Rural Thai Society," *Journal of Asian Studies,* XXVI, no. 4 (August 1968), pp. 788-789.

Chapter 5

BURMA: POLITICAL BREAKDOWN AND MILITARY EXPERIMENTATION WITH ROLE EXPANSION

PART I. THE POLITICAL SETUP

A. The Constitutional Framework

Burma started as an independent polity in 1947 after an intensive political and armed struggle against the British colonial regime and the Japanese occupation forces.[1] From the first, Burma confronted severe internal problems. The political elite had to formulate its ideological credo while being challenged by the almost complete destruction of the country's economic infrastructure and by large-scale guerrilla warfare initiated by the Communists and various ethnic and religious minorities.

The constitution of 1948 was formulated to provide some normative and operational solutions for the political, military, and economic chaos which confronted Burma in 1947-48. The intricacy of the political situation was reflected in the constitution.

It demonstrated the firm resolve to establish a working democratic constitutional framework while responding to the demands of ethnic and religious minorities for direct and more particular representation. The constitution stated that Burma was to have a parliamentary regime. The head of state—the president—had very limited responsibility and authority. One of his main functions was to nominate the prime minister, who would then choose his cabinet.[2] The legislature comprised two houses (or chambers):

1. The Chamber of Deputies (125 in number), to which the cabinet was accountable.
2. The Chamber of Nationalities, with 250 deputies. The deputies in the Chamber of Nationalities were elected on the basis of a fixed (but unequal) quota stipulated for each of the constituent states and for the Burmese

themselves. This reflected the pseudofederal structure of Burma—in which, according to the 1948 constitution, the Union of Burma was to be composed of Burma proper and five constituent states.[3] The heads of these states were both members of the union's cabinet and in charge of the affairs of their states (they could assume other portfolios as well). Each state had a certain (but unequal) autonomy, especially in social services and education. The relationship between the minorities and the central government and, more particularly, the desire to change the constitution in order to achieve more autonomy were among the causes of the military coup d'etat of March 1962.

The normative contents of the constitution showed not only a commitment to a democratic framework but the explicit intention to combine a liberal outlook with moderate socialism. The liberal dimension was expressed by the constitution's commitment to safeguard individual civil rights, individual property rights, and private economic enterprise as long as they did not interfere with the general interest of the public. The socialistic orientation was expressed, inter alia, in the explicit preference given to central economic planning and to nonprofit organizations like cooperatives. The constitution, moreover, stated that all land should be nationalized. In declaring that Burma was to be a secular state, the constitution guaranteed freedom of religious belief. No particular status was given to Buddhism, although its special place in the history of Burma and its contributions to the crystallization of Burma as a nation were emphasized.

The intellectual struggle to synthesize Buddhism and secular political philosophies had begun in the 1920s, if not earlier. The Burmese were compelled to do so, since the nationalistic movement was interwoven with Buddhism as a nationalistic organization (rather than as an internal reform movement).[4] Colonial rule had almost totally destroyed the organizational framework of Buddhism.[5] The effort to rebuild it naturally involved anti-British feelings with nationalistic overtones. If the institutional and ideological identity of the Buddhist renaissance and the national movement had been sustained, the question of combining secular-political concepts and Buddhism would probably not have emerged as a burning issue. However, since the leading role in the struggle against colonial rule was eventually taken over by an elite which defined itself as "secular," it was necessary to seek a principle and a tactical answer concerning the discrepancy between the ideological identity of the elite and the profound religious outlook of the population. The question was thus a problem of calculating the most efficient way to establish a popular base for the political movement and finding principles concerning the cultural character of an independent Burma.

While the British ruled Burma, the urgency of this was not recognized. The emerging national elite was not confronted with an integrated centralistic religious organization, so they could elude the problem. Moreover, the builders of the secular national movement had the advantage of offering their followers a new framework with a comprehensive social mission. Buddhism, or at least Theravada Buddhism (in contrast to Islam and Christianity), always lacked consciousness of social mission and proselytizing fervor, since the question of the *individual's* destiny—the individual who desires to escape from the constant cycle of rebirth in this or other worlds, in human or nonhuman form—is a central concept of Buddhist teaching.

To survey the reasons that the young national elite in Burma were drawn to socialism would be to reiterate, with slight variations, the dramatic story of most of the intellectual elites in the third world. Basically, they turned to socialism in an emotional reaction to the abuses of colonialism and its capitalistic economy. When this reaction engendered embryonic political organizations, socialistic slogans were adopted. These slogans both stated the evils of the colonial regime and mobilized the social classes which had been most harassed by the colonial government. Lenin's characterization of "imperialism as the higher stage of capitalism" was the most favored of the many Marxist ideas. The Burmese were enchanted with it, not only because of its alleged diagnostic power, but also because it convinced them of the inevitability of imperialism's becoming merely a historical episode in the not too remote future. The Russian Revolution, the People's Fronts of the 1930s, only strengthened belief in the rosy future that the radical leftist movement promised the entire world. However, the young political elite (as other elites) did not evolve a comprehensive and systematic conceptual framework on the nature of socialism. Such a theory never has been defined, mainly because of internal hesitations regarding the relationship between Marxism (or other variations of socialism) and Buddhism. The total denial of religion did not solve the problem (the antireligious period was in fact very short).[6] Another reason for the unsophisticated conceptual framework was probably, as Myrdal suggests, the lack in Burma of human resources equivalent to the prominent European intelligentsia who, for several decades, studied, argued, and quibbled about all the philosophical, political, and economic aspects of socialism.[7] Moreover, socialism's appeal derived from the search for an ideological framework which could effect a consensus centered around the anticolonial struggle. In other words, the focus was on the political aspects of socialism—on methods of party organization and mass mobilization, rather than on problems of realization of abstract social and economic concepts.

The conceptualization of socialist principles in Burma changed several times after it was first adopted by the Thakins in the 1930s. In the 1950s the ruling party, under the influence of U Nu, adopted a sort of socialism that was "somewhat in line with the British welfare state model with the addition of large scale nationalization and the cooperative movement. From the standpoint of culture, this choice reflected a philosophy of the golden means, of the middle path which was deeply rooted in U Nu and other nationalist leaders."[8] The mild character of U Nu's socialism was reflected in the constitution itself, where Burma was never explicitly defined as a socialist state.[9] Moreover, in contrast with former attempts to synthesize two different philosophies or to practice Marxist (or social democratic) concepts with the help of Buddhistic terminology, U Nu now made Buddhist philosophy a starting point. He emphasized its originality and its ability to serve as a guide for peace, harmony, and social justice in society. He tried to present Buddhism not only as morally superior to Marxism but as more adequate to the modern world and to the progress of science and technology.[10] This ideological transformation, reaching its peak with the establishment of Buddhism as the state religion after the 1960 election, did not unify Burmese leadership. It alienated still further the underground and legal Marxist groups. It annoyed the officer corps and satisfied neither the lay antisocialist Buddhist groups nor the monks—much less the non-Buddhist minority groups. These last interpreted the new policy as an additional step in "Burmazation" and the abolishment of their autonomy. The issue of cultural and social identity in Burma was thus linked to another fundamental issue: loyalty to the national framework and the sovereignty of the central government. The lack of consensus on these questions was revealed in Burma's complex constitution and in the armed insurgence of ethnic groups.[11]

B. Political Parties and Political Organizations

Three kinds of groups participated in the political process in Burma: (a) political parties and other political organizations, including organizations established by minorities and underground groups; (b) pressure groups to which an opportunity for direct and overt political action was granted officially or unofficially; and (c) pressure groups formally barred by the constitution from political activities which nevertheless chose to be active. During the early period they worked mainly through indirect channels.

Any discussion of parties in Burma must first clarify the nature of the Anti-Fascists People's Freedom League (AFPFL—in Burmese, *PASABALA*). The AFPFL was established in 1944 as the result of Aung San's efforts to unite (or at least to gather) political organizations—excluding some small right-wing and pro-Japanese groups—under one roof.[12] From the first, it was a shaky coalition composed of subcenters of political power that had already attained a certain amount of control over autonomous power resources. The main partners in this coalition were the Socialist Party and the Communist Party—both newly established as formal parties, although their leaders and adherents were veterans on the political scene. The third partner was the People's Voluntary Organization (PVO), a military-political body under Aung San's leadership. This was the latest variation of the defunct Burmese armed forces who had formerly been under Japanese control.

The advantage of the coalition was its nationwide basis. Its great disadvantage, however, was the heterogeneity which, from the beginning, caused disagreement on basic issues and means of action. This situation improved slightly after several withdrawals from the AFPFL in the late 1940s and early 1950s.[13] The league became more ideologically homogeneous after the departure of the extreme left factions. It was thus able to promote, at least temporarily, a consensus on more general targets and means of attaining them.

According to its constitution, the AFPFL was to have two sorts of members or, more specifically, there were two ways it could be joined. The individual could join personally and directly through one of the local party cells, or he could join one of four affiliated associations: (1) the Trade Union Congress of Burma (RUCB); (2) the All Burma Peasant Organization (ABPO); (3) the Federation of Trade Organizations (FT); and (4) the Women's Freedom League (WFL). These bodies had been established by the Socialist Party and were an important asset. Also affiliated with the AFPFL were political organizations formed by ethnic minorities.[14] These were the league's power bases and their support of it gave it a great advantage in its struggle with opposition parties. The strength of the organizations was demonstrated by their quantitative contribution to the league.[15]

Because of its impressive scope of political mobilization (both in terms of quantity and in terms of the main functional groups in the country), as reflected in its success in two elections, the AFPFL was, many felt, the sole non-Communist party in southeast Asia with a strong apparatus on the national and on the local levels. In reality, the league was divided. Its internal conflict stemmed from a combination of ideological policy conflicts and personal frictions. Although the ideological agitation was apparently very great, ideology per se rarely served as a basis for sectional affiliation or loyalty for the rank and file of members. There is much evidence that personal loyalty to heads of opposing sections was the most frequent criterion for assessing the internal balance of power. The formulation of ideologies often only provided a rationalization for the personal animosity of the leaders. And indeed, the league's history between 1948 and 1962 is one of ceaseless crises and internal rifts despite electoral victories.[16] The disputes centered around various issues. The chief ones were (a) internal policy and Burma's cultural and ideological identity, or the problem of a synthesis between socialism and Buddhism; and (b) the definition of national unity together with the means to implement socialism in Burma.

The political center collapsed first from within. The opposition parties, because of their smallness and their internal cleavages, played only a marginal role. There were at least four types of opposition groups in Burma until 1962. The first may be defined as the broadly based opposition parties. Actually, only one party fits this description—the Burma Workers and Peasants Party (BWPP), a

Marxist party established in 1950 after the socialist left wing had seceded from the AFPFL because of disagreement in the government's policy toward the Korean War. Its power was drawn mainly from the urban sector. The BWPP was for many years suspected of being a front for the Burmese Community Party, which had gone underground in 1949.[17]

The "personalistic" parties were the second type of opposition group. They resembled political cliques clustered around one central figure. Rightist opposition parties, such as the Burma Democratic Party (BDP) and the Justice Party, are examples.

The third type comprised ethnic organizations. Their declared policy was to achieve optimum autonomy for their constituent states or even the establishment of sovereign states. Perhaps the most important was the Arakan National United Organization.[18]

The last type was the ad hoc alignment of opposition parties aiming to defeat the AFPFL in elections. Two were formed for the election of 1956.[19]

The various underground organizations included types very similar to those outlined in connection with the opposition camps.[20] For example, in the category of the broader and more universalistic organizations, there were the two Communist factions. One was the Red Flag, headed by Thakin Soe, which went underground in 1946. This smaller faction was considered the more extreme of the Communist parties. The second was the White Flag, which went underground in 1947. This faction, then headed by Thakin Than Tun, was considered more moderate. In the 1950s, it had good relations with the Soviet Communist and the Indian Communist parties, and later also with China. Thakin Soe and his faction were always more isolated in terms of organizational and ideological connections.[21]

Aside from these rebellious groups, there were underground organizations based on ethnic solidarity. The most famous was the Karen National Defense Organization (KNDO).[22] Loose alliances were sometimes formed between the ethnic insurrectionists and the Communists. An additional factor undermining political authority in the early 1950s came from the remnants of the Chinese National Army (KMT), on the one hand, and dacoits, on the other. All these divisions within the opposition groups saved U Nu's government from the total collapse of which it had been in danger since the early 1950s.

We have stressed the heterogeneous character of the AFPFL and the fact that it was composed of different functional groups. Although these groups were formerly a part of the league, they must be regarded primarily as pressure groups or groups with options for separate (or parallel) political activities. One example is the All Burma Peasants Organization, which was supposed to represent the economic interests of the major segment of the Burmese population. Since the beginning of this century, the peasants' main grievance has been the lack of adequate agricultural credit. Indebtedness caused by the peasants' eviction from their lands was concurrent with the emergence of hired laborers. With the collapse of the credit system which had operated during the British rule, mainly through *Chettyars,* the ABPO became the central mediator among the peasants, the government, and the party. Since then, the ABPO has been the backbone of the Socialist Party and later of the AFPFL. No opposition party has ever succeeded in forming a viable rival body. The ABPO's broker activity was relfected in the peasants' exchange of political support for inexpensive—although insufficient—credit.[23] Because of their control of manpower and financial resources, ABPO leaders probably held the strongest power position within the league.[24] However, the strength of this organization did not reflect a political alertness and activism on the part of the peasantry. The focus of power lay in the hands of those who manipulated the ABPO bureaucracy.

In many ways, there were similarities with the trade unions, with the important difference that the latter were far less unified than the ABPO. Their lack of cohesion is best exemplified by the many types of trade unions, both in terms of their legal rights and of their political affiliations.[25] In addition to administrative and functional divisions, the trade unions were hampered by political subdivisions. As a matter of fact, the trade unions (their first national organization, ABTUC, was established by the Thakins in 1940), were initially established as well-defined political bodies by Marxist-oriented leaders. Small wonder that, throughout this period, parties and trade unions were inextricably linked and directly affected by splits within the ruling party. On the eve of the military coup in 1962, all three main leftist parties had their own trade unions.[26]

Between 1948 and 1960, the Burmese trade unions suffered from lack of experience and lack of central organization, and internal splits resulted in divided loyalties. Their "natural" rival—the employers—were much less organized. Although there were already some national, industrial, commercial, and trade organizations whose membership was composed of private employers,[27] none, except perhaps the All Burma Rice Industrialists Association, was an employers' organization. None had attempted to formulate or enunciate a policy defining the employer's stance toward the trade unions or had acted on behalf of its members in collective bargaining. The fact that a substantial number of employers were non-Burmese—i.e., Europeans, Indians, and Chinese—repeatedly relegated them to a position of self-defense and a struggle for survival. They were thus kept effectively from becoming a focus of independent political and economic power, although it is doubtful whether they ever seriously considered seeking such power.

C. Pressure Groups: Students and Intelligentsia

Throughout this period, the peasants' organizations and the trade unions were formally and actually integral parts of the Burmese political order. It would, however, be unforgivable to describe the political events and the Burmese political system without referring to those organizations and associations which pursued direct political activities as a result of their own choice of procedures and objectives rather than because of particular or inevitable circumstances such as those presented by the peasants' organizations, trade unions, and employers' associations. Noteworthy examples are the student organizations and the intelligentsia.

Since its founding, the University of Rangoon has been the focus of demonstrations, strikes, protests, political and ideological ferment. However, until the 1930s these activities did not have any direct political significance, and political agitation per se was sporadic and unorganized.[28] Even after the Rangoon University Student Union was established, it remained a sort of debating club comparable to those of Oxford and Cambridge until 1935. In 1936, when the union was taken over by a small group of socialist and Marxist students, it became a militant political organization. In the subsequent four years, it became the spearhead of the national movement, and its leaders later became a part of Burma's civilian and military elites.[29]

Rifts in the ruling party after independence intensified the political enthusiasm of the students, who were courted by various political factions eager to control this important group.[30] The number of students had tripled following the reductions in tuition and in qualifications for eligibility. But the increase in students resulted in overcrowded classes and in higher failure rates. The University of Rangoon, like other institutions, became the home of thousands of students of whom only the most gifted found adequate and/or prestigious jobs. The gap between potential rewards and academic title grew ever wider. All this strengthened the extremely left leanings of the more activist elements—no more than 2% of the student population.[31] In contrast to the pressure groups active within the framework of the establishment (such as the peasants' organizations and most trade unions), the students became a rich source of cadres for both legal and illegal opposition parties.

Expressions of public and political action by the Burmese intelligentsia can be examined further through the press. The overall circulation of newspapers was very low;[32] newspapers nevertheless varied in outlook and content.[33] A content analysis of press writings up until the military regime indicates that, in the absence of real vocal opposition (at least until 1956), the newspapers and the Journalists Association actually fulfilled most of the functions of a parliamentary opposition and contributed to the pseudodemocratic character of U Nu's Burma. Without a more or less free press, the de facto existence of a one-party system would have been far more conspicuous.[34]

D. Pressure Groups: The Pongyis

Those organizations which found their path to political activity blocked by the constitution must also be considered in any valid modern history of Burma. The pongyis and the military are two examples.

Mehden has suggested that the history of Buddhist involvement in politics (until 1962) be divided into five main stages.[35] The first three involve the pre-independence period and will be very briefly considered here.

The first major period is that of the Burmese kings, including the time of political and military confrontation between the royal court and British imperialism. One characteristic, until the end of the nineteenth century, was what may be termed as "symbiosis" between the royal court and Buddhist religious institutions. The king was a bodhisattva—a future Buddha. Moreover, as the protector of the faith, the king was responsible for the sangha and controlled it through naming and suppressing all heretic and schismatic elements. In this capacity, the kings at times would clash with the sangha. According to the Vinaya, monks were expected to eschew all interest in mundane political activities and devote themselves exclusively to religion. However, the monks, both as individuals and as a collective body, were invariably involved in politics as judges or as consultants to governors and kings. Nevertheless, one can accept Smith's general conclusion that the kings' interference in religion was far more conspicuous and important than the sangha's involvement in political affairs.[36]

The second period, roughly 1900 to 1930, may be described as a time of partnership, if not identity, between the nationalistic movement and Buddhism. The previous stage had ended in severe crises for the sangha, because of the colonial regime's deliberate policy of breaking the sangha hierarchy and annihilating it as an independent center of power. The dominant role played by monks and laymen in organizing the first national movement was definitely a reaction, albeit a belated one, to such British policy. The Buddhist circles established the Young Men's Buddhist Association (**YMBA**) in 1906, and its successor, the General Council of Burmese Associations (**GCBA**), in 1920. Activists in these organizations were, however, laymen recruited from the minute Westernized middle class. The sanghas did not commit themselves to the Buddhist nationalistic infant organization, which perceived religion as a foundation stone and a focus for recruitment against the destructive influence of Christian Western culture. At this stage that organization, in terms of ideological articulation and organizational techniques, was still far from the mass political movements that were later to emerge. The sangha bore the imprint of personalistic and amateurish groups and (in the 1930s) could not compete with the young elite who were applying new concepts of political organization drawn mainly from Marxist doctrine.

The third period is distinguished by an almost total withdrawal of Buddhist groups from any direct political activity. The conservatives, and the pongyis in particular, vacated their positions of power.[37] They were replaced by the Thakins who, until the military regime (and actually even to this day), held key positions in the government and the military. The nonreligious, perhaps even antireligious, phase of the national movement lasted only for about a year or two after Burma had gained independence. Buddhism as an organization, and monks as individuals, had nonetheless entered a new epoch in their relationship with the political authorities.

The fourth stage began with independence. Burma adopted a secular constitution in which Buddhism was not granted any privileged official standing. Moreover, the constitution failed to define clearly its position with respect to the separation between state and church, and the government was inclined to interfere quite actively in clerical affairs. The interference was initiated primarily by U Nu, whose proclaimed intention was to exalt and extol Buddhism. U Nu tried to prevent the sangha from interfering in political decision making and from expressing any opinion on routine issues of state. On the other hand, he pledged to make Buddhism the state religion. Whether he chose to do this from purely opportunistic motives or whether he was compelled to do so because he was a devoted Buddhist is an open question. In any event, it caused the sangha to indulge in direct political activities, especially after independence. The religious elite's renewed interest in political activity was, however, far more the result of external pressure than of internal circumstances.[38]

The fifth stage began after the 1960 election, in which U Nu's party gained a sweeping victory, winning more than 60% of all parliamentary seats. In the following year, U Nu fulfilled his campaign promise to make Buddhism the state religion.[39] Although this period lasted less than two years and was abruptly ended by the military coup, it lasted long enough to heighten even more the political fervor among the ethnic and religious minorities and among the more extreme groups of the sangha—still dissatisfied, despite the high prestige of Buddhism as the official religion and the concessions to the minorities.[40]

In sum, the sangha, as a collective body, rarely assumed permanent institutionalized political roles in the history of Burma. The monks' actual participation was greatly disproportionate to any potential pressures they could have exerted. U Nu's personality and his religious policies certainly neutralized the monks' role in politics to as great an extent as the moral prohibition on mundane activism that is given in Buddhist teachings.

Other types of groups or organizations prohibited from direct political action by the constitution were the military and the civilian bureaucracies. These are perhaps even more relevant, since restrictions on sangha activists were hardly comprehensive. Despite the constitution, the military became a central political factor at the end of the 1950s. As far as the civilian bureaucracy is concerned, the picture is less clear.

Burma's Political Breakdown

To understand the decision-making process properly, one must note the sharp conflict between politicians and administrators.[41] This conflict was not only between two disciplines of thought but also between two different status groups. The politicians were upwardly mobile and intoxicated with their achievements in the struggle for independence. The administrators were frustrated and disappointed by the loss of the relatively prestigious positions which they had achieved under British rule and immediately after independence.[42] On the other hand, the administrators never appeared to the public as an autonomous pressure group, nor did they ever endeavor to enlist public support. Their power thus derived from their control of important key positions and their ability to manipulate the law for their own ends rather than apply it according to its more manifest or literal content. Yet even on this level, there was no evidence of any organized opposition or of any collective planning by the more senior bureaucrats. Their actions were basically unsystematic and uncoordinated, but they nevertheless had an impact on government activities.[43]

E. The Range and Intensity of Political Action

Thus far, we have considered what may be called the formal and static aspects of the political framework in Burma. Let us finish with some remarks about the more dynamic aspects, reflected in the efforts of the political center, until 1962, to control and regulate the social, economic, and political processes within Burma. What best characterizes Burma in this respect is perhaps the great gulf between the political elite's expectations and their actual achievements in incorporating (within the framework of the legitimate responsibilities of the political authorities) a *maximum* number of functions and roles. In practice, the scope of control and regulation by the elite was far more restricted than one would expect, while the implementation of plans involved far greater manipulation of political and naked power than anticipated. The result was overpoliticization of many sectors and the failure of a large number of programs owing to the use of force. Some examples will illustrate the effects of this discrepancy between aspiration and achievement.

The weakness of the last Burmese kings and the deliberate policy of the British long delayed the process of Burmazation of ethnic and religious minorities. Different minorities gained important concessions from the constitution, which promised them a certain autonomy.[44] The government was formally committed to those clauses in the constitution outlining a degree of freedom for these minorities in regulating their own affairs. However, it tried to corrode, by both formal and informal means, this "independence," thereby contradicting the spirit of the agreement in order to accelerate the pace of Burmazation.[45] The Burmese government was not, however, very consistent in its policies toward the minorities, partly because of governmental inefficiency and partly because of the hostile reactions of the minorities themselves—they occasionally resorted to insurrection and violence.

Economic policies and their implementation provide an additional, although less unequivocal, example. The programs formulated by the *Pyidautha* Conference in 1952, as well as others on other occasions, endorsed the nationalization of land and the promotion of a nationalized economic sector. In practice, these plans were altered several times, partly because of administrative inefficiency and partly because of violent resistance by various interest groups.[46] In many cases, considerations behind programs were purely political—for example, the ousting of Indians and Chinese from key positions in import and export trade. Because political manipulation was furthering the political interests of certain groups, progress in nationalization had been only partly realized by 1962.

Another significant manifestation of the government's ambition to extend its sphere of influence and control over the entire Burmese society was its interference in religious affairs. The authorities wanted to introduce order in the almost anarchic structure of the sangha and to improve the sangha's level of scholastic achievement. Indirectly—and according to many observers[47] more important—the objective was to strengthen the government's political power by increasing the identity between the political authorities and Buddhism. A special Ministry for Religious Affairs was established to initiate legislative measures. Among the most important laws were the ones calling for the establishment of a hierarchy of ecclesiastical courts whose main function was to improve monastic discipline, and the law compelling the pongyis to pass certain examinations before being promoted.[48] A special Buddhist university was established to improve the monks' education—which was at its lowest level ever. The supreme efforts to promote Buddhism came with the sixth Great Buddhist Council in 1956 and with the proclamation of Buddhism as the state religion in 1961.[49]

In the first decade following independence, the Burmese leaders were full of good intentions about firmly grounded democratic principles and politics. They tried earnestly to find an optimum position among numerous spheres controlled by the center, using only a minimal amount of power in order to reduce the intensity (but not the scope) of political activity. In practice, things worked out very differently. Violence predominated, there were political arrests and political murders, and private armies became an institutional fact.[50]

PART II. THE MILITARY—INNOVATIONS AND FRUSTRATIONS

A. A Short History of the Burmese Military

The Burmese army originated in the Burma Independence Army (BIA) raised by General Aung San in 1941-42 for a revolt against the British.[51] Before independence, there had been only a few battalions, composed mainly of Karens, Kachins, Chins, and some Burmans. The nucleus of the BIA consisted of thirty men known as the "Thirty Comrades." Almost all of them were students who belonged to the movement founded by Aung San and U Nu that later became a part of the "Tankins," an anti-British, nationalistic, leftist political group. Under the Japanese authorities, the BIA was expanded to include between 20,000 and 30,000 men. It participated in some of the battles launched by the Japanese against the British.[52] By 1944, the relations between the Burmese government established by the Japanese and the Japanese army had drastically deteriorated. The resistance movement, this time against the Japanese, was born, led again by Aung San, who was the defense minister in the Japanese-sponsored Burmese government.

However, at the end of World War II, Aung San's resistance movement was only one of many armed groups in Burma. There were also the Burmese forces which had returned from India with the British army and were mostly remnants of the colonial Burmese battalions. These two forces at first united. However, since many of the British Burmese forces were drawn from minority groups —especially Karens, who were opposed to Burmese nationalism—many deserted the new army and joined their tribesmen, who had already rebelled against the newborn state. In addition, there were two groups of Communist rebels—the Red Flags and the White Flags—as well as the People's Volunteer Organization (PVO), a left-wing oriented militia organized immediately after independence, some of whose men refused to be disarmed.[53]

Despite their brief existence under the Japanese, the BIA and the BNA not only laid the foundation for the post-independence Burmese army but also greatly molded the political structure and party setup of independent Burma.

A second factor which eventually had a tremendous impact on the political system was the vital need to establish a relatively large and strong army, because of the necessity of crushing the various insurgents who, in the first months of independence, controlled de facto almost all of Burma except Rangoon and its vicinity.[54] In 1947, the Burmese army consisted of six regular battalions, fifteen military police battalions, and some thousands of irregulars. The strength of the armed forces has been increasing steadily since. By 1960, the army was up to 25,000; the navy, over 3,000; and the air force, activated in 1953, 3,000. In the late 1960s, the total number was 120,000.[55] The army's combat experience, although limited in scope, was considerable. Some of the enlisted men and many officers had long experience in guerrilla warfare against the British and the Japanese. After independence, the fighting against the insurgents was mainly guerrilla warfare. The basic combat units frequently were the battalion or the company. Hence opportunities to develop tactical and logistic deployment of larger units were quite limited.

The degree and direction of professionalization of the Burmese army were determined by the type of enemy, their strength and tactics, and actual combat experience. They were, of course, also dependent on the kind of manpower put at the army's disposal. Unlike many other ex-colonies, Burma's army and political leaders decided not to use foreign officers in command posts. The British officers were deposed immediately after independence, although a British military mission remained and Burmese officers continued to be sent to Britain for higher training after graduating from the Defence Services Academy. With the British officers deposed, wonderful opportunities opened to the Burmese noncommissioned officers and officers for promotion. However, this situation seems to some extent to have curbed the progress of professionalization. For example, in the first years after independence, a great shortage of officers and NCOs led the military to recruit many students who were actually politically nominated.[56]

On 3 March 1959, the People's Militia Act was passed, prescribing compulsory military service for periods ranging from six to twenty-four months for every man between the ages of eighteen and forty-six; every woman between the ages of eighteen and thirty-six; and every doctor, engineer, or teacher between the ages of eighteen and fifty-six. In fact, this act was never implemented. The armed forces were maintained entirely on a volunteer basis, except for the conscription of a few needed doctors. Terms of enlistment ranged from four to six years, with a commitment to remain in inactive reserve status for a specified period on termination of enlistment. As there was no reserve organization or program, however, this stipulation did not entail any obligation.

Until 1937, the Burmese units were a part of the colonial Indian army and adopted its pattern of social and ethnic composition; that is, the regiments and companies were organized on an ethnic religious basis. The ethnic composition of the army at the outbreak of World War II was the following: Burmese, 12.3%; Karens, 27.8%; Chins, 22.6%; Kachins, 22.9%; and others, 4.3%.[57] After the war, when Aung San asked to unite his BIA forces with the Burmese forces who had fought under British command, he insisted that the army should be organized on what was called the "class battalion basis"; in other words, on an ethnic principle. The object was to establish "pure" Burmese battalions—to counterbalance the battalions, composed mainly of minorities, which were considered disloyal to Burmese nationalism, and to assure the Burmazation of the officer corps.[58] The army was reconstituted in 1949-50. The government's policy favored the acceptance of Burmans in increasing numbers. In 1967 a majority of the men in service were Burmans, although there were still many of other ethnic affiliations, principally Karens, Chins, and Kachins.[59]

The top army leadership contrasts sharply with the bulk of the officer corps recruited in the 1950s and 1960s. Most of the senior officers were the cream of the resistance movement and its political counterpart before 1947. For example, twenty of the twenty-three colonels in key positions during the caretaker regime in 1958-60 had been engaged in politics in the pre-independence period and were nominated by the political elite to military roles.[60]

One of the factors which contributed to the consolidation of the NCO and officer corps as a distinct status group was that the military has been, since independence, the most available channel of social mobility. The military has a considerable advantage, compared to other public institutions, in attracting the most qualified personnel in the country. One main reason for this is the prestige of the military profession. Although there is no direct evidence on this issue, it appears that the attitude of the Burmese people toward the military profession changed, from 1948 to 1962, from a negative to a much more positive one. The role played by the army on the battlefield apparently strengthened the soldier's status in Burmese society after independence.[61] Another inducement was rewards—officers received a considerable salary in comparison to other groups dependent on the government and more or less equivalent in status.[62]

One should also mention the opportunities, at the army's expense, to study and acquire a profession (such as medicine, engineering, or accounting) highly valued in civilian society and to which, in most cases, one could transfer. This greatly attracted the young to the military.

Many of the economic enterprises developed and controlled by the army were apparently viewed by the military as means for securing their own futures. Retirement, in the military services, comes early, and "the army is the promise of a vast reservoir of future well-paid jobs for military personnel, their relatives, and their friends."[63] Political power became, after 1958, another inducement for those with aspirations for mobility. For the senior officers, this balance of rewards meant renewal of the "golden age" before and immediately after independence. The deposed Colonel Maung Maung, the number-three man in Ne Win's first administration, put it in this way:

> After the Second World War was over and we had obtained our independence, the cream of the resistance movement stayed with the Burma army, and most of the rest became politicians. It was irksome to find that those who could not hold their own in the army came, in time, to be our political superiors.[64]

B. Phases of Ideological Development in the Defense Services

In many ways, the Burmese army was an innovator in terms of the role of the military in developing countries. The redefinition of the army's role was certainly directly linked with the economic, political, and ideological crises of the first decade of Burma's independence. These crises troubled the politically conscious military elite no less than did their battle against insurgents. Moreover, the stalemate on the economic and political-ideological levels prevented, in a sense, any "final" victory on the battlefield. In this context, the propensity of the officer corps to expand and enlarge the "classic" roles of the armed forces becomes relevant to our discussion. In other words, one may ask whether the failure of the political elite to mobilize its resources and to "supply" adequate "services" to its operational organs did not lead to the molding of a particular and unorthodox pattern of relations between the military and the civilian society? We shall consider this on two levels: (a) the ideological level; and (b) the application of ideology.

Prior to the 1962 coup, there were six phases of what the military elite itself defined as the "ideology of the defense services."[65] The first two were preideological. The first phase involved BIA and BDA in 1941-43, when ideology was confined to the basic issues of independence and political freedom. The political and social character of the future independent state was a marginal concern. The second phase began with the establishment of a Japanese-sponsored Burmese government in 1944. Greater sophistication in ideological formulation was reflected by according priorities among goals—the most important ones being achieving political freedom, establishing a democratic state, realizing socialistic programs.

In the third and fourth phases, national ideology was rethought and reassessed. The third phase (1948-55) was defined by the military itself as a "period of ideological gestation"; and the fourth (1956-57) as a "period of thorough study and discussion of the ideology for the defense services." For this purpose, a special conference was called in 1956 to which all commanding officers were invited.

The last two phases were those in which a new version of an ideology was consolidated and the methods for its application spelled out. The army called the fifth the "first phase of ideological development." The sixth and last phase was that in which the specific role of the defense services was finally formulated.[66]

At the Mehtila conference, it was stated that

> Man's endeavour to build a society set free at last from anxieties over food, clothing, shelter, and the ability to enjoy life's spiritual satisfaction as well, fully convinced of the sanctity, dignity and essential goodness of life, must proceed from the premise of a faith only in a politico-economic system based on the eternal principles of justice, liberty and equality. This is our belief. We would rather give up life than give up this belief. In order to achieve the establishment of such a society, we have resolved to uphold this belief forever in this sovereign independent republic of the Union of Burma.[67]

An outsider reading this document may be surprised that military leaders defined this period as the first phase of an autonomous ideological development. Even the participants at the conference emphasized that the declaration was in essence a repetition in "simple" language of three fundamental documents: (1) the Burmese Declaration of Independence; (2) the first address to parliament by the first president of the union; (3) the Constitution of the Union of Burma.

An answer may be found elsewhere in the document. Feeling that some more specific formulation of means and aims should be presented, its authors stated that "now [68] the time has come to determine precisely and clearly the role and attitude of the Defence Services in the second phase of ideological development." The reasoning behind this is both interesting and typical: "For the Defence Services simply to accept the National Ideology without giving thought to their role and defining this attitude is to develop a strategy without devising the tactics." What is implied here by "role" and "attitude"? The document assumes this question by presenting a clear order of priorities: "to restore peace and the rule of law—first. To implement democracy—second. To establish a socialist economy—third." These three objectives are viewed as interdependent:

> To establish a socialist economy, democracy is a prerequisite: for democracy to flourish, law and order is essential. Without peace and the rule of law, no country can be a democratic one. In an undemocratic country, a socialist economy can never be established—a totalitarian government will impose only a rigid economic system which will deny the right of private property.[69]

The definition of socialism is of great interest. In addition to the general and classic definition—"to build up a society in which there will be no exploitation of man by man" or to institute a "planned economy," the document states the ultimate problems of the Burmese economy:

> The Union's economy is based on agriculture, but the methods of production are outmoded, and consequently our production capacity is limited. Small industry is not sufficiently developed to provide adequate consumer goods for all citizens. Therefore, the main feature of the national economic policy should be to modernize the basic agricultural economy, and secondly to develop local industries commensurate with the natural and human resources of the country. This will require deliberate and thoughtful planning. In the process of development this state-controlled economy may appear not to differ from state capitalism. But it should be noted, at the same time, that the state will continue to encourage those private enterprises which contribute to increased national productivity.[70]

Two important items should be noted. First, the military as such and before the coup felt it necessary to formulate its own ideology which, although based on the national ideology, was labelled the "Ideology of the Defence Services." Second, this ideology was all-embracing, including many areas of private and public activities.[71] However, in the 1950s the focuses of cleavage between the military and the political elites became numerous and included many intellectual and practical fields.[72]

In contrast to U Nu's strongly religious orientation, the military elite could almost be described as vigorously antitraditional, although not to the same extent antireligious. Ne Win did not hesitate to suspend, after the 1962 coup, the decree making Buddhism the state religion, despite the fact that U Nu considered this decree the most important development of the last decade in Burma. Ne Win also dissolved the executive and general council of the Buddha Sasana Council.[73] The second military government also abolished the observance of the Buddhist sabbath enacted by the previous government. This had entailed the closing of all government offices on a different day each week, causing considerable confusion in the business community. In addition, the military regime abolished the ban on cattle slaughter, which is anathema to the Buddhist.

In spite of these extreme acts, in those days the military elite could by no means be defined, or its acts interpreted, as reflecting a militant antireligious attitude. The military's attitude could be more properly characterized as favoring an institutional separation between state and church and simultaneously encouraging a national culture based on a synthesis of the basic tenets of Buddhism and socialism.[74]

Another source of antagonism between the military and civilians was the concept of government. Perhaps there is no other sphere in Burmese life with which the military leaders were more dissatisfied than the process and patterns of decision making at every level of government. They felt that inefficiency, corruption, and political considerations—instead of rational and professional criteria—characterized governmental operations, often with serious consequences for the nation. These were among the main charges in the military's opposition to the U Nu government. They are not really ideological in character but refer mainly to administrative practices which are means of achieving ideological ends. However, there is evidence that this extremely critical attitude was rooted in a basic disagreement about concepts and images of ideal government.[75] For example, the army constantly tried to preserve and strengthen the authority of the central government apparatus against local political leaders who used to interfere in the activities of government officials. The army favored a return to the power system of having village headmen and deputy commissioners. It thus increasingly clashed with the AFPFL representatives.

The issue of economic planning was a source of conflict as well. The official ideological declaration of the defense services refers very seriously to the problems of economic planning and to specific priorities in capital investment. Some clear indications of basic differences in this field between the attitudes of the military leaders and of the political leaders can be seen in the statement, made by Aung Gyi, after the coup d'etat in March 1962: "The economic program to be formulated gradually by the new regime will be cautious and more practical. We do not want to indulge in big dreams."[76] In more concrete terms, this meant a return to the policies of the caretaker government, which placed greater emphasis on increasing agricultural production and less on industrial development.[77]

The basic antagonisms were by no means confined to above mentioned areas. Another area where the policy of the government was opposed, and ostensibly, at least, provided the ultimate stimulus for the recent coup d'etat, was in the relationship between the constituent states and the central government. The last coup d'etat was justified by the contention that U Nu was inclined to give greater concessions to the constituent states, especially to the Shan state.

The preceding remarks may not allay all doubts about the military elite's sincerity in its ideological rationalization of the military's role in Burma. However, these doubts may well be eliminated by considering the actual events of 1958-60.

C. The Application of the National Ideology of the Defence Services: 1958-60

In retrospect, the efforts to elaborate a specific ideological identity for the defense services were apparently largely propelled by a desire for innovation —albeit a general, pragmatic one. In the early 1950s, Burma's military leaders had demonstrated those entrepreneurial qualities, which were to be so evident under Ne Win's first government, that greatly influenced the military's ideological development. They can be perceived in the economic, and to a much lesser degree in the political and educational, spheres.

The army's first steps into the realm of economic action were very modest.[78] In 1950, the Ministry of Defence created the Defence Service Institute (DSI), a nonprofit association designed to supply consumer goods to soldiers through a department store—and to undermine the black market. All profit was to go toward promoting the welfare of the defense services' personnel. The next step, still very modest, was the establishment in 1951 of a book and stationery store, open to all, subsequently enlarged and then named Ava House. The Ava bookstore was a model for future, more widespread ventures into public enterprise, the development of which now accelerated. In 1953, the International Trading House was established to deal with government contracts. In 1956, the Burma Fisheries was formed. By 1957, the DSI had grown from a general store to a three-branch commercial agency which supplied goods to the armed forces and to the general public.

Economic activity was confined mainly to purchasing and selling consumers' goods without interfering with economic policy per se. "The military did not participate in the long-term planning as annual budgeting processes, either as participating staff at the interdepartmental review level or at the policy-making level."[79]

In 1958, under the caretaker government, the DSI became the largest and most powerful business organization in Burma. Its subsidiary concerns dominated the vital fields of banking, shipping, construction, and fishing. Its holdings included Rangoon's largest department store, the largest automobile service station, a bus line, a radio assembly factory, a motor workshop, and a factory producing shoes and boots for the army. The DSI also became the nation's largest importer, controlling trade in coal and coke and holding agencies for the various automobile manufacturers. In addition, the DSI entered the world of tourism and hotels.[80] All profits were reinvested in the expanding concerns. As a nonprofit organization, the institute received sizable tax exemptions not enjoyed by its competitors.[81] Military enterprise as part of a nonprofit public corporation agreed with the economic objectives encouraged by U Nu's government of promoting cooperatives and nonprofit enterprises—which, until 1958, had received only lip service. The Burmese army thus revealed a capacity to apply abstract ideas systematically and comprehensively. Furthermore, its innovative spirit was expressed in its willingness to embark on new projects.[82] In fact, most investment capital in this period was provided by the DSI.[83]

Although the army maintained that it did not intend to compete with or displace private enterprises, private businessmen grew increasingly suspicious of the military's objectives. The majority of the Burmese mercantile community did not completely believe in the army's good faith.[84] Even the cooperative movement felt it had been trumped. The new government headed by U Nu, reelected in 1960, also was apprehensive. To tighten civilian control over the military-economic sector, the legal status of the DSI was modified, and most DSI enterprises were taken over by the Burma Economic Development Corporation (BEDC).[85] This newly established corporation was expected to help finance, coordinate, supervise, and assist all activities of the organized corporate bodies.[86] The BEDC had seven members; the general managers of the Union Bank and ministerial secretaries were included ex officio. The corporation members and the chairmen were military men.[87] Thus, although the military shared control of the corporation with civilians, the military's overall influence on economic policies was heightened owing to the broader fields now covered by the new corporation. The BEDC received new economic resources to promote economic development, but the military, through its strategic position in the corporation, could direct and regulate its course, and, no less important, it could provide jobs and economic rewards for its retired and active NCOs and officers.[88]

While building the economic empire, the military elite by no means overlooked the importance of accumulating popular support outside the conventional channels of the political parties. Political activities were not unfamiliar to the senior officers; before 1948 many had belonged to the young nationalist elite. Within the framework of the BIA, the officers played roles that were more political than military.

Furthermore, in the first years after independence, senior officers like Ne Win and Aung San played clearly political roles.[89] A more definitely institutionalized division of labor existed in the urban political areas. In the provinces, because of the long struggle against insurgents, regional commanders often assumed administrative and political functions—which inevitably resulted in clashes between them and party representatives.

In a period of severe political crises—on the eve of the first Ne Win government—the military unwillingly was dragged into the arena of internal political feuds where the chief political factions were trying hard to win the army's sympathies. More senior officers, in fact, sympathized with the Swe-Nyein faction of the AFPFL than with U Nu's faction. The army also had reservations about U Nu's policy toward the insurgents and the NUF. All this worried U Nu and his followers, who feared that the armed forces would help the Swe-Nyein faction in the forthcoming elections. The Union Party also suspected the various paramilitary organizations, which were not under the control of the chief of staff and the Ministry of Defence. Very much feared were the police, the Union Military Police, and the Village Guards (Pyusautis) under the control of the minister of the interior. The efforts to purge the military failed, but verbal encounters were frequent, particularly following a declaration by some leaders of U Nu's party that the army was the "public enemy number one." The "stable" and "clean" factions of the AFPFL were on the verge of an armed clash.[90] This conflict ended with U Nu's resignation and the military's creation of the caretaker government.

Just as it had in the economic field, the military sought to pave new ways in the political sphere. By declining to identify with any political faction, it hoped to gather support in another form. It established a countrywide movement called the National Solidarity Association (NSA or *Kyant Khaing Ye Ahphwes*). Its official purpose was to fight economic and armed insurgence and to inculcate in the people of Burma the values of law and order and competitive democracy. However, one of the undeclared aims of the NSA movement, which appealed mainly to ex-servicemen, was to encourage independent candidates to run for parliament and to generate popular support for them. The army leaders apparently hoped that such a body of independent professional men—of the sort who served in various capacities in the caretaker regime—could be used to influence the outcome of the legislative process.[91] The NSA was not dissolved after U Nu took over the reins of government in April 1960, but remained in army hands. The army's original intention—that the NSA be a mass movement—was abandoned. With U Nu's return to power, the organization became much more elitist in character, an educating rather than action oriented organization.[92]

Until the March 1962 coup, the educational and ideological training of the Burmese army was of a limited nature in comparison to its functions in the country's economy and even with its indirect influence on political life. The army was mainly concerned with agricultural training. It established an agricultural vocational training center, whose aim was to instruct soldiers in agriculture, animal husbandry, tractor driving, and maintenance.[93] The army also provided training for civil service personnel. During Ne Win's first term, the man in charge of military training conducted a special school for public administration.

These two educational services indicate the range of nonmilitary education and training given by the military to the wider Burmese society. Ideological indoctrination was apparently limited to the military itself and perhaps extended to the NSA as well.

One prominent result of these diversified activities was a considerable increase in the infiltration of officers into civilian posts. This was due less to a deliberate policy of posting officers and ex-officers to key positions within the civilian sector than to the expansion of military roles. The greatest opportunity arose, of course, under the caretaker government, when about 150 officers were shifted to civilian posts.[94] A sizable proportion of these were drawn from the senior ranks. At U Nu's request, senior officers later remained in civilian posts. In addition, a number retained civilian posts at their own request and subsequently resigned from military service.

The army's pledge to return to the barracks after the election of February 1960 was duly honored. Since then, many hypotheses and speculations have been published about the reasons the army leaders kept their word despite their disappointment in U Nu's victory and internal pressure to disregard their pledge and to remain at the helm of the government. Some observers have attributed the military's retreat to disappointment. The military's great effort to restore law and authority had resulted in growing resentment and unpopularity within the population—who presumably preferred the permissiveness and tolerance of U Nu's regime to the brusqueness of army rule.[95] Because of its inability or unwillingness to institute a new political organization affiliated with it, the army was unable to maintain its close relationship with key groups in the population. This resulted in an ever expanding communication gap and growing unpopularity. The army may also have been reluctant to compete for popularity in the conventional political channels with the political parties. It did not want to abandon its professional image and adopt that of the politician whom it so despised. The fear of intensifying divisions within the army was also a factor that encouraged Ne Win to abide by his promise.

A further factor may be added. The military elite was not yet ready, psychologically or ideologically, to establish a prolonged military regime. It was willing to give the politicians another chance to prove the superiority of the democratic mechanism. In any event, the military's withdrawal must be seen as conditional; the democratic regime was on probation and was to improve and prove itself. The army did not completely abandon its power in the civilian sectors. Through the BEDC, it directly substantially controlled the Burmese economy and could eventually indirectly influence decision making in other spheres. Compared to other armies which managed to achieve what the Burmese army had, its return to the barracks was certainly an outstanding and unique act. Even in this respect the Burmese senior officers were innovators. However, the withdrawal was not unanimously accepted by all senior officers, and after U Nu's return to power the army was divided into three groups. The first, composed mostly of young officers, looked reluctantly at the army's retreat from politics and considered it a blatant error. The second group argued that the army should not interfere in politics in any way. The third group saw "the army performing limited, but still essential roles in national development."[96]

The "probation period" for the civilian elite lasted two years. In March 1962, the officers finally concluded that the politicians had no intention—or ability—of changing themselves. The officers were disturbed by: (a) the concessions U Nu promised to the minorities—which the army considered to be the final step leading to the dissolution of the union; (b) the rapid succession of economic crises; (c) the proclamation of Buddhism as the state religion; (d) the inefficiency of the administration; and (e) the progressive disintegration of the ruling party.[97]

D. The Military as a Political Elite and the Consolidation of Power

With the coup d'etat, the military elite entered a new phase of ideological deliberation, distinguished by a relatively higher degree of depth, articulation, and specification of the normative principles intended as guiding lines for Burmese society on its way toward progress. Army ideologists tried to define the "revolutionary philosophy" of Burmese socialism. Its uniqueness was established by contrasting the philosophy of the newly established *Lanzin* Party (Burma Socialist Programme Party—BSPP) with those of the Communist and of the Social Democratic parties.

In an official publication dealing with this issue, the military leadership contended that five vital differences existed between the BSPP and the so-called rightist Social Democratic parties and the Communist parties throughout the world.

1. The social democrats arbitrarily discarded the texts and treatises of Marxism-Leninism and relied entirely on those written by bourgeois reformists. On the other hand, Communists generally depended on Marxism-Leninism as the only source of their knowledge and thought, the arsenal of their ideology, the guide to their actions and the repository of their hopes. The BSPP, however, studied the texts and treatises of the Marxist-Leninists and the non-Marxist-Leninists alike. In no area—political, economic, or other—was study restricted to a particular view. The BSPP was guided by a philosophy of humanism on the system of dialectical objective realism. In the center of the BSPP *Weltanschauung* was a correlation of man and his material environment. The environment provided the conditions in which thinking, sentient men (the citizenry) decided, invented, and acted.

2. A Social Democratic Party permitted its members freedom of faith and worship. It would, however, draw no clear border between religion and politics and often deliberately confounded the two. A Communist Party knew neither religious faith nor worship, whereas the BSPP allowed full freedom of conscience and religion.

3. A Social Democratic Party could profess to be the party of the working people, but it actually drew its strength from those classes or strata of society where bourgeois habits lingered. A Communist Party was the party of the workers, and more especially of the industrial workers. But the BSPP was the political party of all the working people in the Union of Burma, of all races and religions—the peasants in the fields, the workers in the factories, the toiling poor, the progressive intelligentsia, and the intellectuals.

4. In the matter of political leadership, a Social Democratic Party had no clear class orientation. As a result, the BSPP maintained, the leadership fell into the hands of the bourgeois gentry, who used the working class as a means of augmenting their own position. The BSPP firmly believed that, in a socialist society, the rule of the working people must prevail. In this case, the BSPP admittedly shared the views of the Communists.

5. A Social Democratic Party was vague in defining the way progress operated in the history of human society and was enamoured of reformism —without any philosophy resting on an objective view of the realities of life. The Communist Party believed that the history of human society showed a constant advance toward a classless society where the state had withered away. The BSPP believed that, in the history of human society, the material world and the society of men were in a state of constant flux. The BSPP believed in the laws of dialectics, i.e., the laws of motion and change of all phenomena. It also believed that the lot of man in his society could and had to be improved by his working in fruitful cooperation with his fellow men. To the BSPP no economic, political, or social treatise was infallible. The quest for and the development of ideologies, systems, and programs to promote the welfare of society must always continue.

Man and his interests should never be sacrificed in pursuit of any dogmatic theory.[98]

The alleged distinctiveness of this ideological formulation was achieved by oversimplifications and sweeping generalizations about the ideologies of the social democrats and the Communists, and hazy elaborations of the character of Burmese socialism. No wonder the translation of these vague slogans into concrete programs was confronted by serious obstacles and required great improvisational skill! Actually, built-in rationalization for such improvisations was provided by the very belief in a pragmatic and nondoctrinaire attitude.

If some of the general ideas were to be implemented, key groups within the population would have had to favor them and potential as well as real opposition groups would have had to be neutralized. The military revolution, however, resulted in a complete disintegration of the fragile balance of power within the old political center. The military had, therefore, to reconstruct a new political center and to redetermine the balance of power and the functions of various organizations. It also had to reassess the policy toward the periphery, peasants, workers, and minorities. In building a new political center, it had to allocate new roles to those organizations which would be permitted to survive.

As the role of "backbone of the new center" had been granted de facto—if not de jure—to the military, the military's role had first to be defined under the new political conditions. One can learn about the new concept of the military's role from, inter alia, speeches delivered on various occasions by senior officers. For example, Brigadier San Ye (vice chief of staff), in his address to the cadets of the Hmawbi Burma Army Officers Training School, said:

> In the training that they had just concluded, the officer cadets were taught not only the arts of warfare, but also how they could serve the working people in the promotion of the people's economic, social, and educational interests. This indeed, is a revolutionary change even for an army which has its genesis in a people's revolution against colonialism and imperialism and for the people's freedom and independence, as the Burma Army.

Furthermore:

> The new concept of the role of the army is exactly contrary to the opposite one thought in the colonial days as the ideal to be nutured and cherished by an army. It was thought that politics was to be eschewed as no part of a soldier's training. That this "ideal" is wrong and most harmful to a people, needs no great perspicacity to see.[99]

The new concept thus called for total politization of the army and its being molded into an instrument for the construction of a socialist state. In this task the auxiliary role was assigned to a civilian organization, whose main function was to enlist support from key civilian groups. This organization emerged in several phases, since a reorganization of the entire political order was necessary.

The first step was divulged about three months after the coup. On 4 July, the Revolutionary Council (RC) made it known that it proposed to constitute a new political organization or party. Before this, feverish negotiations had been held between the RC and the leaders of the old parties in order to find a common framework, but only the NUF would accept. As a result, the military leaders decided to go their own way and establish a cadre party without any foundation in the old parties.[100] The various leading positions of the new party (the Burma Socialist Programme Party—BSPP) were allocated to members of the RC.[101] For two years after the coup, the civilian parties continued to function (with some restrictions) alongside the BSPP. In March 1964, the RC promulgated the National Solidarity Protection Law, which immediately went into effect, dissolving all political organizations. This law further required all nonpolitical organizations, including religious associations, to be registered with the government. The *Lanzin* Party was initially planned, at least for a transitional period, to be a cadre party. The Revolutionary Council stated that "since the party is to be organized as a cadre party during the first stage it will be necessary to screen the candidate membership applications which had been submitted with diverse motivations."[102] Obviously, the nucleus of the cadre was members of the armed forces.[103]

Concomitant with establishing the BSPP, the RC was active in developing additional types of frameworks of political and administrative action among peasants and workers. In May 1964, the Security and Administrative Committees (SAC) were established,[104] to replace the NSA. The SAC were composed of military personnel.[105] The officers in charge were eventually to become full-fledged civil servants. A nucleus for a new type of bureaucracy was thereby created. The SAC were to form a link between the government and the people in the periphery, coordinating the roles of different government departments responsible both for keeping law and order and for properly distributing commercial goods, although a more specific function was to allocate loans to peasants.[106] The next step was the proposed organization of peasants' councils to ensure political control in this sensitive sector.[107]

These councils were supposed to be the first tier in a hierarchy of three proposed layers in the legislative process.[108] Similar institutional frameworks were designed for the urban workers. In May 1964, the RC announced that it intended to set up the Burmese Way of Socialism Workers Units to establish a better system of organization for the workers. According to the declaration, under the new organization and system there would be effective control and utilization of manpower and labor and the elimination of exploitation—all conducive to greatly improved quality and productivity. Furthermore, the system would enable the units to be quickly converted into national defense units, defending the state in time of war and as effectively constructing it in times of peace.[109] A full-scale campaign of political ideological indoctrination was also launched. The dissemination of the BSPP's ideological platform, "the system of correlation of man and environment," was primarily aimed at neutralizing hostile groups in the small middle class, civil service, students, and the sangha, and at resocializing friendly elements among the army, workers, and peasants.[110]

With the establishment of the Central People's Peasants Council (CPPC) and the Central People's Workers Council (CPWC), which were presented as the "bulwark of the Socialist Democratic State of Burma," the RC initiated political statements and programs whose aim was to reconcile the RC with various opposition groups. Thirty-two opposition leaders, including U Nu, were released from prison, where they had been since 1962. The RC then invited them to participate in the Internal Unity Advisory Board, to make suggestions about either amending the old constitution, which was in fact suspended at that moment, or drawing up a completely new one.[111] The background to these dramatic gestures was the severe economic crisis and the failure to crush the subversive activities of the Communist and other minority groups.[112] The political dialogue with opposition leaders failed, ending with U Nu's flight first to India and later to Thailand, where he allegedly tried to organize armed resistance to Ne Win's regime.[113]

In another field, an effort was made to reform Rangoon University with three objectives: (a) to adjust the curriculum to the needs of Burmese society as defined by the ideological platform of the RC; (b) to raid the academic level and to expel all unqualified students; and (c) to remove all subversive elements from among the students or, if this was impossible, to minimize their influence.[114] These reforms began to be effected after lengthy discussions at a series of seminars on higher education held in April 1964. With minor modifications, the recommendations made there were later incorporated in the new system of university education with the opening of new universities and institutions in November 1964. The most important features of the new system, as far as implementing the principles of "Burma's Way to Socialism" (BWS) were concerned, were: (a) to redefine the aims of the university, so that it would train and produce the specialists necessary for improving all fields of socioeconomic activities inspired by socialism and imbue the students with a socialist moral outlook; (b) to give precedence to science and professional education; (c) to change the curriculum, especially in subjects like history, economics, and philosophy; and (d) to adopt the Burmese language as the medium of instruction.

This educational policy, especially as reflected in (d), was actually part of a more comprehensive plan aimed at the almost total dissociation of Burma from foreign—both Western and Eastern—influence. This plan was manifested in the closing of a substantial number of English-language dailies and journals—this began in U Nu's period but reached extreme dimensions after 1962.[115] Through these and other measures,[116] the RC hoped, the universities and institutions would become a vital sector of the national economy—their activities would be in line with the needs of the socialist economy planned for Burma.

The RC confronted far greater difficulties when trying to tighten control over the sangha. There were two distinct levels in the religious policy pursued by the military regime: the ideological-philosophical level; and the level of politics and power relations. On the ideological level, the military continued in the old tradition, striving for a "reasonable" synthesis between non-Buddhist philosophical ideas and certain Buddhist principles.[117] The results of this intellectual endeavor were published, as *The System of Correlation of Man and His Environment,* in January 1963. In this document, otherwise full of commonplace ideas and logical inconsistencies, the use of several concepts of traditional Buddhist thought are interwoven with appropriate *Pali* terminology. The document adopts the Buddhist distinctions of the natural world *(Okasaloka),* the animal world *(Sattaloka),* and the phenomenal world *(Sankharaloka)* in describing relations between the material and metaphysical worlds.[118] These distinctions are, however, negligible in the bulk of Buddhist philosophical principles—which this document completely ignored. No attention was paid to the Buddhist belief in the existence of spiritual being, to the doctrine of the "Wheel of Rebirth," or to the assertion that man is unable to direct his own destiny but is limited by his karma.[119] In fact, the formulators of the RC ideology suggested secular answers to most problems of human existence. For example, they presented basically materialist and pseudo-Marxist concepts of history and of man ("man matters most," "man is the master and captain of history"). They defined spiritual happiness without any reference to religious concepts or images.[120]

In the political sphere, the RC's policy was much clearer. The military was hostile to U Nu's religious policy and considered the proclamation of Buddhism as the state religion a serious error, since it caused the minorities to be more—and unnecessarily—alienated. "There was a strong feeling among the military that the country was in the hands of a religious obscurantist whose policies had the effect of disturbing national unity."[121]

The RC was expected to modify U Nu's religious policy. Indeed, immediately after the coup, many laws enacted in the U Nu period were suspended but, by and large, the RC adopted a fairly cautious policy. The state religion provision became a dead letter without, however, being explicitly rejected. Ne Win was torn between the conviction that religion and politics should be separated and the feeling that the RC should occupy itself with religion to construct a new Burma according to the basic ideological outlines set forth in "Burma's Way to Socialism." Although the latter approach inevitably led to a confrontation between the RC and the sangha, it eventually prevailed. It was noticeable in intensive propaganda against popular cults (like the *nat* worship), and the reorganization of the sangha (viewed by the RC as a parasitic and unproductive element)[122] granting it a status similar to that of other political and social organizations. These measures brought about a number of incidents which the RC and the sangha largely resolved through mutually acceptable compromise.

The Communist underground, the students, and the sangha, all focal points of opposition, troubled the RC mainly because they were composed of people in elite social positions, although they did not endanger Burma's existence or its recognized borders and population composition. However, the ethnic minorities explicitly expressed their desire for more autonomy and in some cases even complete separation from the union. This, with its undercurrent of violence, was a real danger to the union. Until 1962, Burma's governments had continued the traditional policy pursued by the Burmese kings: the Burmazation of minorities and their absorption and assimilation into Buddhist-Burmese society. In the final stages of his rule, U Nu was compelled to respond to certain demands from the minorities about rights beyond those guaranteed by the constitution. The military cited these same concessions as a major reason for the coup—after which there was no doubt that the new government would nullify them and assume a tougher stance toward the minorities. In January 1964, the RC announced the decision to have one set of laws for all Burmese states in the union.

To the guerrilla warfare led by the Red and White Flags and the various minority groups, the army responded with severe countermeasures—but with only partial success. The situation in the beginning of the 1970s was substantially the same as in the early 1960s after the army took over.[123]

Besides legal, administrative, and military measures to tighten control over ethnic and cultural minorities, the RC also explicitly encouraged the promotion of indigenous languages, folklore, literature, and religious beliefs. In this respect, the RC accomplished far more than the preceding governments.

Previous citations from "Burma's Way to Socialism" may have indicated the basic outlines of the RC's economic policy. Some illustrations from the economic field will help concretize them.

The main objectives of the RC's economic policy were to end all direct foreign investment; to nationalize all industries, particularly oil and rice; and to nationalize all trade and banks except for small retail stores.[124] The rationale was provided by arguing that the coexistence of private and public enterprise was an economic and social evil in which the previous government indulged. It is interesting that, to legitimize its dramatic intentions, the RC resorted not only to secular-ideological arguments but also to Buddhist thinking.[125]

Enactment of this extreme economic nationalism was slowed down by passive resistance from those primarily interested in maintaining an economic status quo and by insufficient professional manpower or adequate administrative infrastructure. Implementing the economic programs involved many compromises, and sometimes the RC was compelled to retract former announcements.[126] Nevertheless, the basic outlines of the policy were carried through, despite severe internal disputes that ended in an internal purge of the RC. The immediate effects of the economic reforms were rather negative. Burma's gross domestic product (in constant prices) declined, both the volume and value of exports fell, and agricultural production was reduced. There were nevertheless a number of contingent achievements, such as an increase in foreign exchange resources resulting from curtailing imports.[127] Most of the economic activity during RC rule was concentrated in the industrial and commercial sectors.[128] Relatively little was accomplished in the politically most sensitive sector—the rural—despite various programs of agrarian reform. Peasant frustration grew, centered around indebtedness, the need to improve markets, and rising prices.[129]

E. Summary and Conclusions

Burma's structural features and political processes can be summarized in terms of the achievements and failures of the Burmese elite and its ability to maintain its organizational framework and the existing social-political arrangements while consolidating its authority—which was constantly challenged, particularly by various sectors of the country's heterogeneous periphery. The greatest obstacle to satisfactory integration of political action in the center with that at the local community was the government's inability to crush its most violent vocal opponents, whether Communist insurrectionists or minority groups. True, despite twenty years of armed struggle, the insurrectionists never succeeded in annihilating governmental administrative and political action in Burma's most important administrative and geographic centers. But in the more remote places, they occasionally disrupted the government's efforts to stabilize and pacify the population. Such regions were mostly populated by ethnic minorities who resented attempts to incorporate them fully into the Burmese national framework. In the eyes of these minority groups, the question of national sovereignty and autonomy within Burma had not yet been solved.

Thus, despite being a Buddhist society—one that preaches against violence and killing—Burma became in actuality an extremely violent society. However, this must be viewed as a type of deviant subculture, for the intentions of the leaders were obviously quite different. The constitution was liberal in spirit and democratic in its recommendations. All parties—including the ruling party—were to be instruments by which the executive would seek to implement the government's plans and programs. This was the theoretical formulation, but the practice was quite different. Party organizations were very vague, especially for those in the middle and lower groups and on the local community level. In the rural sector, party organizations had almost no meaning at all. The parties' representatives deliberately used traditional communication channels to introduce new ideas, to safeguard political loyalty. Almost nowhere did a local party organization replace the traditional elite, for most of those nominated by the party or by a government representative already occupied a prominent position in the traditional rural structure.[130] The government and the political elites endeavored to combine new ideas and organizational techniques within existing frameworks. Sometimes they established a substantial level of stability and cooperation between the government and the frustrated sectors in the periphery. The greatest weakness (excluding objective impediments) was that it was not part of a comprehensive and deliberate policy orienting the entire country toward a modern political setup within the traditional hierarchy of power. The dominant mood of the AFPFL, despite its desires, was that of an elite party rather than a mass movement, and the social composition of the political elite showed this mood.

The question is, however, whether what happened in Burma can be termed political modernization or whether the events described were only symptoms and attributes of other kinds of political development and change. We have suggested that political development is the "simple" institutionalization and deinstitutionalization of political processes. We have proposed political modernization (in addition to the indexes of political development) be linked to radical changes in social groupings freed from previous particularistic affiliations that succeed in establishing connections, loyalties, and commitments beyond the particularistic ascribed group. If this is an acceptable criterion (although certainly not the sole one) for assessing the extent of modernization in a polity, what happened in pre-1962 Burma can be described as at most political *development*. Moreover, in many respects it may even be defined as political involution.[131] In the period we have described, Burma was in a transitional stage typical of many developing societies, a stage when political changes are mainly expressed by the institutionalization of political organization, by the introduction of constitutional legal organs and universal law. Although not complete, the achievements in this sphere (insurrection is the most extreme expression of rejection of the legal institutional framework) were nonetheless great in comparison to the relative failure of the Burmese elite to reach a more positive balance between the "parochial" and "participation" orientations in the political process. The parochial orientation prevailed throughout almost the entire country.

This incomplete institutionalization of the political framework and of the new national legal basis for economic and social advance conditioned the degree of central authority activity in the different sectors. The limited role of the free-floating voters in the political game and the fact that an important number of those competing for political support were bound by unyielding ascriptive ties resulted in an intensive use of rewards to bribe potential supporters and eventually, as a last resort, in the use of naked, brutal power by opposition groups. A permanent state of institutional instability, a lack of control over human and economic resources, insufficient consensus about basic aims and ad hoc issues and methods—all are evidence of the weakness of Burma's social and political center in the 1960s.

In Chapter 1, four prototypes were outlined to differentiate between armies in terms of the direction and the intensity of their propensity to intervene in political affairs.[132] It seems to us that Burma can be traced to prototype B, which *overemphasizes the integrative and the pattern maintenance* aspects of its social system to the detriment of the more technological and logistic aspects. In Burma, the emphasis on cohesiveness and normative patterns was of a unique character. In terms of ideological articulation and its practical implication, the Burmese army belonged to the type defined as the *ideological entrepreneurial military establishment*.[133] Even before the caretaker government was formed and much more so afterward, the Burmese army manifested entrepreneurial traits, accompanied by adroit ideological formulation, over a wide range of activities, from the economic sphere (where they are most conspicuous) to the political, and to a lesser extent to the educational socialization, spheres.

The army's desire to intervene in domestic affairs was tremendous. The army's ideological entrepreneurial orientation only intensified it. The stimulus was a direct result of the large gap between the prevailing civilian ideology (whose successful application would have required revolutionary change in the process of mobilization and allocation of rewards), the unstable political system, the lack of political solidarity, and inadequate psychological readiness to change. The military elite considered itself an "agent of modernization and nation building" and was therefore particularly sensitive to this discrepancy. Unable to give the military services adequate manpower, budgets, or political support, the political elite failed to provide and maintain a workable framework for mobilization. Thus the military gradually became involved in productive entrepreneurial activities of its own and wound up by finally taking over political power. Before the 1960 election, the military leaders were hesitant and lacked confidence in their ability to concretize a new basis for national consensus. They chose to abdicate. Later it appeared that the only possible means to transform the military rule into civilian rule would be by the civilianization of the military leaders themselves.

Finally, it seems that what the army is doing in Burma is more than a simple rebellion or even an ideological rebellion, since the military elite is not interested in reviving or reintroducing an idealized society. On the other hand, it is doubtful that the 1962 coup approached a total revolution or a revolution which intended to supplement the entire structure of values and recast the entire division of labor.[134] At this stage in its evolution, the Burmese revolution may perhaps be most appropriately labeled, in spite of all innovations, a "simple revolution," a revolution with an ideology limited to the change of only a limited number of values. It affects the political order largely by its establishment of a one-party state. In the economic sphere, no fundamental changes in policy are evident. The RC admitted that it was only implementing the principles formulated in the constitution of 1948. Nevertheless, in methods, rate, and temperament, some substantial changes have been made. This balance of achievements and failures in Burma is not unique. It is an example of the fundamental weakness of most military establishments. The army's unlimited ability to solve problems of the order of those with which the Burmese army is dealing is no more than a myth. And yet, the prospects of restoring civilian rule remain very remote. Equipped with its homemade brand of ideology, the military is convinced of its own diagnostic and therapeutic qualities.

NOTES

1. It would be superfluous to open the analysis of Burma with a historical introduction dealing with the emergence of the Burmese national movement. As we are dealing primarily with civil-military relations, we need not present the historical panorama in its entirety. However, we shall refer to historical events whenever necessary. For Thailand, there were substantial reasons for presenting historical background.

The following books and papers deal with general and detailed historical events as well as with basic facts about the geography, population, economy, and religions of Burma: J. S. Furnivall, *The Governance of Modern Burma*, 2nd ed. (New York: Institute of Pacific Relations, 1960); J. S. Furnivall, *An Introduction to the Political Economy of Burma* (Rangoon: People's Literature Committee and House, 1957); Aye Hlaing, "Trends of Economic Growth and Income Distribution in Burma 1870-1946," *Journal of the Burma Research Society*, XLVII (June 1946), part I, pp. 89-148; Manning Nash, *The Golden Road to Modernity: Village Life in Contemporary Burma* (New York: Wiley & Son, 1965); Lucian W. Pye, *Politics, Personality and Nation Building: Burma's Search for Identity* (New Haven: Yale University Press, 1962); Josef Silverstein, "Burma," in *Government and Politics of Southeast Asia*, ed. M. G. Kahin (Ithaca, N.Y.: Cornell University Press, 1959), pp. 75-182; Donald E. Smith, *Religion and Politics in Burma* (Princeton University Press, 1965); Hugh Tinker, *The Union of Burma* (Oxford: Oxford University Press, 1961); Frank N. Trager, *Building a Welfare State in Burma 1948-1956*, (New York: Institute of Pacific Relations, 1956); Louis J. Walinsky, *Economic Development in Burma 1955-1960* (New York: Twentieth Century Fund, 1962); John F. Cady, *A History of Modern Burma* (Ithaca, N.Y.: Cornell University Press, 1958).

2. For more details, see Furnivall, *Government,* pp. 48-55; Silverstein, "Burma," pp. 103-110.

3. The Kahin state, the Karen state, the Chine special divisions, the Span state, and the Kayah state.

4. E. Sarkisyanz, *Buddhist Backgrounds of the Burmese Revolution* (The Hague: Martinus Nijhoff, 1965), pp. 217-218. See also Martin Rudner, "Traditionalism and Socialism in Burma's Political Development," in *Socialism and Tradition*, eds. S. N. Eisenstadt and Y. Azmon (New York: Humanities Press, 1973), pp. 112-115.

5. On the status and functions of Buddhism in the pre-British period, see Cady, *History;* Tinker, *Union.*

6. Even in the most Marxist period of Burma's nationalism, among the Thakins there were traditional elements. The famous Burmese author Thakin Kudaw Hmine fulfilled a crucial role. For details see E. Sarkisyanz, "On the Place of U Nu's Buddhist Socialism in Burma's History of Ideas," in *Studies on Asia,* ed. R. K. Sakai (Lincoln: University of Nebraska Press, 1961), pp. 56-58. See also Rudner, "Traditionalism," pp. 115-116; and Sarkisyanz, *Buddhist Backgrounds,* pp. 128-129.

7. G. Myrdal, *Asian Drama: An Inquiry Into the Poverty of Nations* (New York: Pantheon, 1968), I, p. 373.

8. Mya Maung, "Socialism and Economic Development of Burma," *Asian Survey,* IV, no. 12 (December 1964), p. 1185.

9. For the "dialogue" between Buddhism and socialism in the first decade of Burma's independence, see Richard Butwell, *U Nu of Burma* (Stanford: Stanford University Press, 1963); Sarkiyanz, *Buddhist Backgrounds,* pp. 189-191, 199-200; Rudner, "Traditionalism," pp. 117-122; E. Leach, "Buddhism in the Post-Colonial Order in Burma and Ceylon," *Daedalus,* (Winter 1973), pp. 31-53.

10. U Nu, "Political Ideology of the AFPFL," *Burma Weekly Bulletin,* VI, no. 43 (6 February 1958), pp. 373-376.

11. See J. Silverstein, "The Federal Dilemma in Burma," *Far Eastern Survey,* XXVIII, no. 7 (July 1959), pp. 97-105.

12. See Silverstein, "Burma," pp. 94-100; Tinker, *Union,* chs. 1, 2; Furnivall, *Governance,* pp. 55-61; Maung Maung, *Burma and General Ne Win* (London: Asia Publishing House, 1969), ch. 6.

13. The Communists left first. In 1946, a part of the PVO joined them in the underground. In 1951, the left-wing faction of the Socialist Party left the league.

14. The United Hill People's Organization; All Shan States Organization, Shan States Peasants' Organization; Kachin National Congress.

15. Thus, for example, in 1958 the AFPFL had 1,368,014 members, 848,331 of whom were members of one of the affiliated associations (ABPU—550,050 members; TUCB—140,584 members; ETO—100,243 members; WFL—57,331 members). The absolute power of these organizations was doubled by these members' double vote, one for the league and the other for the affiliated association. See Silverstein, "Burma," p. 116, and Furnivall, *Governance,* pp. 114-115.

16. For the deterioration of the AFPFL, see Sein Win, *The Split Story* (Rangoon, Burma: The Guardian Ltd., 1959); E. N. Trager, *Burma: From Kingdom to Republic* (New York: Praeger, 1966), ch. 8; J. Silverstein, "Politics, Parties and the National Elections in Burma," *Far Eastern Survey,* XXV, no. 12 (December 1956), pp. 180-184.

17. For the policies of the BWPP and its dispute with the AFPFL, see G. Fairbairn, "Aspects of the Burmese Political Scene," *Pacific Affairs,* XXIX, no. 3 (September 1956), pp. 215-222.

18. Other examples were the People's Economic Cultural Organization and the Pawngyaung National Democratic Front.

19. The All Opposition Alliance (AOA) was formed in August 1955, with twelve parties and political organizations from the right to the extreme left. It could not exist for more than a few months and split into two. The left wing, headed by the BWPP, established the National United Front (NUF), while the other group formed the Burma Nationalist Bloc (BNB).

20. For a general description of the rebels in the early 1950s, see Trager, *Burma,* chs. 5-6.

21. For a detailed account of the various Communist factions, see J. H. Badgley, "The Communist Parties of Burma," in *The Communist Revolution in Asia: Tactics, Goals and Achievements,* ed. R. A. Scalapino (Englewood Cliffs, N.J.: Prentice-Hall, 1965), pp. 290-308.

22. There were similar organizations among the Shans, the Kachins (KIA), the Mons (MNDO) and the Kayahs. According to an official report, there were 5,485 insurgents in 1966; White Flag Communists, 700; Red Flag Communists, 209; Karens, 1,695; Shans, 274; Koumintang, 2,317; Mujahdis, 290. See Union of Burma, *Is Trust Vindicated?* (Rangoon: Director of Information and Broadcasting, 1960), p. 35.

23. Tinker, *Union,* pp. 231-232, 241-242, 646. For an illustration of how political support is mobilized, see M. Nash, "Party Building in Upper Burma," *Asian Survey,* III, no. 4 (April 1963), pp. 198-201.

24. This strength was reflected in their command of the armed units, known for some time as the Peace Guerillas, Tinker, *Union,* pp. 63, 236.

25. See International Labor Organization, *The Trade Union Situation in Burma* (Geneva: International Labor Organization, 1962), p. 32. In 1961, there were about 200,000 union members, but 64,520 belonged to 173 registered unions. Ibid., p. 37.

26. U Nu's Union Party controlled the Union of Burma Labor Organizations. A great part of the TUCB followed its leader, U Ba Swe, who after the split formed the "stable" faction. The third union was the BTUC, under the BWPP's control since the 1950s.

27. These included: (1) the Council of Burma Industries; (2) the Union of Burma Chamber of Commerce and Industry; (3) the Federation of Trades Organization; (4) the Industrial and Commercial Council; (5) the Burma Chamber of Commerce; and (6) the All Burma Rice Industrialists Association.

28. J. Silverstein, "Burmese Student Politics in a Changing Society," *Daedalus* (Winter 1968), pp. 275-276; J. Silverstein, "Burmese and Malaysian Student Politics: A Preliminary Comparative Inquiry," *Journal of Southeast Asian Studies,* I, no. 1 (March 1970), pp. 4-9.

29. The behavior of the Burmese students was not unusual in south and southeast Asia. One can find similar characteristics and activities among their student counterparts in India, Ceylon, Vietnam, Cambodia, and Singapore. See Philip G. Altbach, "Student Movements in Historical Perspective: The Asian Case," *Journal of Southeast Asian Studies,* I, no. 1 (March 1970), pp. 74-84.

30. See J. Silverstein and J. Wohl, "University Students and Politics in Burma," *Pacific Affairs,* XXXVII, no. 1 (Spring 1964), p. 53.

31. For the distribution of the students by religious, social, and political organizations and other demographic data, see ibid., pp. 57-59.

32. The newspapers with the largest circulations until 1962 were *The Nation* (in English), about 10,000 copies per day; *Hanthawaddy* (in Burmese), about 15,000 per day. See Tinker, *Union,* p. 20.

33. Eleven daily in Burmese, six in English, seven for the Indian population, and five in Chinese.

34. Tinker, *Union,* p. 78; Silverstein, "Burma," p. 125.

35. F. R. von der Mehden, "Buddhism and Politics in Burma," *Antioch Review,* XXI, no. 2 (Summer 1961), pp. 166-175; T. V. Sathyamurthy, "Aspects of Burmese," pp. 28-30.

36. Smith, *Religion,* p. 23. See also Leach, "Buddhism," pp. 55-56; S. J. Tambiah, "The Resistance and Transformation of Tradition in Southeast Asia, With Special Reference to Thailand," *Daedalus* (Winter 1973), pp. 56-62.

37. See Smith, *Religion,* ch. 3; F. R. von der Mehden, *Religion and Nationalism in Southeast Asiaa* (Madison: University of Wisconsin Press, 1968), pp. 80-82, 147-165. However, a few militant monks continued to participate in politics, collaborating particularly with the students; see Silverstein, "Burmese Student Politics," p. 280.

38. Smith, *Religion,* ch. 5. Sarkisyanz emphasizes that the leaders of the sangha, for example, Sayadaw U Nanda Thami, many times declared their lack of interest in politics. Individual monks, however, were very active in politics after independence. See Sarkisyanz, *Buddhist Background,* pp. 201-202.

39. See excerpts from the State Religion Promotion Act of 1961, in Mehden, *Religion,* pp. 103-107.

40. For later developments in what may be defined as the sixth stage, see below in the discussion of Ne Win's policy toward the sangha after 1962.

41. J. F. Guyot, "Bureaucratic Transformation in Burma," *Asian Bureaucratic Systems Emerged from the British Imperial Tradition,* ed. R. Braibanti (Chapel Hill, N.C.: Duke University Press, 1961), p. 428.

42. For some instructive notes about the social profile of the pre-war civil servants, see ibid., pp. 419-427.

43. For a general discussion of the civil service and especially its failure to respond to the challenge of modernization, see ibid., pp. 408-419; J. F. Guyot, "The 'Clerk Mentality' in Burmese Education," in *Man, State and Society in Contemporary Southeast Asia,* ed. R. O. Tilman (New York: Praeger, 1969), pp. 215-217.

44. See Silverstein, "Federal Dilemma," pp. 97-105.

45. For example, since Burmese was the official language and the only one taught in schools from the middle grades upward, the minorities became dependent on familiarity with the official language for much of their education and all of their higher training. More direct and concrete pressure to the same effect stemmed from unofficial encouragement of the missionary activities of Buddhist monks.

46. Walinsky, *Economic Development,* part IV.

47. Michael I. Mendelsohn, "Buddhism and the Burmese Establishment," *Archives des sociologie des religions* no. 17 (1964), pp. 85-88; Mehden, *Religion,* pp. 163-164. The anarchic situation was such that certain monasteries gained the reputation of being haunts or bogus monks who were in reality dacoits and petty criminals sheltering under the Yellow Robe (*Eastern World,* January 1958, p. 17).

48. The council of the Ecclesiastical Assembly was supposed to be composed of leading *sayadows* (authorities on Vinaya law and procedure). This plan was rejected by some heads of various monasteries. See *Eastern World,* January 1958, pp. 17-18.

49. See Smith, *Religion,* ch. 5; Mehden, *Religion,* pp. 97-98; Mendelsohn, "Buddhism," pp. 89-92.

50. These phenomena involve not only the insurrection but violence within the establishment framework as well. These kinds of acts became very common during the great split of the AFPFL.

51. See Traver N. Depuy, "Burma and Its Army: A Contrast in Motivations and Characteristics," *Antioch Review,* XX, no. 4 (Winter 1960-61), pp. 428-440; Tinker, *Union,* pp. 2-23; D. Guyot, "The Burmese Independence Army: A Political Movement in Military Garb," in *Southeast Asia in World War II,* ed. J. Silverstein (New Haven: Yale University, Monograph Series, no. 7, Southeast Asia Studies, 1966), p. 31.

52. At a later stage it was called the "Burma National Army" (BNA). See also D. Guyot, "Burmese Army," pp. 60-61; Ba Maw, *Breakthrough in Burma* (New Haven: Yale University Press, 1968), chs. 5, 6, 8; Maung Maung, *Burma,* pp. 93-160.

53. See Tinker, *Union,* pp. 34-61. See also F. R. von der Mehden, "Politics and the Military in Burma," in *The Military and Politics in Five Developing Nations,* ed. J. P. Lovell (Kensington, Md.: American Institution for Research in Social Systems, 1970), p. 206.

54. Butwell, "Burmese Political Development," pp. 134-135; Maung Maung, *Burma,* pp. 203-233.

55. American University, *Area Handbook for Burma,* (Washington, D.C.: United States Government Printing Office, 1968), p. 335.

56. Another reason for the shortage was the desertion of many NCOs and officers who belonged to the minorities. Two principal training facilities turn out officers for the three

services. The Defence Services Academy has a four-year course and is the professional school for regular officers. An officers' training school conducts a six-month course to train "emergency" or reserve officers, see ibid., p. 334. See also Mehden, "Politics," p. 208.

57. John S. Furnivall, *Colonial Policy and Practice: A Comparative Study of British and Netherland India* (Cambridge: Cambridge University Press, 1948), p. 184.

58. One minority with very great representation in the armed forces is the Anglo-Burman. The chief of the air force and some colonels have Anglo-Burman origins. See Mehden, "Politics," p. 200.

59. American University, *Area Handbook*, p. 333.

60. Union of Burma, *Trust*, p. 561. About the common background of the officers, see also Badgley, "Burma's Political Crises," *Pacific Affairs*, XXVI, no. 4 (December 1958), pp. 344-350; Maung Maung, *Burma's Constitution* (The Hague: Martinus Nijhoff, 1959), p. 144. See also Mehden, "Politics," p. 209; Guyot, "Bureaucratic Transformation," pp. 430-432.

61. It is interesting that the civilian government tried constantly to fight the flourishing of militarism and the military cult. One indication of this is that, in the Burmese army, there is no inflation of military ranks. Ne Win is only a lieutenant general; commanders of divisions are only brigadiers, etc.; whereas in Thailand there are seventy-two full generals. See Tinker, *Union*, p. 328. On the high prestige of officers in the provinces, see Badgley, *Politics Among Burmans: A Study of Intermediary Leaders* (Ohio University Center for International Studies, Southeast Asia Program, 1970, no. 15), pp. 73-75. In 1972, Colonel Tin U was reported to have been promoted to brigadier. It was the first such promotion in *ten* years. See Jon A. Wiant, "Burma: Loosening Up on the Tiger's Tail," *Asian Survey*, XIII, no. 2 (February 1973), p. 180.

62. *The Area Handbook for Burma* notes several inducements that added to the attraction of a military career: "medical care, retirement and survivor benefits. A variety of supplementary allowances for quarters, rations, families, special skills, and hazardous duty could substantially augment basic rates to attractive levels well above the civilian norm" (pp. 339-340).

63. See Walinsky, *Economic Development*, p. 261.

64. Quoted by Butwell, "Civilians and Soldiers in Burma," Sakai, *Studies on Asia*, p. 74.

65. Union of Burma, *Trust*, p. 533.

66. Ibid., p. 533.

67. Ibid., p. 534.

68. When the caretaker government was in power.

69. Ibid., p. 536.

70. Ibid., p. 540.

71. It is interesting that the army issued a journal called *The Open Mind*, which "aims to disseminate modern thought in various subjects, and to stimulate discussions and diversified interest among the government servants and others of leadership standing" (quoted in D. Wolfstone, "The Burmese Army Experiment," *Far Eastern Economic Review*, 12 February 1960, p. 356). The journal contained diversified international writings. Among the articles republished were Rostow's "Non-Communist Manifesto" and articles by such writers as Aldous Huxley, Viscount Montgomery, and Albert Einstein. The army director of education and psychological warfare issued a list of recommended reading for army officers that includes Marx, Engels, Lenin, Stalin, Bertrand Russell, Djilas, Grossman, Koestler, Cole, Howard Fast, Strachey, and Narayan.

72. Butwell, "Civilians," p. 77. See also Butwell, "The Four Failures of U Nu's Second Premiership," *Asian Survey*, II, no. 1 (March 1962), pp. 3-11.

73. *Asian Recorder*, June 25-July 1, 1962.

74. One of the most serious efforts made so far in Burma to synthesize Buddhism and Marxism was by the psychological warfare department of the army, which published a booklet dealing with this issue. See Smith, *Religion,* p. 132. In April 1962, the government announced the reconstruction of the Union Culture Council, "to strengthen traditional national culture and patriotism which are considered to be vital for the country's march towards the goal of socialism." See the *Asian Recorder,* May 14-20, 1962. See also Butwell, "Four Failures," p. 4; New York *Times,* 15 March 1962, and 18 March 1962.

75. Pye, *Politics,* p. 246.

76. New York *Times,* 8 March 1962.

77. Butwell, "Civilians," p. 77. For the policy of the second Ne Win government, see New York *Times,* 18 March 1962; and Butwell, "Four Failures," pp. 3-4.

78. See S. C. Banerji, "The BEDC Enterprises," *Far Eastern Economic Review,* XXXIX, no. 7 (14 February 1963), pp. 301-302; T. V. Tai, "The Role of the Military in the Developing Nations of South and Southeast Asia with Special Reference to Pakistan, Burma and Thailand" (Ph.D. diss., University of Virginia, 1965).

79. L. J. Walinsky, "The Role of the Military in Development Planning: Burma," in *Man, State,* ed. Tilman, pp. 341-342.

80. See, Union of Burma, *Trust,* p. 229.

81. The New York *Times,* 25 September 1960. Between 1952 and 1958, the DSI department store alone was able to contribute K 200,000 ($40,000) to the army welfare fund, and in 1959 it gave over K 7,200,000 ($1,400,000) to the command and brigade branches. The DSI enterprises were so successful because they were greatly encouraged by the government, receiving exemptions from all duties, such as customs duties, port fees, and sales taxes. The government also provided credit facilities and contracts for government business. See Walinsky, "Role of Military," p. 344.

82. The DSI did not hesitate to establish partnership with foreign investors, particularly with Israeli firms (in shipping and construction).

83. Considering the economic activities of the military, one should also consider the continuous increase in the defense budget. The following figures indicate a very substantial increase in defense after the takeover in 1962.

Percentages of total government expenditures for defense: 1950, 24%; 1951, 26%; 1952, 29%; 1953, 32%; 1954, 29%; 1955, 26%; 1956, 27%; 1957, 28%; 1958, 28%; 1964/5, 31.4%; 1965/6, 51.3%; 1966/7, 45.5%. Sources: figures until 1958 from Economic Commission for Asia and the Far East, *Economic Survey of Asia and the Far East, 1960* (Bangkok: Economic Commission for Asia and the Far East, 1961), table 38, p. 83; subsequent figures from American University, *Area Handbook,* p. 332.

84. The private sector was especially hurt by the crackdown on "economic insurgents" and by the fact that the regime tried to cut down the price level by having the army go into competition with businessmen.

85. However, Walinsky states, "Prime Minister U Nu, perhaps because he desired to direct the military's energies into constructive channels, perhaps because he sought allies within their ranks, encouraged Brigadier Aung Gyi to continue expansion of the DSI's economic activities and program and even negotiated a huge development credit with Mainland China, in the utilization of which Aung Gyi and DSI would obviously participate in major degree" ("Role of Military," p. 345).

86. Banerji, "BEDC," p. 302.

87. Wolfstone, "Burmese Army," pp. 296-299.

88. Walinsky, *Economic Development,* p. 261. After Brigadier Aung Gyi had been forced to resign, the BECD was actually wound up. The subsidiary firms were parceled out among the relevant boards and departments of the government. See *Forward,* 22 September 1963, p. 4; see also J. Guyot, "Bureaucratic Transformation," p. 401.

Burma's Political Breakdown [181]

89. Other military officers who played important political roles were Brigadier Aung Gyi and Brigadier Kyaw Zaw. See J. Guyot, "Bureaucratic Transformation," p. 427; Maung Maung, *Burma*, pp. 214-227.

90. "Civilians and Soldiers," p. 60.

91. Ibid. See also Mehden, "Politics," p. 225.

92. In 1961 U Nu ordered the central executive committee to disband on the grounds that the need for NSA was over. It is worth mentioning that the NSA was not the sole instrument for indoctrination. The army's psychological warfare department was in charge of cleaning the administration of corruption and strengthening its morale.

93. The Burmese army paid special attention to resettling veterans on land when they go on pension. This project entailed establishment of cooperative settlements, with the help of Israeli experts. See Union of Burma, *Trust*, pp. 37-39.

94. Cady, *History*, p. 494. Burmese officers in Burma's civil service were thus more numerous than Thai officers in Thai's civil service. See J. Guyot, "Bureaucratic Transformation," pp. 410-411.

95. E. Hagen, *On the Theory of Social Change* (Homewood, Ill.: Dorsey Press, 1962), p. 460. See also R. Butwell and F. R. von der Mehden, "The 1960 Election in Burma," *Pacific Affairs*, XXXIII (June 1960), p. 146.

96. See Lucian W. Pye, "The Army in Burma Politics," in *The Role of the Military in Underdeveloped Countries*, ed. J. J. Johnson (Princeton: Princeton University Press, 1962), p. 250. Twelve high-ranking officers—two brigadiers and ten colonels—had to take up careers as diplomats, businessmen, and politicians. Though no one dared to say so officially, it became clear that the announcement of Ne Win's decision to return his office to U Nu ended a struggle for power within the armed forces. See Mehden, "Politics," p. 221; J. Guyot, "Bureaucratic Transformation," p. 434.

97. For a detailed description of the events of 1960-62 from the point of view of Ne Win and his fellow officers, see Maung Maung, *Burma*, chs. 8-9. See also *Forward*, 15 April 1965, p. 3.

98. *Forward*, III, no. 3 (15 September 1964), pp. 4-6. For more opinions and citations of Ne Win statements after 1962, see Maung Maung, *Burma*, pp. 300-306.

99. *The Guardian*, 18 October 1964. A official publication dealing with the organizational and ideological foundations of the *Lanzin* Party devotes a special paragraph to the building of the People's Armed Forces. Among other things, the document states that "the present socialist revolution was launched with the Armed Forces as a basis. With the support of the power of the Armed Forces, the Revolutionary Council undertook the revolution as representative of the people to do away with the power of landlords and capitalists and to set up revolutionary power. The Armed Forces were born in political struggles and have gone through various armed revolutions. But at one time their notion of the role of the Armed Forces was that 'politics is no business of soldiers. Economic and social affairs are not the work of the Armed Forces; our sole duty is to defend the country.' Because of this narrow view of the role of the Armed Forces, they almost lost their revolutionary heritage and were about to disintegrate in political factional struggles" (Union of Burma, The Burma Socialist Programme Party Central Organizing Committee, *Party Seminar 1965*, February 1966, pp. 152-153).

100. Trager, *Burma*, ch. 9. For criteria of recruitment, see J. Silverstein, "Burma Socialist Program Party and Its Rivals: A One Plus Party System," *Journal of Southeast Asian History*, VIII, no. 1 (March 1967), pp. 12-13. For the official stand, see *Party Seminar 1965*, pp. 132-138.

101. In 1965, the RC included the following: chairman, General Ne Win; vice chairman, Brigadier Tin Pe; secretary, Brigadier San Yu; joint secretary, Colonel Than Sein; and

Colonel Kyaw Soe, Colonel Hla Han, Colonel Thaung Kyi, Colonel Maung Shwe, and Colonel Maung Lwin. See *Party Seminar 1965,* p. 123; J. H. Badgley, "Two Styles of Military Rule: Thailand and Burma," *Government and Opposition,* IV, no. 1 (Winter 1969), p. 107.

102. See *Party Seminar 1965,* pp. 128-130, 135-141, 144-152.

103. For example, the RC reported that "today (1965), out of a total of 99,638 candidate members in the Party, 35, 638 are servicemen. This shows that the Armed Forces are nondescript Armed Forces but are becoming transformed into revolutionary Armed Forces with political convictions. The members of the Armed Forces are systematically getting their orientation in the Burmese way to socialism" (ibid., p. 151).

104. Silverstein, "Burma Socialist Program," p. 15.

105. *Far Eastern Review Year Book, 1966,* p. 9; J. Guyot, "Clerk Mentality," p. 220.

106. The SAC very frequently were under very strong pressure because of the burden of excessive responsibilities. J. F. ·Guyot, "Political Involution in Burma," *Journal of Comparative Administration,* II (1970), p. 316. For the scope of penetration of officers into local government affairs, see Badgley, *Politics,* p. 74.

107. *The Guardian,* 21 June 1965. In 1969, after a long period of preparation, the RC established the Central People's Peasant Council (CPPC). For the structure, the composition of members, and the discussion held in its first national meeting, see J. Silverstein, "Burma: Political Dialogue in Burma: A New Turn on the Road to Socialism?" *Asian Survey,* X, no. 2 (February 1970), pp. 136-137.

108. The motives behind these policies were spelled out in the editorial of the RC's official paper, *The Working People's Daily:* "Still the residence of the overwhelming majority of the population, the basic economic unit of production and construction, the basic territorial level of administration, and consequently, the most important unit of political organization—the village—attracts the greater consideration in national life. The political climate (after independence) continued to promote the process of social disintegration of the village. It is from such social and political ruins that the village must be reconstructed" (23 January 1966).

109. *The Guardian,* 7 May 1964. After four years, the central organization of the People's Workers Council came into being. Like the Central People's Peasants Council, it was headed by military officers. See Silverstein, "Burma Political Dialogue," p. 387.

110. In July 1963, the Central School of Political Science was established to train party cadre leaders. In addition, all institutions where civil service personnel were trained held courses devoted to the study of the fundamental principles of the *Lanzin* Party ideology. The same policy was adapted for the teachers training course (*Forward,* 15 January 1965; *The Working People's Daily,* 25 June 1965), and the seminars for peasants and workers (*The Guardian,* February 1965; *The Working People's Daily,* November 8-9, 1964). For a list of seminars and publications between 1963 and 1965, see *Party Seminar 1965,* pp. 125, 131-132.

111. In April 1972, the Constitutional Drafting Commission made public the first draft of the new constitution. The final draft was approved by the Central Committee of the BSPP in mid-1973, by the BSPP's second congress in October 1973 and a referendum in December. On March 2, 1974, U Nu Win announced that the RC was returning power to the People's Assembly. U Nu Win was elected as president. The People's Assembly elected also a 28-member state council—the highest authority in the country—and an 18-man cabinet headed by Sein Win. See *Asia Research Bulletin,* III, no. 10 (March 31, 1974), p. 2539 B.

112. For more details, especially on U Nu's resolute stand calling for Ne Win to resign, and for the restoration of the democratic regime, see R. Butwell, "U Nu's Second Comeback Try," *Asian Survey,* IX, no. 11 (November 1964), pp. 870-871; Silverstein, "Burma Political Dialogue," pp. 131-134, 140-147.

113. D. Davies, "What's New, U Nu?," *Far Eastern Economic Review* (August 1969), pp. 530-532.

114. See Trager, *Burma,* ch. 9. See also Silverstein, "Burmese and Malaysian Student Politics," p. 9; J. F. Cady, "Burma's Military Dictatorship," *Asian Studies,* III, no. 3 (1965), pp. 504-506.

115. "During the *Pasabala* the circulation of English language newspapers stood at about one third that of Burmese language newspapers and this proportion held for the Caretaker period as well. With U Nu's return to power English language circulation dropped to one quarter of the Burmese rate and with the Revolutionary Government the ratio fell further to about one sixth" (J. Guyot, "Political Involution," p. 304).

116. Ibid. For more details on educational reform in primary and high schools, see Tai, "Role of Military," p. 379; Cady, "Burma's Military," pp. 506-507; Badgley, "Two Styles of Rule," p. 112.

117. Attempts at synthesis were expressed in the symbolic-visual-level "by the requirement that students, civil servants and other modern elements of civil society invest themselves in the traditional *longyi* and *gaungbaung* while the military flaunted their modernity by wearing trousers" (J. Guyot, "Political Involution," p. 314).

118. See Smith, *Religion,* p. 29; Trager, *Burma,* pp. 210-211.

119. See Smith, *Religion,* p. 291.

120. Ibid., pp. 292-294.

121. Ibid., p. 281.

122. See, for example, the Independence Day broadcast of General Ne Win, *Forward,* I, no. 12 (4 January 1963). Cited in Maung Maung, *Burma,* p. 308. Nevertheless, Ne Win used religious holidays or festivals, like the *Pwe,* for political mobilization. See editorial, *The Guardian,* 6 January 1965.

123. See Cady, "Burma's Military," pp. 502-504; R. A. Holmes, "Burmese Domestic Policy: The Politics of Burmanization," *Asian Survey,* VII, no. 3 (April 1967), pp. 193-197; *Far Eastern Economic Review* (25 April 1968), pp. 223-225; J. F. Badgley, "The Union of Burma: Age Twenty-Two," *Asian Survey,* XI, no. 2 (February 1971), pp. 150-152; P. Fulham, "Burma Guards Her Secrets," *Far Eastern Economic Review* (3 March 1966), pp. 404-405; F. N. Trager, "Burma: 1967—A Better Ending than Beginning," *Asian Survey,* VIII, no. 2 (February 1968), p. 114. However, immediately after the 1962 takeover, there was a sincere attempt by the RC to negotiate with the insurgents. In order to provide a proper climate, the RC declared general amnesty. For the description of the negotiations with the insurgents, see Maung Maung, op. cit., pp. 300-313; Holmes, "Burmese Policy," pp. 193-197. These negotiations also involved the foreign relations of Burma, especially with China. For the complex foreign relations with Burma, see Cady, op. cit., pp. 507-510; Trager, "Burma: 1967," pp. 112-114; Silverstein, "Burma Political Dialogue," pp. 138-148.

124. The "modernization" of the economy was actually linked with the Burmazation of the economy. It involved the expulsion of all foreigners, especially Indians. The cadres of the *Lanzin* Party assisted administratively in acts of nationalization and demonetization. See Holmes, "Burmese Policy," pp. 188-193; Walinsky, "Role of Military," pp. 346-350; Silverstein, "Burma Socialist Program," p. 13.

125. Mya Maung, "Socialism," p. 1190. See also Bechert's statement that nationalization of business and of the land is just as much "traditional" as it is "Marxist," cited in Leach, "Buddhism," p. 43.

126. For details, see J. Silverstein, "First Steps on the Burmese Way to Socialism," *Asian Survey,* IV, no. 2 (February 1964), pp. 717-719.

127. New York *Times,* 19 January 1968.

128. For methods of mobilizing workers into brigades and for the new constitution for

the industrial workers, see J. Silverstein, "Ne Win's Revolution Considered," *Asian Survey,* VI, no. 2 (February 1966), p. 99; *The Working People's Daily,* 7 May 1964 and 30 April 1964.

129. See *Far Eastern Economic Year Book, 1964* (Hong Kong: Far Eastern Economic Review, 1965), p. 102.

130. Party organization as a link between the center and the periphery was complemented by additional important frameworks, as, for example, the Burma civil service and a network of private businesses. See, J. Guyot, "Political Involution," p. 314. For some illustrations of the use of traditional frameworks for political means or of the traditional character of modern political frameworks, see Badgley, *Politics,* pp. 74-76.

131. As suggested by Guyot, following Geertz. J. Guyot, "Political Involution," p. 318.

132. See above.

133. See above.

134. C. Johnson, *Revolutionary Change* (Boston: Little, Brown, 1966), p. 137.

Chapter 6

BURMA: THE VULNERABLE POINTS IN THE STRATIFICATION ORDER

A. INTRODUCTION

We have already noted, in discussing stratification in Thailand, that dealing with social stratification is vital for a better understanding of power structure and the principles of resource allocation and a more comprehensive view of the structural and normative obstacles confronting development and modernization. The discussion of change in social stratification enables us also to look at the society from a wider historical perspective than would a discussion of civil-military relations in a specific period.

We shall thus review some of the changes that have taken place in the stratification of Burmese society since the 1930s and determine to what extent signs of a more modern class structure can be discerned and of what it consists.

Developing countries have great difficulty in creating conditions conducive to the rapid modernization of their economies and societies. To effect such modernization is a common goal of both civilian and military regimes, though their style and mode of action may be different. Many of these countries —including Burma—are fairly pluralistic ethnically, linguistically, and religiously, and ethnic and religious affiliations are related to occupational category, political status, and geographic concentration. This interferes with the attainment of a high level of national integration and the emergence of a modern, open class structure devoid of particularistic elements at various stratificational stages of the hierarchy. Obviously, it is not the only obstacle. There also is the interaction between town and country, the Westernized elite and the traditional sectors, the vast economic and cultural disparity between different strata—all problems that are no less important than the interrelation of the minorities and their interaction with the dominant sector.

The vulnerable spots of a developing, heterogeneous society, especially one that contains numerous particularistic ethnic enclaves, are best revealed by an examination of (a) the scope and rate of change in the occupational structure and the economic differential between different social strata; (b) the real potential for social and economic mobility and the aspiration of the various sectors of the population; and (c) the extent to which any changes in these variables tend to obscure the identity between ethnic and ecological affiliation and occupation and prestige categories, and whether they have led to psychological, normative, and structural conditions that stimulate greater interaction among different status groups.

As far as is known, no comprehensive study has been conducted in Burma on these issues. As a modest substitute, we have examined the data published at various times, and usually compiled for different purposes than those with which we are concerned here. Nevertheless, this rather fragmentary material can cast some light on our problems. It discusses changes in occupational structure and the process of urbanization. It also includes some rather sketchy information on mobility patterns and social image and status symbols, as well as on the social hierarchy and the stratification of the population of Burma, mainly until the 1962 military coup.

B. SOME ASPECTS OF STRATIFICATION IN THE COLONIAL PERIOD

We shall refer mainly to the post-independence period, but our point of departure will be the last decade of British rule in Burma. Although some changes in the stratification order occurred during the British period, these were marginal; only the most important need be mentioned.

Let us first present some of the findings of the 1931 census, the last published under British rule.[1] The occupational distribution in that census shows that agriculture and forestry was the dominant occupational category, involving 69.9% of the population. The other two categories with some significance were industry, mainly processing rice and other foodstuffs, with 10.7%, and trade, with 9.0%. The agricultural population was divided into three broad categories:[2] (1) owner cultivators, 38% of the principal workers; (2) tenant cultivators, 22%; and (3) agricultural laborers, 40%.

By 1931, about 62% of all persons engaged in agriculture were landless. This was because, beginning in the nineteenth century, to acquire land, seeds, and other means of production, the peasants had to borrow heavily. Very few succeeded in paying their debts and eventually many were evicted from their lands. Thus, for example, in 1936 the Chettyars (the main moneylenders in

Burma) owned approximately 2,500,000 of the 10,000,000 acres of rice land in the thirteen leading rice-growing districts. By 1939, the total farm acreage left to cultivators was 59% in lower Burma, 32% in upper Burma, and 49% in the country as a whole.[3] The overwhelming majority of the labor force lived in rural areas and engaged in farming, and most of it consisted of rural proletariat. Most of the urban population—as much as 75% of the urban labor force, was engaged in processing and supplying materials in industry, transportation, and trade. About 12% was classified as in administration, public security, and the free professions.[4]

In a colonial society—particularly a multiethnic one, such as Burma became with the influx of Indians and Chinese after the British conquest—the occupational structure of the population alone means little unless it is related to ethnic distribution. During the British period, businesses in Burma needing large amounts of capital—like mining enterprises, teak harvesting and marketing, much of the rice trade, and most commercial banking—were in the hands of British or other European companies. These also controlled most of the imports and internal services, such as transportation and electric power. Some import and export businesses were owned by Indians and Chinese, who also distributed most imported consumer goods. As a rule, there was no place in business for the Burmese, except as laborers, clerks, small merchants, or small "industrialists." On the whole, the economy was primitive.

The export industries run by the British were modern and efficient, as was the transportaiton system needed for them. But there was no other industry except cottage industries, with limited output.

In 1931, the ethnic composition of the population of Burma was as follows: Burmese, 65.7%; other indigenous groups, 24.6%; Indian, 7.0%; Indo-Burmese, 1.2%; Chinese, 1.3%; Europeans, 0.2%.

Table 6.1 shows the relationships between ethnic origin and occupational structure in 1931. In agriculture, trade, and industry, the Burmese, 56% of the total employment figure, were represented more or less according to their numbers. They were, however, underrepresented in mining, transport, public security forces, and public administration. They were surprisingly overrepresented in the professions and liberal arts, probably because the Buddhist monks were classified in this category.[5]

The Chinese, on the other hand, only 15% of the total of employed persons, were overrepresented in mining, industry, and transportation—and still more in trade. This was even more marked among the Indians born outside Burma, whose share in the total employment was only 8% but who made up 43.4% of the public security forces, 43.2% of the transportation sector, 36.3% of the mining sector, and 26.6% of public administration. By the 1930s, this applied to other categories as well. The Chinese and the Indians held rather important

TABLE 6.1: LABOR FORCE PARTICIPANTS BY RACE AND OCCUPATION IN BURMA, 1931 (in percentages)

	All Races	Burmese	Other Indigenous Races	Chinese	Indians Born in Burma	Indians Born outside Burma	Indo-Burmese Races	Europeans and Allied Races	Anglo-Indian	Other Races
All occupations	100.0	55.8	32.1	1.5	1.6	7.9	0.9	0.1	0.1	—
Farming	100.0	56.7	38.0	0.5	1.6	2.5	0.7	—	—	—
Mining	100.0	33.5	15.0	9.8	1.0	36.3	0.3	1.4	0.4	—
Industry	100.0	56.7	24.1	2.3	1.1	14.7	0.9	0.1	0.1	—
Transport	100.0	40.5	8.3	2.6	2.5	43.2	1.5	0.6	0.6	0.1
Trade	100.0	59.2	14.1	6.9	1.6	15.6	2.2	0.1	0.1	0.1
Public forces	100.0	31.3	15.9	0.3	2.0	43.4	0.8	5.8	0.5	—
Public administration	100.0	37.4	25.5	1.3	2.3	26.6	1.9	0.8	1.7	0.1
Professional and liberal arts	100.0	67.1	24.8	0.7	0.8	4.4	0.8	0.5	0.6	0.1

SOURCE: Surider K. Mehta, "The Labor Force in Urban Burma and Rangoon: A Comparative Study" (Ph.D. dissertation, University of Chicago, 1959), p. 399.

positions in most occupations and places offering exposure to new ideas —generally known as the by-products of modernization. "An ethnic division of labour placed the Burmese at the bottom of the ladder, concentrating them in the agricultural and extractive sectors of the economy, tying them to money lent by small capitalists, and binding their welfare to the fluctuations of the world market in rice."[6]

The percentage of Burmese engaged in agriculture in the early 1950s was 62.7% (in comparison to 69.6% in 1931),[7] in spite of the population growth. The professional category went down from 3.2% in 1931 to 1.2% in 1953-54, and though it must be remembered that "one of the most important categories relates to persons in religious orders who were included under the professional group in the pre-war census, but were omitted from the occupational classification altogether as being institutional persons in the later census,"[8] its share evidently did not go up. The only significant increase was in the administration sector. The number of civil servants grew in absolute and in relative terms.[9] Clearly, since the 1930s no significant change occurred in the occupational structure, and symptoms of stagnation and even of regression may be discerned when Burma is compared with typical industrialized societies.

The economic sector distribution of employment status of the labor force is also relevant. In this respect, Burmese statistics distinguish among: (1) hired workers in the private sector; (2) hired workers in the government sector; (3) self-employed workers; and (4) unpaid workers.

In 1953-54, the farmers were divided almost equally between private landowners (36.8%) and hired workers (32%).[10] It is difficult to compare these figures with the 1931 figures, where an additional distinction was made between tenants and laborers, but dependents or unpaid family workers were not listed separately.[11] Nevertheless, the percentage of "own-account" workers in agriculture remained largely stable. Hired laborers in the private sector also constituted the majority of persons employed in mining and in crafts. Hence, in the three occupations of the rural sector—farming, mining, and crafts—there were significantly more hired laborers than "own-account" workers. When all occupations are taken into account, 40.1% (including the private and government sectors) were hired workers and 35.7% self-employed. Moreover, considering that 24.2% were unpaid family workers, many of whom should probably be classified among the self-employed, the proportion of hired laborers is still impressive.

One conclusion is that, in rural sectors, a great reservoir of candidates for geographic and even vertical mobility existed. In the 1930s large manpower resources for political and ideological manipulation were concentrated in the rural areas. This class of people could, at least theoretically, have exerted great pressure on the political center. Since independence, this segment of the population has become the focus of political recruitment by rival political parties and movements.

In principle, the situation in the cities was similar. There were more employees than self-employed, although, as in the rural sector, the difference was not big. As many as 42.8% of the professionals were government employees. Only 25.5% worked in private firms, while the rest were self-employed. The proportions were about the same among the managerial workers. Trade, on the other hand, was heavily concentrated in the hands of private merchants—79.8% in 1953-54.[12]

Unfortunately, no systematic data are available on the relationships between the ethnic and occupational structure after Burma became independent. However, radical changes have taken place since, mainly because of the departure of Europeans and Indians.

In principle and in practice, the economic and political policy of the Burmese government promoted Burmazation and nationalization of the economy. Nationalization, mostly directed toward large foreign-controlled business enterprises and, after the 1962 coup, toward small businesses, was at first a cover for the Burmazation policy.[13]

In sum, in the 1950s, the Burmese labor force in both the urban and rural sectors was composed mainly of hired laborers, small traders, craftsmen, and civil servants. The Burmese were conspicuously absent from the middle class, which until the late 1950s consisted of Chinese and Indians.[14]

C. URBANIZATION AND MODERNIZATION

Students of the relationship between stratification and modernization attach great importance to the well-known desirable and the undesirable effects of urbanization in developing countries. The undesirable effects, for example, include the disruptive tendencies resulting from large-scale and rapid urbanization when large unskilled masses cannot be integrated—at least in the short run—economically, socially, or politically. We shall try to examine to what extent such apprehensions are justified for Burma.[15]

Urbanization in Burma was a rather slow and restricted process. Moreover, although it began as early as the beginning of the nineteenth century, there seem to have been some trends in the opposite direction (see Table 6.2). The proportion of the urban population went down during the first quarter of the twentieth century and was restored to its former size only in the late 1940s and early 1950s, when large numbers moved to the towns—at least 756,000 in 1948-52, and about 127,000 in 1953.[16] The early urban decrease was largely due to expansions of the rural sector brought about by the transfer of some of

Burma's Stratification Order

TABLE 6.2: URBAN AND TOTAL POPULATION IN BURMA, 1891-1953 (in thousands)

	Total Population	Total Population	Percentage
1891	947	7,722	12.3
1901	991	10,491	9.5
1911	1,127	12,115	9.3
1921	1,292	13,212	9.8
1931	1,520	14,667	10.4
1941	–	16,824	–
1953	2,579	19,045	13.5

SOURCE: R. M. Sundrum, "Urbanization: The Burmese Experience," *Journal of Burma Research Society*, XL (June 1957), part I, table 111.

the indigenous population from the towns to uncultivated areas in the provinces. It might have been greater still if there had not been a simultaneous invasion of the towns by Indians and Chinese. The trend was reversed when agriculture suffered heavily in the economic depression of the 1930s, when farmers sank into debt, were evicted from their land, and again moved into the cities. This movement was sustained until World War II. As the cities were, at least economically, unprepared to absorb such massive immigration, this had many repercussions on the administration and the political apparatus.

It would be misleading to describe the process of urbanization generally without stressing the prominent role played by Rangoon. Table 6.3 shows its rapid growth compared with the other three big cities (Mandalay, Moulmein, and Bassein) after 1891. By 1953, Rangoon had 737,000 inhabitants—one-quarter of the total urban population of Burma. Again, the cities and towns of Burma, notably Rangoon, attracted not only the indigenous races but also and primarily Indians and Chinese.[17] In 1931, the indigenous races accounted for only 59% of the urban population; not until 1953 did they constitute 84%, more or less equivalent to their weight in the total population.[18] However, as late as 1953 the so-called exogenous groups made up about 30%. In 1931, these constituted 65% of Rangoon's population.

TABLE 6.3: POPULATION GROWTH IN RANGOON AND OTHER CITIES (in thousands)

Census	Rangoon Population	Secondary Towns Average Populations	Ratio
1891	180.3	91.5	1.97
1901	234.9	91.4	2.57
1911	293.3	77.7	3.57
1921	342.0	84.3	4.06
1931	400.4	86.4	4.63
1953	737.1	122.2	6.03

SOURCE: R. M. Sundrum, "Urbanization: The Burmese Experience," *Journal of Burma Research Society*, XL (June 1957), table ix.

Urbanization in Burma (especially the growth of Rangoon) is reminiscent of urbanization patterns in other societies of southeast Asia and underdeveloped countries.[19] In several respects, the starting point was the same in many Asian countries. The royal cities formed the core of urbanization. However, the process and its consequences were widely divergent, primarily because in the developing countries, urbanization occurred under a colonial regime. The bland assumption that colonial rule curbed urbanization is misguided, but since the entire economic development of the colonies was geared to the specific interests of an alien metropolis, these interests and their underlying ideology were naturally reflected in urbanization. For example, the British had a literal policy for Indian and Chinese immigration into Burma, because they considered the Indians and the Chinese best suited for administrative, military, and economic functions.

A characteristic feature of urbanization in southeast Asia is the emergence of what have been called "primate cities." The primate city predominates over the other cities and towns of a country; it is many times larger than the next-largest city. This kind of city also exists in Europe (London, Copenhagen, etc.). However, the Asian primate city was developed by foreigners. Its rate of growth was conditioned by colonial policy rather than by the interests of the colony. The impact of the metropolis was both in its physical outlay and in the composition of its population. The result was that the alienation and estrangement between the primate city and other cities—not to mention the rural sector—were far greater than those between European "primate cities" and their hinterlands. Small wonder, then, that these cities "failed to perform their natural function (in and for their own countries), in such a way as to be commercial centres of internal trade, financial centres for internal transactions or even as cultural clearing ground."[20] Moreover, because of foreign dominance, native industrial enterprise was unable to establish itself.

D. INCOME DISTRIBUTION IN POST-INDEPENDENCE BURMA

A more comprehensive picture of Burmese class structure may be obtained by studying income distribution and its development. It must be remembered that, in the 1950s, Burma was one of the poorest countries in southeast Asia. In 1957, Burma ranked as the 113.5th among 122 countries in terms of GNP per capita—$57 a year.[21] Table 6.4 presents both the aggregate and average *annual* incomes of various occupations in 1953-54. The lowest income was K. 377 ($75), earned by the service occupation; the highest was K. 1,420 ($284) earned by administrative employees—about four times as much. The total average income was K. 592 ($118).[22]

TABLE 6.4: OCCUPATIONAL CLASSIFICATION OF PERSONAL INCOMES IN BURMA, 1953-54

Occupations	Total Income (in Millions of Kyats)	Average Income (Kyats)
Professions	131	1,193
Managerial	277	1,420
Sales	514	638
Farming	1,805	539
Mining	32	754
Transport	177	755
Crafts	467	567
Services	332	377
Miscellaneous	35	1,311
Total	3,710	592

SOURCE: R. M. Sundrum, *Census Data on the Labour Force and Income Distribution in Burma* (Department of Economics, Statistics and Commerce, University of Rangoon, 1958), table xvii.

It seems that, after the 1930s, real income decreased.[23] With regard to the income distribution in the rural and urban sectors, two points should be noted.[24] In every occupational category, wages in the cities were higher than in the rural areas—the ratio being approximately 1 : 2. Second, the highest income span was between civil servants and services employees, with a ratio of 1 : 3.5; in the urban areas, the highest differential was between civil servants and farmers, with a ratio of 1 : 3.[25]

The income differentials among occupations, sectors, and sexes are only one income aspect of social differentiation. Another important one is the relative size of each income category. Table 6.5 provides instructive information on the urban distribution sector in 1957.[26] In dollars, two-fifths of the urban working population earned less than $157.50; more than half, less than $210; and more than 85% less than $420 per annum (or $35 per month).[27] From all this, certain conclusions follow.

Burma, in the 1950s and 1960s, ranked at the bottom of the scale in standard of living as measured by per capita income.

In most occupations, the real average income had not risen since the beginning of the 1940s; in some, it seems to have actually gone down.

The average income differential between the highest and lowest occupational categories was about one to four, and between the extreme income groups the span was, of course, much greater. The income of a judge, for example, was about K. 3,000 ($600), and that of an unsilled worker about K. 90 per month, a ratio of 1 : 30.

For all occupations, the income level in the cities was twice that in the rural areas. The income level of men was twice that of women.

TABLE 6.5: URBAN POPULATION BY INCOME GROUPS IN BURMA, 1957

Average Annual Income	Percent of Total Sample	Persons Above the Age of 11 Who Did Some Work During the Year (thousands)
Total	100.0	1,108.7
Under K. 250	8.8	97.2
K. 250-K. 499	14.9	164.9
K. 500-K. 749	17.2	190.6
K. 750-K. 999	12.2	134.4
K. 1,000-K. 1,999	32.9	364.2
K. 2,000-K. 2,999	6.3	70.0
K. 3,000-K. 3,999	3.9	43.1
K. 4,000-K. 4,999	1.2	13.3
K. 5,000-K. 7,499	1.4	15.9
K. 7,500 and over	1.0	11.5

SOURCE: Walinsky, *Economic Development in Burma 1955-1960* (New York: The Twentieth Century Fund, 1962), table 3, p. 37.

Employees in government-public sectors earned a higher income than private employees or even self-employed persons.

The annual income of more than 62% of the urban labor force was between K. 500 and K. 1,999 ($100-$400). According to Walinsky, that part of the population which may be defined as belonging to the middle class (earning more than $2,000 per year) in 1957 consisted of less than 0.5% of the population. From an economic aspect, the social differentiation in the 1950s was thus practically the same as in the 1930s, the only difference being in the changed relationship between the economic-occupational and ethnic compositions. The Indians and Chinese were ousted from their positions in trade and administration, but only a very small segment of the population, the new elite which emerged after Burma achieved its independence, reaped the benefits of this.[28]

E. PATTERNS OF SOCIAL MOBILITY

We have presented some basic statistical data. Although those are indispensable for any analysis of stratification, the cultural and symbolic manifestations of the stratificational order must also be considered. Some, especially those associated with mobility and the components of prestige and status, will be discussed here.

The channels of mobility in Burma, even in the pre-British period, were never governed by rigid religious norms. Nor were there any other moral sanctions that prescribed a rigid stratified system in terms of the quality and the number of alternatives open to individuals and groups. "Social place, in the hierarchical and in the spatial sense, was not fixed. There was fluidity, change, intrigue, and the rise and fall of royal and individual fortunes."[29] This substantial conceptual flexibility conflicted with the cruel reality, especially after the British conquest. Channels of mobility were for all practical purposes nonexistent. The Burmese did not and could not move into the modern spheres of the economy. They were also restricted politically by the obstacles the British raised to a broadly based national movement. Those who nevertheless chose a political career were left with few career openings. At most they could attain cabinet posts lacking any real responsibilities. "The ambitious only had one direction in which to turn, one avenue of possible advance—towards the domain of officialdom."[30] Indeed, the prewar Indian civil service, and especially the Provincial Civil Service, provided an opportunity, although a very limited one, to a small elite of Westernized Burmese, many of them Anglo-Burmese.[31]

After a decade or more of independence and the rise of a new civilian political elite, the principal channels of mobility had changed little. After as well as before the coup, the peasantry, the small traders, and the few industrial workers had gained little scope for economic expansion. The only slight signs of new mobility were discernible in the bureaucracy—the traditional channel of mobility. Most opportunities came with its expansion and diversification. Some measure of change also came about when the various political parties active prior to the coup established a bureaucratic apparatus of their own.

There is even less information on the possible effects of the bureaucratic nature of the channels of mobility and social aspiration, the conception of the ideal pattern of social stratification, than is available on the effective class structure. Study of "status bases and symbols" and prestige of various occupations in the Burmese society shows the relative absence of sanctified and institutionalized ascriptive status variables and criteria. The relative flexibility and universalistic flavors of the status images are reflected in some of the key concepts used in descriptions of power relations and evaluation of personal prestige and social position.

One of the key concepts is *Awza*.

Awza is a function of relationship, the important thing being that in every group there is someone who has *Awza*. The components of *Awza* include the characteristics we would normally associate with power: influence and prestige—among them respectability, wisdom and knowledge, a degree of religiosity, a commanding presence and skill and ease in handling authority. *Awza* also implies a likeable personality, a touch of modesty, and usually considerable sex appeal. Wealth in itself may not be absolutely essential, but one must give the impression of not being worried about matters of daily living, of being able to live beyond one's visible means, or best of all, of having no visible means of support but still living comfortably.[32]

Nash refers to this concept in conjunction with two others, *Pon* and *Gon,* and contends that only all three together properly define the relationship among power, influence, and authority. *Pon*

> means power to carry out plans, to bend others to one's will, to move destiny to one's advantage. The *Awza* of a man with *Pon* stems from his *personal* [italics added] powers, his marked and conspicuous abilities to succeed in this world.... It connotes a sterling personal character of special religious learning or piety, or even the trait of impartiality in disputes. *Pon* and *Awza* are power dimensions of social relations. *Gon* is the moral content.[33]

The interesting thing in these definitions is their particularistic and ascriptive element. They are far from being so dominant as similar concepts would be in the terminology of power relations in, for instance, the traditional society of India or in feudal societies. To a great extent, the qualities to which these concepts refer are personal. Although authority is necessary for them to be realized, their authority does not necessarily derive from a traditional power position, despite the importance of such position in traditional Burmese society.

The value which Burmese accord to *Awza* and *Gon* implies a great respect for the exercise of power and the authority to exercise it. "There are few cultures that attach greater importance to power as a value than the Burmese. Consideration of power and status so permeate even social relationships in Burma that life tends to become highly politicized."[34]

These qualities are intensified by the loose structure of the society, and they are very highly evaluated as a means of exchange and accumulation of power and prestige.[35]

Awza and *Gon* are, however, certainly not the only social determinants of Burmese society. At least two other criteria are present. One is traditional and the other is a direct result of modernization. The traditional criterion is the concept of accumulated *merit* for the attainment of religious goals.

> The goal toward which all Buddhists are struggling is the escape from the constant cycle of rebirth in this or other worlds, in human or non-human form. The goal of Nirvana, or more immediately of rebirth in a higher state in the next existence, is balanced by a fear of hell or rebirth in a "lower" existence or non-human form. Progress toward eternal bliss is independent upon the store of Karma which in turn is dependent upon the merit or demerit earned by one's actions in this existence.[36]

The importance attached to this criterion, especially in traditional sectors, explains the reverential attitude to monks. Their social status is not based on economic and political preeminence, in the instrumental, narrow meaning of these terms, but rather on their "association with popular religious values, ideals, and concepts or morality. In the monks' observance of religious vows and precepts . . . the Burmese have a visible, living example of life which, according to their view, is so full of merit and as free from sin as is possible in this world."[37] The monks' social status, at least for believers, also stems from their significant role as a literate elite, versed in Burmese and *Pali* scriptures, in transmitting cultural values to the young.[38]

The modern criterion is education. Since the British conquest of Burma and the establishment of a modern administration, education has become the most promising avenue for social mobility.[39] Because a college degree was once the best and virtually only means for social and economic advancement, many parents urged their children to go to college regardless of whether they were qualified and whether their studies prepared them for the more technical jobs available. High school and university education became so highly regarded that "the university students who failed their examination continued to try year after year,"[40] until they acquired the title to which they aspired. The prestige was not, however, for education as such but only for education as a means for entering the administration. The status of academicians was not very high and apparently decreased after independence.[41] The esteem in which education was held was not coupled with an equally high regard for the skills of the specialist.

It is within the framework of these expectations and norms that the clashes between the students and university authorities since 1920 may be partially explained. Aside from the purely political nature of these conflicts, demands that the enrollment criteria and requirements for academic titles be lowered are still an acute issue.[42] Education is still viewed as a means of access to administrative jobs. Research on occupational choices among the university students of Rangoon and Mandalay, conducted in 1962, showed that the overwhelming majority were interested in working in the government of in the private sector. Only 10% wished to pursue a scientific career.[43] However, the prestige of education has decreased sharply since the establishment of the military elite. This is apparently related to changes in the conceptions of the role the educated should perform in a socialistic country.

In a letter to the editor of the *Working People's Daily,* a student of Rangoon University contended that "nowadays voices of contempt are as loud against graduates as against capitalists. Graduates are often alleged as easy-going bourgeois and opportunists and that they have not better intelligence and general knowledge than an ordinary man in the street."[44] There can be no doubt that the emphasis on the importance of degrees and of charismatic qualities such as *Awza* and *Gon* testifies to the existence of some universalistic elements both in reality and in the status images of the Burmese society (especially in the Westernized sector). This helps explain why entrepreneurship traditionally had a low status in the Burmese social structure. Traders were considered socially inferior to those who served the king, ordinary civic employers, and even cultivators. This attitude was further strengthened by colonial rule and by socialist criticism of capitalism.[45]

This is an appropriate place to present some of the data about literacy and the Burmese educational system. Literacy is rather more widespread in Burma than in most other countries in southeast Asia and is more or less the same as in Thailand.[46] Approximately 80% of all males and 40% of all females are literate, without significant differences between the rural and urban sectors (especially among males), in the Burmese language.[47] This high rate is not maintained for other languages (particularly English), and the women lag far behind (see Table 6.6). In 1953, the figures for those able to read and write in languages other than (and in addition to) Burmese were 14.1% for men and 5.3% for women.

To what extent did literacy rise during the 1960s?[48] The percentage of literate males was relatively high (53%) at the beginning of the century. The most dramatic increase was in the female population—from 6% in 1901 to 40% in 1960.[49]

The vague uses of the concept of literacy and the unreliability of some of the figures could lead to a distorted picture of the situation. In order to visualize the scene more fully, we must go beyond the dichotomy of illiterate and literate people.

A survey conducted in 253 towns in 1953 found that 63% of the urban population aged twenty-five and over did not finish primary school and many were illiterate. Approximately 36% graduated from secondary schools and only

TABLE 6.6: LITERACY IN BURMESE AND OTHER LANGUAGES, BY SEX FOR POPULATION FIVE YEARS OF AGE AND OVER, URBAN BURMA, 1953

Language	Total	Male	Female
Total	100.0	100.0	100.0
Total literate	66.3	80.5	51.5
Burmese only	51.0	57.9	43.8
Burmese and other languages	9.8	14.1	5.3
Other languages	5.5	8.5	2.4
Illiterate	33.7	19.5	48.5

SOURCE: Mehta, *The Labor Force in Burma and Rangoon*, Table 24, p. 107.

1.2% from higher institutions, including the higher stages of secondary schools and the universities.[50] In this respect, the educational attainment in Thailand was already higher than in Burma.[51]

In the rural sector, the situation was obviously worse. More than 83% were actually illiterate or had received fewer than four years of primary school education. Only 17% had attended school for seven years. One reason was the fact that in that period education was not compulsory. It is thus no wonder that only 20% of the pupils enrolled in grade 1 (and they were only 60% of all those between five and seven) actually completed the four years of primary schooling.[52] One may assume that the situation has improved since 1953. The number of pupils enrolled in primary schools had increased from about 400,000 in 1950-51 to 1.7 million in 1962-63.[53] Yet even at the later date, only about 10,000 of 30,000 villages had primary schools. Some villages were even without Phongge Kyang or monastic schools.[54] About 70% of those finishing primary schools received a secondary education; approximately 15% of all boys and 6% of all girls at the age of eleven were enrolled in a fifth year of study.[55] There has been a substantial increase in the number of students, despite the introduction of fees for secondary education in 1959.[56]

A great proportion of secondary schools in the 1950s and the beginning of the 1960s were general secondary schools. We assume that only 2% of those enrolled in secondary schools afterward attended technical and vocational schools. The significance is clear: The educational system was unable to supply anything but a negligible percentage of the technological manpower required for economic development. The secondary education system merely contributed to an already overstaffed bureaucracy. Moreover, the emerging manpower was not too well qualified, since only a small percentage passed the matriculation examinations.[57]

The commitment of Burma's leaders to socialism, and their well meant, though unsuccessful, attempt to build a welfare state *(pyidautha)*, at least normatively helped to blur potential and real differences and to legitimize universalistic channels of mobility. Moreover, they tried to belittle and deprecate the economic component of social status. It would nevertheless be wrong to describe Burma as a country totally lacking any distinct status group. Most status groups are a legacy of colonial rule or have emerged in the course of modernization, while some are founded on subjective status images. The colonial legacy is reflected in the significant distinction made between "Westernism" and adherents of traditional culture—which also includes some in-between groups. In colonial times, the most highly respected occupational and economic functions tended to be concentrated in the bureaucracy and the military; this certainly reinforced the internal cohesion of the Westernized group.

The party bureaucracy attracted social groups placed between the Westernized and the traditional groups. Although the politicians who came from such intermediate groups were in many respects closer to the intelligentsia and the higher civil servants, they did not necessarily mitigate the conflict with the Westernness or help to bridge the difference. In fact, if there was any conflict with class overtones, it was precisely between politicians and the administration.[58] The administrative elite apparently had attained considerable internal solidarity as a result of two internally contradictory developments: their achievements, especially under British rule; and their frustration as "natives" whose way to the top power positions was barred. The distinctiveness and sense of alienation of this status group was not diminished by independence, for it was unable to realize its old aspirations and it was gradually ousted from most key positions. Parallel to this development, the process of Burmazation of the Burma Civil Service in the 1950s was accelerated, since the vacuum created by the forced retirement of British and Indian officials enabled junior members to attain upward mobility. Mobility, however, did not bring with it more power and prestige. These resources were monopolized earlier by the political elite and later by the military officers.[59]

The political elite was much less cohesive and integrated than the administrative elite. Incessant rifts were caused by personal ambitions and intensive political and ideological differences of opinion. Though as an intermediate group, in terms of exposure to Western culture, it was able to act as broker between the top leaders and the "masses," this role did not contribute to its subjective sense of unity and solidarity.

By and large, no other status groups can be discerned. Below the national elite, the social order was fairly undifferentiated. There was hardly a stratification approaching a class structure. People were not class conscious; nor did they organize as separate classes politically or in more diffuse nonpolitical settings. However, monks constituted a distinct, though not homogeneous, group from an institutional and in some respects also from a political point of view. Before 1962, they had gone a long way, compared with the urban proletariat or the peasantry, toward independent political organization. Both the trade unions and the farmers' organization served more as political tools in the hands of the political elite than as a focus of class consolidation. Some of the complex reasons for this may be sought in Burma's political heritage. The lack of confrontation between exploited employees and employers—in the West, such confrontations led to militant trade unions and employers' organizations—may also be partly responsible. In Burma, the public services and joint government and private ventures were the only ones with strong trade unions—whose activities were curbed by law.

The 1962 coup, which was followed by a serious attempt to redistribute power and prestige, did not change this situation substantially. Moreover, to a certain extent, there was a change for the worse. The monopoly over political and economic resources became more absolute and extreme, while social and economic differentiation was reduced owing to the policy which imposed on the Burmese society far-reaching economic equality by lowering the standard of living of almost the whole population and nationalizing the entire private economic sector.

F. SUMMARY AND CONCLUSIONS

We have outlined some characteristics of the Burmese class structure. Occupational structure and its modification during the last three or four decades seem especially important, as is the income distribution among various occupational groups. The differentiation and cooperation of the different elites, the settings in which they function, the qualification for admission, and the patterns of mobility—comparing the standard of aspirations with the channels available—have been described. The internal cohesiveness of the social strata insofar as distinct self-conscious entities are concerned has been examined. The main question now is: What conclusions may we draw? What are the positive and constructive aspects? Where are the vulnerable points, especially in terms of the ability of the political center to cope with the serious problems it has confronted since independence?

We have suggested that one of the main problems of many developing countries is that of overcoming the pattern of institutional pluralism that emerged (for various historical reasons) and then approaching a pattern of social and cultural pluralism (if the society is a heterogenous one). "Institutional pluralism" has been defined as one characterized by the coexistence of antagonistic institutional systems where contacts between groups are largely restricted to purely instrumental matters. The "social pluralistic" society has been defined as that type in which the interaction between social groups, especially on informal levels, is restricted by manifest (at least) latent norms which are largely accepted by the potential role incumbents. To maintain this kind of order, certain conditions conducive to voluntary *partial* segregation and the isolation of the various groups must be promoted. Social pluralism may be contingent on the propensity and the acknowledged right of groups to manifest distinctive identities and at the same time to accept procedures regulating intergroup contacts. It is also vital that many partial overlappings of points of contact between status groups emerge to blunt any sharp edges of potential or real social fissures. From a societal point of view, institutional dispersion is required—at least a partial dispersion of the various segments of the population in different economic and occupational categories. From the standpoint of the individual, this means an increased number of incumbents of noncongruent status profiles.

Since none of the research which has served as sources for our analysis was designed primarily to test our theory, we must be careful in making statements. At best, some tentative conclusions may be drawn.[60]

First, the population of Burma split into two main parts. There is the small elite concentrated in the governmental administration, in the party bureaucracy, and in the military; and there are the peasants, small traders, businessmen, and hired laborers. In between the two groups is a very small group of middle-class and skilled workers.

Second, although the average income level is exceedingly low, the discrepancy between the earnings of those in the highest and of those in the lowest categories was very important, at least until 1962.

Third, the modern elite is small and its internal differentiation, although limited, shows a great degree of internal antagonism. Before the coup, the adversary groups were chiefly administrators, various politicians, and students. The extent of autonomy and freedom of action of the various elite groups was quite limited, owing to the absence of frameworks of action beyond the governmental bureaucracy, the military, and the underdeveloped party bureaucracy. In other words, the weakness of the opposition parties and the trade unions, the small number of independent economic organizations, and the limited size of the academic community and professional organizations made it difficult for elites to develop in opposition and to be institutionalized in relatively independent power positions. This had many repercussions on the already limited ability of the political and social center to cope with economic and political problems.

Fourth, despite both the universalistic criteria which made for acceptance into the various elite groups and the not insignificant de facto mobility, channels for upward mobility were few and limited to a number of branches in the political and governmental bureaucracy. This enabled the ruling elite to exert a great deal of influence in channeling desirable (upwardly mobile) recruits. On the other hand, the limited number of open avenues for mobility created a permanent pressure from the unemployed or underemployed high school and university graduates.

Fifth, if we do not consider the ethnic minorities, crystallized class oriented organizations were very rare. To the extent that they existed, one of the important criteria for membership was type of education received and the amount of exposure to Western culture. This overlaps only partly with the distinction between the urban and the rural sectors. The majority of the urban population was very similar, in those respects, to the rural population. Burma no longer may be described as a society exhibiting manifest clear-cut institutional pluralism. The class structure is actually in a state of extensive flux. Burma must first and foremost achieve a more institutionalized differentiation of those beneath the elites. If this can be attained, the difficulties in establishing bridges between the elites and the population would be less salient, as the number of noncongruent status groups would be increased and these would be in a position to serve as intermediaries between the elites and the more sophisticated differentiated population.

NOTES

1. For the occupational composition in 1911 and 1921, see Surider K. Mehta, "The Labor Force in Urban Burma and Rangoon: A Comparative Study," (Ph.D. diss., University of Chicago, 1959), p. 52; and R. M. Sundrum, *A Note on Comparison of Occupational Data in the 1921 and 1931 Censuses* (Department of Economics Statistics and Commerce, University of Rangoon, 1957), Economic paper no. 4, table 8.

2. See R. M. Sundrum, "Census Data on the Labour Force and the Income Distribution in Burma" (Department of Economics, Statistics and Commerce, University of Rangoon, 1958), table 13.

3. Mya Maung, "Cultural Values and Economic Change," *Asian Survey*, IV, no. 3 (March 1964), pp. 757-769.

4. R. M. Sundrum, "Urbanization: The Burmese Experience," *Journal of Burma Research Society*, XI (June 1957), part I, table 18.

5. Sundrum, "Census Data," p. 17.

6. Manning Nash, "Southeast Asian Society, Dual or Multiple?," *Journal of Asian Studies*, XXIII, no. 3 (May 1964), p. 413.

7. Sundrum, "Census Data," table 9.

8. Ibid., p. 17.

9. According to one source, the number of clerks increased to 250,000, three times the prewar figure. See Hugh Tinker, *The Union of Burma* (London: Oxford University Press, 1961), p. 156.

10. The rest were unpaid family workers and presumably more or less equally divided between these two categories.

11. Sundrum, "Census Data," table 14, p. 17.

12. Mehta, "Labor Force," pp. 45-46.

13. For data on Burmazation of the higher civil service in 1910-60, see J. F. Guyot, "Bureaucratic Transformation in Burma," in *Asian Bureaucratic Systems Emergent from the British Imperial Tradition*, ed. R. Braibanti (Chapel Hill, N.C.: Duke University Press, 1961), p. 376.

14. For evaluation of the importance of the indigenous middle class, see I. Adelman and C. T. Morris, *Society, Politics and Economic Development* (Baltimore, Md.: Johns Hopkins, 1967), pp. 30-33.

15. See, for example, G. Myrdal, *Asian Drama* (New York: Pantheon, 1968), p. 470; G. Breese, *Urbanization in Newly Developing Countries* (Englewood Cliffs, N.J.: Prentice-Hall, 1966), pp. 44-46.

16. Sundrum, "Urbanization," p. 123.

17. Ibid., table xiii.

18. Not only minority groups but also the more educated tended to concentrate in the cities, particularly in Rangoon. In the 1930s, two-thirds of those with a college and higher degree and one-fourth of those with degrees in engineering, education, law, and medicine lived in Rangoon. See J. F. Guyot, "Political Involution in Burma," *Journal of Comparative Administration,* II (1970), p. 312.

19. For a comparative analysis of patterns of urbanization in Europe and developing countries, see Gideon Sjoberg, *The Pre-Industrial City: Past and Present* (New York: Free Press of Glencoe, 1965); for comparative data on urbanization see Adelman and Morris, *Society,* pp. 25-27.

20. Sundrum, "Urbanization," pp. 111-112.

21. B. M. Russett et al., *World Handbook of Political and Social Indicators* (New Haven and London: Yale University PRess, 1964), pp. 155-157.

22. $1 = K. 5.

23. These findings refer to national averages. See also Tinker, *Union,* p. 155.

24. For further details, see L. J. Walinsky, *Economic Development in Burma, 1955-1960* (New York: The Twentieth Century Fund, 1962), p. 37.

25. Sundrum, "Census Data," table vii.

26. The 1957 census gathered data on population and cottage industries in 252 centers classified as townships, including 708,000 households, with a total population of close to 3.3 million. Data on income were taken from a sample of 1.1 million persons, aged eleven years or more, gainfully employed for at least some time during the year of the census.

27. For further information, see F. N. Trager, *Building a Welfare State in Burma, 1948-1956* (New York: Institute of Pacific Relations, 1956), p. 73; Josef Silverstein, "Problems in Burma: Economic, Political and Diplomatic," *Asian Survey,* VII, no. 2 (February 1967), p. 120. There is no reliable information about salaries in the mid-sixties, but both their level and their purchasing power decreased substantially; see Guyot, "Bureaucratic Transformation," n. 135.

28. R. A. Holmes, "Burmese Domestic Policy: The Politics of Burmanization," *Asian Survey,* VII, no. 3 (March 1967), pp. 188-197.

29. Nash, "Southeast Asian Society," p. 418.

30. Lucian W. Pye, *Politics, Personality and Nation Building: Burma's Search for Identity* (New Haven: Yale University Press, 1962), p. 63.

31. See Guyot, "Bureaucratic Transformation," pp. 366-381.

32. Pye, *Politics,* p. 147.

33. M. Nash, "Party Building in Upper Burma," *Asian Survey,* III, no. 4 (April 1963), p. 147.

34. Pye, *Politics,* p. 146; see also J. Badgley, *Politics among Burmans: A Study of Intermediary Leaders* (Athens, Ohio: University, Center for International Studies, Southeast Asia Program), 1970, no. 15. Badgley observed that "in Lower Chindwin a good machinist who is also a superior organizer for the Buddhist Layman's association is elevated in the eyes of the community. Were he also talented as a political party organizer, one could be certain that he is a community leader of considerable influence" (p. 24). For further discussion, see pp. 24-32, 72-74.

35. For the importance of these qualities and their impact on everyday life, see M. Nash, *The Golden Road to Modernity: Village Life in Contemporary Burma* (New York: Wiley, 1965), chs. 3, 7; and Nash, "Party Building."

36. David E. Pfanner and J. Ingersoll, "Theravada Buddhism and Village Economic Behavior: A Burmese and Thai Comparison," *Journal of Asian Studies,* XXI, no. 3 (May 1962), p. 343; and Mya Maung, "Cultural Values," p. 759.

37. Pfanner and Ingersoll, "Theravada Buddhism."

38. Ibid., pp. 344, 349. The importance of the religious component of social status is demonstrated by the fact that many of the voluntary associations, especially in the provinces, are religious bodies engaged in promoting religious education and charity activities. See Badgley, *Politics*, pp. 19, 20-21, 34-35.

39. Higher education differentiated between the higher civil servants and the politicians, and, at the later stage, between the politicians and the military officers. See Guyot, "Bureaucratic Transformation," pp. 430-431. For the importance of education among the urban leaders as against rural leaders, see Badgley, *Politics*, p. 77.

40. Josef Silverstein and Julian Wohl, "University Students and Politics in Burma," *Pacific Affairs*, XXXVII, no. 1 (Spring 1964), p. 54.

41. Josef Fischer, *Universities in Southeast Asia* (Columbus: Ohio State University Press, 1964), p. 29.

42. See Nyi Nyi, "The Development of University Education in Burma," *Journal of Burmese Research Society*, XLVII (June 1964), pp. 12-76; Silverstein and Wohl, "University Students"; Fischer, *Universities*.

43. Silverstein and Wohl, "University Students," table 1, p. 56.

44. *The Working People's Daily*, 31 August 1965.

45. However, the businessman's low prestige stems mainly from religious norms. In daily life, especially in the provinces until 1962, businessmen were rather influential and often this was reflected in their political power. See Badgley, *Politics*, pp. 61, 79.

46. Myrdal, *Asian Drama*, p. 1672.

47. The definition of literacy is rather complicated. See ibid., p. 1670.

48. Ibid., p. 1674.

49. Deutsch estimates that the rate of growth between 1931 and 1954 was 0.7% per year. See Karl Deutsch, "Social Mobilization and Political Development," *American Political Science Review*, LV, no. 3 (September 1961), pp. 510-511. See also Karl Deutsch, "Toward an Inventory of Basic Trends and Patterns in Comparative and International Politics," *American Political Science Review*, LIV, no. 1 (March 1960), pp. 40, 56.

50. The school system in Burma involves roughly four years of primary school, three years of middle secondary school, an additional two years of secondary schooling and technical training, and finally universities and other higher institutions including upper vocational and technical schools. See Myrdal, *Asian Drama*, p. 1698; see also Mehta, "Labor Force," table 26, p. 112.

51. Myrdal, *Asian Drama*, p. 1684.

52. Ibid., p. 1718.

53. Ibid., p. 1713.

54. M. Nash, "Education in a New Nation: The Village School in Upper Burma," *International Journal of Comparative Sociology*, II, no. 2 (September 1961), p. 138.

55. Myrdal, *Asian Drama*, p. 1748.

56. Ibid., p. 1744.

57. J. Fischer, *Universities*, table 12, p. 116; see also Nyi Nyi, "Development," p. 42.

58. For a detailed analysis of the clash, see Pye, *Politics*, pp. 77-79. See also Guyot, "Bureaucratic Transformation," pp. 433-438; and Guyot, "The 'Clerk Mentality' in Burmese Education," in *Man, State and Society in Contemporary Southeast Asia*, ed. R. O. Tilmon (New York: Praeger, 1969), pp. 213-214.

59. The junior generation of the Civil Servant was different in social composition and political loyalties from the more senior members; see Guyot, "Bureaucratic Transformation," pp. 419-425.

60. If minorities are included, our statement must be modified. Without ignoring the effects of the interaction between ethnic minorities and the Burmese majority on the class structure, we feel this issue is related rather to the vulnerability of the political structure and the problem of national identity.

Chapter 7

SOME NOTES ON ECONOMIC DEVELOPMENT AND VALUE PREDISPOSITION IN BURMA AND THAILAND

A. INTRODUCTION

One of the most common criteria for evaluating the success of a political regime is its achievements in the sphere of economics, measured by increased growth. One may express some doubt about the overall relevance of this economic criterion for the more comprehensive evaluation of societies and political regimes. However, our main purpose here is to present, or more exactly to illustrate, some of the similarities and dissimilarities between Burma and Thailand in economic development and economic policies. In addition, we shall refer to some background factors which influence economic activities—especially what may be called religious-normative predispositions to economic activities.

The two chief similarities between Burma and Thailand are in (1) the geography, natural resources, and demographic composition of their labor forces; and (2) the predominance of an identical normative background which influences daily life, including activities which have economic significance and implication—i.e., the Buddhist religion and cultural tradition.

The dissimilarities manifest themselves in at least two spheres. (1) Contact with the West occurred under different circumstances. In Burma, it was through occupation and colonial rule. In Thailand, Western penetration had been gradual and selective. More important, it was accomplished without the loss of sovereignty and without a sharp clash between the Western and indigenous cultures. (2) The basic political-economic philosophies of the Thai and Burmese ruling elites are different. The post-independent society in Burma initially had a socialist-democratic orientation and eventually shifted to a more authoritarian socialism. Thailand had basically a bureaucratic-capitalistic outlook. The two countries differ in additional important spheres—for example, the internal security conditions and the administrative infrastructure.

B. BUDDHISM AND ECONOMIC DEVELOPMENT

Many students of Burma and Thailand have emphasized the crucial role of Buddhism in the everyday life of these societies. It would thus be interesting to see whether there is consensus among the scholars and to what extent, if at all, the Burmese situation differs from the Thai. More comprehensive and systematic data than are available are needed if this problem is to be considered adequately. Most descriptions concerned with this issue are drawn from the rural sector, i.e., the sector in which the individual is far less exposed to new alternatives and thereby not compelled to make those decisions demanded by the urban sector.

The flexibility or rigidity of the religious value system with regard to structural and functional changes in the economic structure must be investigated. To what extent does Buddhism shape and direct economic activities on various levels and in different contexts? To what extent does Buddhism clearly define alternatives and options theoretically available to the individual and the collective group? The data available about Burma indicate that it would be fallacious to consider Buddhism as inimical to econonic development, although some manifestations of such an attitude may be found. This is expressed, for example, in the form of allocation of income for household and financial commitments, religious rituals, and merit offerings. The chief merit offerings in terms of financial outlay are the initiation and ordination ceremonies for youths entering manhood and the annual robe-giving ceremonies at each monastic school.[1] However, the impact and influence of the Burmese Buddhist monks on economic activities are not directly felt. The monks do not participate directly in any sort of economic activity, since economic assets are forbidden to them as individuals or as a group. Their impact derives from their role as consumers of a portion of the population's already negligible income. Monks symbolize an ideal way of life and share only partially the consumption and investment patterns of laymen in such a way as to undermine saving for short- or long-term investments. Buddhism does not oppose the accumulation of property as long as it is dedicated to merit.

The limitations imposed by Buddhism on the number of alternatives and options are reflected, at least theoretically, in occupational choice. The true believer would not engage in hunting or fishing. He would also avoid, whenever possible, being a butcher, stock breeder, fowl keeper, or soldier—occupations which involve deliberately taking life. Such activities would eventually worsen chances for a favorable rebirth.[2] Aside from these occupations, all others are *neutral* from the religious point of view. The emphasis is on neutrality, since, by comparison with the negative value of certain occupations, a "positive normative urging to do the world's work with dedication" is difficult to find in Buddhist writings.[3]

Buddhism sets another restriction on modern economic activities, namely, the extreme stress on individualism that "has the effects of inhibiting the formation of groups above the domestic level of organization, of inhibiting the allowance of wide swings in a person's reaction to authority (without force accompanying it), group effort, cooperation and the formation of organizations not tied to a concrete individual."[4] Nash perceives this as a liability, for economic growth is clearly tied to efficient, hierarchical organizations that rely on functional, task oriented authority.

Nevertheless, the more flexible elements in Buddhism cannot be ignored. For example, there is hardly any relationship between religious roles and the technology employed in production (except where such technology involves the taking of life).[5] For many years, the Burmese peasant willingly grew new crops, although he was quite conservative in his choice of methods of production (which did not stem from religious sanctions). We have already noted the relative absence of rigid hierarchical status images, reflecting openness and reluctance to rank occupations as well as the avoidance of rigid categorization. This phenomenon is apparently connected with the great emphasis on the individual. This same attitude is reflected in the legitimation of an individual's efforts to improve his position (not necessarily economically). Moreover, success depends first and foremost on individual capacities and not on transcendental entities, on social restriction, or on ascribed status. "So, change, if individuals perceive opportunities, is easily permissible in the individually centered religion with its meagre perspective and proscriptive moral code."[6]

Corroboration of these observations can be found in research dealing with Thailand, especially its rural sector. Like the Burmese peasants, the Thai peasants also did not exploit the opportunities which became available when the international market was opened to the Thai major agricultural product, rice. Unlike those in Japan, the local and national elites of Thailand did not show any willingness to indulge in economic entrepreneurship at the beginning of the twentieth century.[7] Thai entrepreneurs came from the minority Chinese community. The Chinese showed an enormous capability for filling in the vacuum in the economic exchange system between the international market and the Thai periphery created by the Thais' reluctance to enter the more modern economic sector.

As in the case of Burma, some students of Thailand assume that merit making, in both countries a fundamental religious norm, is at least partially responsible for the inability of the Thai farmers to save and accumulate wealth.

Although the real economic price of this religious practice is not clear, even the most cautious scholars agree that, as far as the majority of the peasants are concerned, the merit-making practices make it objectively difficult to save money and to reinvest it in the limited means of production.[8] Moreover, there is much evidence that the poor peasants spent relatively more than the rich as a result of the fixed and rigid price of many ritual activities.[9] The surpluses accumulated by the richer peasants are seldom reinvested productively. They are usually used for "extravagant" funeral rituals or to buy jewelry.[10]

What obtains for Burma applies to Thailand as well. In spite of some accumulation of wealth in the wats, the clergy has no real economic power which may be exchanged either in the political or in the social market.[11] In this context, the undoubtedly negative impact of the enormous number of *pongyies* on the composition and efficiency of the labor force is noteworthy. Although the number of all lifetime and temporary *pongyies* is not definite, it is clear that quantitatively their potential share in labor force is quite impressive. Their estimated number is between 65,000 and 230,000.[12]

In spite of the great similarity found so far in the impacts of Buddhism on economic activities in Burma and Thailand, it is difficult to draw unequivocal conclusions. An important step would be to distinguish between the logical implications of the Buddhist doctrine with regard to economic activities, on the one hand, and the real and practical impact of religious ritual on patterns of economic activities, on the other.

With regard to the Buddhist doctrine per se, some scholars note its internal contradictions, or as Jacobs puts it, the existence of both positive and negative incentives for economic activities. It is difficult to find, in the doctrine, symptoms of apathy toward work. Buddhism actually encourages the individual to work hard and to be thrifty. Moreover, "man, through a doctrine of free will, is allowed, and even sanctioned, within broad limitations, considerable freedom in the pursuit of economic interest to really make himself."[13] On the other hand, the Buddhist doctrine does place important limitations on material pursuits to prevent pure economic desire from becoming an end in itself. The main reason is that "a technological environment, with its ever-rising material temptations, which a priori, on religious grounds, can never satisfy those who live in that environment, inevitably will lead to social conflict, perhaps even the destruction of the social order unless technologically engendered desires are controlled by Buddhist or secular diffused-religious concern for morality."[14]

Ayal suggests a more negative interpretation of the Buddhist doctrine with regard to its impact on economic activities. He points out that the Buddhist tradition clearly tends not to bestow high priority on social aims that can be realized only by intensive economic development. Second, only very restrained and reserved legitimacy is given to personal entrepreneurial characteristics, for

Economic Development and Value Predisposition [211]

example "to accumulate capital, to work systematically and diligently, to cooperate in organizing effort in pursuance of goals and to innovate."[15] However, the routine religious activities, as embodied in merit making, do prevent economic savings and the productive use of savings.[16] There is no conclusive evidence that, had there been economic surpluses, they would have been used in a more rational way.

Thus, in spite of its negative implications (especially in routine religious practices), Buddhist doctrine allows a significant place for more than one interpretation of religious norms with regard to economic enterprise. The modern political and cultural elites had the opportunity to encourage and promote the positive elements of a modern economic system.

C. FACTS AND BASIC TRENDS IN THE ECONOMIC DEVELOPMENT OF BURMA

Burma's economic wealth is based first on its export potential of rice and then on the export potential of teak, oil products, and different metals (tungsten, tin, zinc). Another possible advantage is the fact that Burma is still an underpopulated country. In the 1950s, the population density was seventy-three persons per square mile with a population of about 18.5 million.[17] There are several estimates of the annual population growth; the most accurate is about 1.5% per year.[18] This modest growth is apparently a result of the balance of birth and death rates, both among the highest in the world.[19] Some scholars nevertheless maintain that even this population growth is rapid in comparison, for example, with the rate of increase in rice production. According to this interpretation, the balance is negative and Burma faces the danger that, within the next twenty years, it will cease to be a rice-exporting country.[20]

The general features of the Burmese labor force are very similar to those of other underdeveloped countries. A typical characteristic is the labor force distribution among industries.[21] In spite of the differences between the categories of "industry" and "occupation," the resulting distributions are very similar, particularly when examined with regard to the distribution among primary, secondary, and tertiary industries. About 63.5% are engaged in primary industries, approximately 10% in secondary industries (construction, manufacturing, transport, and electricity), and about 25% in tertiary industries.[22] These figures show a markedly low level of industrial development in Burma. Burma's backwardness in this respect is even more visible when the low level of specialization of those working in the secondary and tertiary industries is taken into account. Most of these workers are unskilled or small traders. In fact, the Burmese economy could not even absorb the flow of workers into the secondary and tertiary industries. This reaffirms that Burma is overurbanized in relation to its degree of economic development.

Indirect but impressive evidence of the massive flow of people into the cities is presented in Table 7.1. A relatively high percentage of the labor force in Rangoon were newcomers to the city in 1953. For example, 70% of those belonging to the labor force in 1953 had been living in Rangoon for over ten years, 39% had been there from one to five years. These figures may yield some important insights about the difficulties entailed in efforts to modernize the Burmese economy.

The economic revolution in Burma began with the British occupation.[23] From 1885 to 1941, the population of lower Burma grew from about four million to roughly nine million people. At the same time, the rice acreage grew from about four million to some ten million. The rise in rice exports was proportionately much greater (in percentage as well as in absolute tons) during the latter period. Exports rose from some 400,000 tons in 1865 and only 520,000 tons in 1881 and 817,000 tons in 1891. By 1921, exports tripled to 2.5 million tons. By 1941, more than three million tons were exported. Burma had become the leading commercial agricultural nation. Moreover, in the 1920s and 1930s there was considerable construction and development of railways, roads, inland waterways, and embankments. This development, however, also involved serious social disintegration, as the peasants were compelled to borrow heavily.

The indexes presented by Walinsky indicate the extent of economic development from the late 1930s to the eve of the coup.[24] Burma showed some progress in terms of gross domestic product when measured in *constant* prices. However, when this is translated into output per capita in *constant* prices, it is clear that Burma did not reach (in the 1950s) the level of output that she had attained in 1938-39. The lag is about 15%. The same applies to consumption per capita. The reasons for this are multiple and diverse. One main one was apparently the destruction of the agriculture and marketing systems during the Japanese occupation and the British withdrawal. Many peasants had no choice but to return to a subsistence economy. Not until the early 1950s did agriculture recover.

TABLE 7.1: DISTRIBUTION OF POPULATION BY YEARS OF CONTINUOUS RESIDENCE BY SEX–RANGOON 1953 (in percentages)

Length of Residence	Total	Male	Female
Under 1 year	7.2	7.1	7.4
1-5 years	38.8	38.9	38.8
6-10 years	24.0	23.7	24.3
11 years and over	30.0	30.0	24.5

SOURCE: Richard W. Redick, "A Demographic and Ecological Study of Rangoon" (Ph.D. dissertation, University of Chicago, 1961), table 3.

TABLE 7.2: LABOR FORCE CLASSIFIED ACCORDING TO EMPLOYMENT STATUS IN BURMA, 1953-54 (in percentages)

	Urban	Rural
Private	41.7	38.6
Government	13.3	1.5
Own account	39.9	35.7
Unpaid	6.1	24.2
Total	100.0	100.0

SOURCE: R. M. Sundrum, *A Comparison of Occupational Data in the 1921 and 1931 Census,* University of Rangoon, 1957, table iii.

The economy at the end of World War II was essentially in the hands of aliens. The impact on the labor force distribution among the various sectors is difficult to assess. In any event, a substantial change occurred after 1953-54. The figures for these years (see Table 7.2) show that the public sectors were reasonably small. It may be assumed that the number of wage earners (in the private and governmental sectors), who in 1953-54 formed 55% of the total urban labor force, increased substantially.

Additional evidence about the proportional weight of wage earners is in Table 7.3. The high figure of wage earners in the rural sector—39%—is a direct result of the peasants' eviction from their land because of indebtedness. The Burmese government tried to alleviate the peasants' distress but "even with the stupendous assistance of the government in recent years the grip of the money-lenders on the Burmese economic life is far from being removed. The problem of indebtedness, agricultural indebtedness in particular, has remained unsolved in Burma."[25]

One measure by the government for coping with the peasants' problems was the nationalization of land and the establishment of cooperatives. From 1940 to 1961, the number of cooperative societies grew from 2,047 to the phenomenally high figure of 11,865. However, only about 40% of these societies were, in 1960-66, actually working societies. Although the government used the Department of the Cooperative Societies and the State Agriculture Department

TABLE 7.3: WORKERS GETTING INCOME, 1953-54 (in percentages)

Source of Income	Urban	Rural
Wages and salaries	53.5	38.7
Other sources	37.1	35.6
Mixed	3.2	3.0
No income	6.2	22.7
Total	100.0	100.0

SOURCE: R. M. Sundrum, *A Comparison of Occupational Data,* table iv.

to allocate credit to the peasants, this policy was not particularly effective in stimulating efforts to improve agricultural yields.[26]

Like many other emerging countries, Burma dedicated attention and resources to the development of industry. We must distinguish here between industry and cottage industry. The latter was owned almost only by families.[27] Industry was also in private hands, but it was generally owned by individuals or partners (about 95%).[28] Family firms of the cottage industry type were considered more efficient, and a great deal of the industrial development in the 1950s and 1960s has been attributed to this sector.[29] Furthermore, they were more efficient despite the obstacles that the private entrepreneur had to overcome in a basically hostile climate.[30]

Generally, the achievements of U Nu's government should not simply be dismissed. Total output increased at an average of 5% per year, and per capita output by 4% per year. Agricultural acreage and output were also substantially increased, forestry and mining partly restored, and transportation and communication largely rehabilitated. Nevertheless, the efforts "failed to achieve the degree of success which it could and should have reached. It was the failure to achieve what was practicable under the circumstances, rather than the failure to achieve at all, that was the real measure of the failure of the AFPFL leadership."[31]

The partial success in a few sectors and partial failures in many others can be attributed to any number of factors—for example, unstable internal security, over which the civilian (or the military) government had very little objective command. This is common knowledge. Nevertheless, it is also true, as has been noted by many, that security problems were used as a cover for the inefficiency (at all levels) of officials in charge of economic development. However, the success or failure should also be measured against the declared objectives and plans and their realistic possibility. Different experts hold that the economic objectives were bombastic and pretentious and could never have been realized —even in the ten years hoped for and promised by the U Nu government.[32] The ambition of these plans is even more exaggerated by the administration's inefficiency and lack of experience. The government completely failed to establish discipline, responsibility, and standards of hard work and sacrifice among its civil servants. Moreover, it tried to adjust the colonial administrative structure to the country's new needs and objectives, both at the periphery and at the superstructure in the center—i.e., to frameworks that were intended to guide and direct overall economic activities.[33]

Probably, contrary to expectation, Burma under U Nu's rule by and large did not suffer from a shortage of capital. The problem was rather the willingness and commitment to raise the money and to use it according to the proposed plans.[34] Thus a grave obstacle to economic development in 1948-58 was the political elite itself, particularly its inability or lack of desire to separate public administration from political bossism and nepotism. The absence of a constructive and responsible opposition only intensified the blurring of the functions of the political apparatus with administrative functions. Many observers point to a psychological block on decision making after policies had been declared. The leadership is often described as being composed of people characterized "by indecision, lack of critical acumen, by the desire for unanimity and the wish to avoid conflict, even when doing so meant knuckling down to undisciplined employee groups, demonstrators, troublemakers or insurgents."[35]

To the extent that status groups with entrepreneurial qualities existed in the past, their members came from ethnic and religious minorities. The groups' distinctiveness became their greatest drawback, as one of the government's main objectives was the Burmazation of the economy. However, although their initiative was disrupted efficiently, no immediate or equivalent substitute for them was found.

One proclaimed reason for the 1962 coup by General Ne Win and his colleagues was the grave deterioration of the economic situation. The officers' diagnosis was the same as the one suggested in 1958. However, in 1962 the officers made a much more radical and unconventional prescription for the Burmese economic malaise. It had already been tested between 1958 and 1960, but then it was offered to the population in a mild form. After 1962, the economic prescription was enforced on a large scale and, at least in the beginning, in an uncompromising and systematic way.

Generally, the major difference between the two periods of military regime is that, during the first, the military gave great leeway to private enterprise. The official policy was that "the private trade sector had top priority to be followed by semi-governmental organizations, such as the Joint Venture Corporation. The last in this order of priority were the state trading organizations."[36]

The second Ne Win government was completely different from the first, especially after Colonel Aung Gye had been dismissed from the Revolutionary Council in February 1963. The essence of its policy would henceforth be the nearly total nationalization of economic resources and services, excluding agriculture, indigenous petty trade, and manufacture. The RC announced the nationalization of marketing of rice, of all import and export trade, and of private banks and industries.[37] The Burma Economic Development Corporation and its thirty-nine subsidiary companies were also transferred to government departments. Joint ventures were liquidated. The nationalization policy supplemented the older policy of Burmazation. In 1964, all Indian and Chinese businessmen were driven out. In planning, the greatest emphasis was on increased capital investment for development of the public sector.[38] The almost immediate results of this policy were devastating. The authorities were soon compelled to ration rice and other foods—in spite of the fact that Burma was the world's leading exporter of rice, which earned three-fourths of its foreign exchange.[39]

No basic improvement in the economic situation could be discerned in the second half of the 1960s. Nationalization continued, although there were signs of hesitation and frustration; even the failures of the RC were publicly acknowledged.[40] The gravity of the economic situation was one of the main reasons that the RC approached the deposed leaders of the premilitary regime to begin a new political dialogue.[41]

There was a significant practical, but not ideological, change at the beginning of the 1970s. For example, it was decided by the RC in 1970 to eliminate the twenty-two state corporations which controlled all trade and manufacturing.[42] The RC also reemphasized the importance and contribution of the cooperatives to the national economy. Bureaucratic control on cooperatives was slightly lessened and they became in effect a front for the activities of various entrepreneurs and for the reintroduction of economic competition—which had disappeared almost totally in the 1960s.[43]

D. FACTS AND BASIC TRENDS IN THE ECONOMIC DEVELOPMENT OF THAILAND

Although Thailand seems to be lagging behind Burma in natural resources, it still has plenty of coal, tungsten, ore, salt, and cement. Moreover, Thailand has a better capacity for extracting and using its natural resources.[44] Thailand is less fortunate than Burma in population density. In the 1950s, the density was 132 per square mile,[45] and in the cultivated areas, 550 per square mile.[46] Nevertheless, demographers warn that this ideal situation cannot long continue because there is an annual population increase of 3%.[47] They predict that the rate of production may not catch up with population growth.[48]

"The 1960 population census estimated the total number of employed persons, 11 years of age and over, to be 13.7 million. The majority of employed persons, or at least 82%, were rural agricultural workers, 11% were engaged in trade and services sectors and about 4% worked in the manufacturing and mining sectors."[49] More detailed data are presented in a 1968 survey,[50] which describes 79% as still engaged in agriculture (a much higher percentage than in Burma). Trade and services are next in importance, but both of them include less than 7% of the labor force.[51]

This picture of the Thai labor force does not differ in principle from the situation in the 1950s in Burma. But, as a result of the RC's nationalization and Burmazation policies, some changes occurred in the labor force composition after 1962. A comparison of the 1968 survey with a similar one made in 1954 discloses some interesting changes in the Thai labor force as well. In 1954, 88% of the population were engaged in agriculture, 8% more than in 1968. On the other hand, there was an increase of 2.5% in trade.[52] These figures show, at least indirectly, the growth of the manpower reservoir from immigration to urban centers. In Thailand, the process of urbanization has been very restrained and gradual. The percent of the urban population was, in the 1960s, one of the lowest in the world.[53] The economic and political stability and the relatively high level of law and order (up to the late 1960s) balances, in a crucial way, the "pull-drive" of the cities and towns. However, the metropolitan area of Bangkok-Thomburi should be perceived as a separate category. This, like Rangoon, is a classic primate city.[54] The great portion of urban growth in Thailand is due to this area's growth.[55]

The year 1855, when the Bowning Treaty was signed, is commonly designated as a turning point in the history of Thailand's economic growth. One direct consequence of the Bowning Treaty was the integration of Thai agriculture (especially rice) in the world economy, followed by gradual monetization of the Thai economy.[56] The almost exclusive concentration on agriculture (as opposed to industry) was expressed by a substantial increase in the cultivated areas, although not in productivity. The area under rice cultivation at the time of the Bowning Treaty amounted to 5,800,000 rai; by 1964, it had increased to 40 million rai.[57] In spite of some increase in productivity, the share of agriculture in the gross national product was decreasing. In 1965, it reached 33%.[58] The real drive for industrialization began when the government enacted the Promotion of Industrialization Investment Act in 1954.[59] Its increasing awareness that rice production was reaching peak while the growth rate of population was still rapidly increasing drove the political elite to change its list of priorities somewhat. The relatively accelerated rate of industrial development was indicated by the more general economic growth (see Table 7.4).

The rate of growth should also be examined in light of the fact that, at the end of World War II, Thailand's economic situation was very bad. The country

TABLE 7.4: INDEXES OF TOTAL AND PER CAPITA GROSS NATIONAL PRODUCT IN THAILAND (1958 = 100)

	'53	'54	'56	'57	'58	'59	'60	'61	'62	'63	'64	'65
Total	88	96	99	99		110	122	127	134	147	161	171
Per Capita	102	105	105	102		107	115	116	119	127	134	139

SOURCE: Tominaga et al., "The Modernization and the Industrialization of Thai Society," *East Asian Cultural Studies,* VII, p. 12.

was disconnected, for three to four years, from all its economic ties, while most of its foreign exchange reserves were blocked in England. Until 1947, rice export was under the strict control of the Allies.[60] Thailand regained economic autonomy after the 1947 coup, which brought Phibun back to power. The extreme nationalistic and anti-Communist policies of the new government ensured United States aid.[61] The real boom occurred, however, with the outbreak of the Korean War in 1951.[62] With the end of the Korean War, Thailand experienced a rather sharp recession and inflationary tendencies. Its recovery was helped by the International Bank, whose experts formulated, in 1955-56, a new economic policy.[63] A new push to the Thai economy came with Sarit and the Six-Year National Economic Development (1961-66).[64] Although there are some reservations with regard to the desired effect of the Six-Year Plan,[65] there is no doubt that rapid economic growth was a main feature of Sarit's rule.[66]

In sum, Thai economic policies since 1947 have been basically successful. Their success is rather impressive in comparison to the economic disaster that Burma experienced during the 1960s. Thailand certainly had several advantages over Burma: social and political stability; law and order in the major parts of the periphery; and benevolent foreign aid. Thai economic development was not, however, successful to the same degree in all the economic areas. The most retarded sector continued to be agriculture. Production did not catch up with population growth. There was a "gradual increase of tenancy and indebtedness —phenomena due to increasing pressure of population on land."[67] The traditional means of production and the peasants' lack of motivation are not solely to blame for the relative retardation of agriculture. A substantial part of the stagnation can be attributed to corruption and inefficiency of the administration in charge of agricultural economic plans.

In the industrial sector, there was clearly a dual economy. Besides the traditional small-scale industry, a new modern economic sector controlled by government ministries and subsidiary organizations emerged in the 1960s. While the small-scale industry was ethnically mixed and included Chinese and Thais, the other was controlled exclusively by Thais. Its establishment was historically related to the eagerness of the Thai power elite to remove the Chinese monopoly on the economy. The governmental control of the modern economic sector did not encourage private initiative—certainly not when the main "private" beneficiaries were the members of the military-bureaucratic elite. This specific combination of bureaucratic control and semiprivate entrepreneurship has been one of the main reasons for the inability of the industrial sectors, in spite of their growth, to respond effectively to the urgent needs of the Thai economy and demography. For example, they did not respond to the need to increase the absorption capacity of the urban sector. Referring to these problems, Wit states

Economic Development and Value Predisposition [219]

that the Thai economy faces a bleak future because of four almost unavoidable developments: (1) a deterioration in the favorable ratio between natural resources and population; (2) a change for the worse in the international market for traditional export products; (3) the growth of a more variegated consumer society with a higher level of aspiration; and (4) a greater need by the government for financial resources for security measures and improvement of social services.[68]

Finally, we should comment on the validity of comparing the respective economic achievements of Burma and Thailand. Myrdal testifies that the comparison is very difficult; unless a great deal of caution is exercised, one can very easily come to distorted and even absurd conclusions.[69] Even reliance on conventional economic indexes is dangerous and may be misleading, as, for example, with the measurement of the growth of real output per head. Observing Table 7.5, one could conclude that Burma exhibited by far the faster rate of growth. Myrdal, however, adds immediately that "several comments are in order regarding the apparent record of Burma." For one thing, there is doubt about the reliability of the real aggregate product estimates. Myrdal finally concludes "that it was probably premature at the end of the 1950's to class Burma as an economy well on the way toward economic success."[70] He adds that "the most one can say regarding over-all economic growth in Burma is that, while the evidence is mixed, there is a strong probability that stagnation or even a decline has occurred in recent years."[71]

One can find corroboration for the generally advantaged position of Thailand in the economic sphere in all of the comparative survyes which include Burma and Thailand—for example, in the works of Adelman and Morris, Russett and his associates, and, of course, Myrdal. Thailand's advantageous position is very striking in such important spheres as the growth of real output per head, average yearly income per head,[72] the growth of the national product per capita,[73] and in a long list of indexes presented in Adelman and Morris.[74]

We have not intended to present any systematic comparative survey of the economic policies of Burma and Thailand and to analyze the reasons for their success or failure. Nevertheless, the above remarks complement the previous chapters in two ways. First, the data presented provide at least some basic illustration for those who would like to test the success of the regimes in economic terms. Second, after having focused the discussion on the *elites'* political and ideological attitudes, we have referred to the cultural-ideological predisposition of the population *at large* to economic entrepreneurial and innovative activities. Some echoes of these conclusions will be heard in the last chapter.

TABLE 7.5: GROWTH OF REAL OUTPUT PER HEAD (Index: 1952 = 100)

Country	1950	1951	1952	1953	1954	1955	1956	1957	1958	1959	1960
Pakistan	103.9	100.9	100	103.0	103.5	100.0	105.2	104.3	102.2	103.0	105.6
India	96.9	97.7	100	103.9	104.7	104.7	107.8	104.3	109.4	109.0	114.5
Indonesia	–	98.5	100	104.9	111.5	113.4	114.1	120.2	113.3	111.6	...
Burma	86.8	95.8	100	105.5	107.6	112.1	114.1	123.9	117.1	122.6	128.4
Philippines	93.6	94.8	100	104.6	106.7	111.6	113.5	115.0	115.9	119.3	119.0
Thailand	116.0	110.7	100	98.3	94.1	105.5	101.3	96.1	89.4	98.8	102.1
Ceylon	89.7	95.5	100	96.4	96.6	100.2	92.5	95.9	92.3	100.9	104.7
Italy	92.9	98.1	100	107.7	114.0	120.5	125.0	131.2	137.7	147.3	157.1
United Kingdom	98.9	100.9	100	104.0	108.1	110.2	113.2	114.1	112.8	114.8	118.3
Sweden	98.3	97.9	100	101.9	107.6	110.6	113.3	116.6	117.2	122.2	126.7
United States	94.7	99.2	100	101.9	97.9	104.1	105.1	104.2	100.4	105.8	106.3

SOURCE: Myrdal, *Asian Drama* (New York: Pantheon, 1968), p. 486.

NOTES

1. During 1950-60, in a village of 150 houses in the Pequ district, where the average annual net disposable family cash income was calculated at about $200, an average of 4%-6% of net disposable cash income after production costs was spent for religious purposes. See D. E. Pfanner and J. Ingersoll, "Theravada Buddhism and Village Economic Behavior: A Burmese and Thai Comparison," *Journal of Asian Studies*, XXI, no. 3 (May 1962), pp. 347-348. Nash reports that religious demands are about 14% of the annual outlay of a rich family, about 4% of a moderate family's outlay, and about 2% of a poor family's outlay. See M. Nash, *The Golden Road to Modernity: Village Life in Contemporary Burma* (New York: Wiley, 1965), p. 160. Pfanner contends that, although "on the surface this figure may not seem to represent a large proportion of income or expenditure it does become significant when compared with the proportion of income saved or invested in economically advanced countries, or with allocation of surplus income beyond subsistence" ("Theravada Buddhism," p. 348).
2. Nash, *Golden Road*, p. 157.
3. Ibid., p. 160.
4. Ibid., p. 161.
5. Ibid., p. 162; Pfanner and Ingersoll, "Theravada Buddhism," pp. 345-394.
6. Ibid., Pfanner and Ingersoll, "Theravada Buddhism."
7. E. Ayal, "Value Systems and Economic Development in Japan and Thailand," *Journal of Social Issues*, XIX, no. 1 (January 1963), pp. 37-38, 40-44.
8. On the basis of 1953 data, Blanchard reports that the religious cash expenses of the average Thai family per year was 10% of the total cash income. See *Thailand: Its People; Its Society; Its Culture,* ed. W. Blanchard (New Haven: Human Relations Areas Files Press, 1957), p. 115. For more examples, see Pfanner and Ingersoll, "Theravada Buddhism," p. 356; Moerman, "Ban Ping's Temple: The Centre of a 'Loosely Structured' Society," in *Anthropological Studies in Theravada Buddhism*, ed. M. Nash (New Haven: Yale University Press, 1966), pp. 150-155.
9. Pfanner and Ingersoll, "Theravada Buddhism," p. 357.
10. H. K. Kaufman, "Bangkhuad: A Community Study in Thailand" (Ithaca, N.Y.: Monograph of Association for Asian Studies, Cornell University Press, 1960), p. 69.
11. For a detailed explanation, see N. Jacobs, *Modernization without Development: Thailand as an Asian Case Study* (New York: Praeger, 1971), pp. 220-234. For examples from individual villages see Kaufman, "Bangkhuad," pp. 102-104.
12. Evers and Silcock estimate that the number of *pongyies* in the rainy season each year is about 250,000. H. D. Evers and T. H. Silcock, "Elites Selection," in *Thailand, Social and Economic Studies in Development*, ed. T. H. Silcock (Canberra: Australian National University Press, 1966), p. 49. The New York *Times* cites the same figure but adds that one should also take into account 75,000 studying in the 20,944 monasteries (20 May 1968). Moerman reports about 160,000 monks and 95,000 novices in 1960. Kaufman reports about 165,000 monks and 70,000 novices in 20,000 wats in 1954 ("Bagkhuad," p. 100).
13. Jacobs, *Modernization*, p. 302. See also G. Wijeyewardene, "Some Aspects of Rural Life in Thailand," in Silcock, *Thailand*, pp. 81-82.
14. Jacobs, *Modernization*, p. 303.

15. Ayal, "Value Systems," p. 31. A similar approach is in D. E. Smith, *Religion and Politics in Burma* (Princeton: Princeton University Press, 1965), pp. 323-325. A more balanced approach can be found in Nash's notes about the validity of Weber's thesis with regard to Buddhism's effects on economic activities. Nash, *Golden Road* pp. 156-157. An extreme view is expressed by Leach: "The Ethic of Buddhism is fundamentally at variance with the spirit of capitalism" (E. Leach, "Buddhism in the Post-Colonial Order in Burma and Ceylon," *Daedalus,* Winter 1973, p. 49).

16. Pfanner and Ingersoll, "Theravada Buddhism," p. 356. Interesting evidence of the possibility of encouraging the sangha to participate in economic development is the *Mahachula longkorn* project in Thailand. The project is two-pronged. "One program sends out to the provinces for working periods of one or two years monk-volunteers." The second part does the converse: "For a period of usually two months it brings to Bangkok suitable volunteer-monks from the provinces for intensive training and then returns them to their old wats and villages so that they can initiate community development projects." See S. J. Tambiah, "The Persistence and Transformation of Tradition in Southeast Asia, With Special Reference to Thailand," *Daedalus* (Winter 1973), pp. 71-72.

17. S. K. Mehta, "The Labor Force in Urban Burma and Rangoon, 1953" (Ph.D. diss., University of Chicago, 1954), p. 36.

18. L. W. Pye, "The Politics of Southeast Asia," in *The Politics of the Developing Areas,* eds. Gabriel A. Almond and James S. Coleman (Princeton: Princeton University Press, 1960), table 2, p. 101.

19. The crude birth rate in 1953 was 49.2 per 1,000 and the crude death rate was 33.5 per 1,000. See Mehta, "Labor Force," pp. 36-37.

20. A. A. Wichman, "Burma: Agriculture, Population, and Buddhism," *American Journal of Economics and Sociology,* XXIV, no. 1 (January 1965), pp. 74-76.

21. Partial data from 1965 note similar proportions. *Far Eastern Economic Review Year Book* (Hong Kong: Far Eastern Economic Review, 1965), p. 96.

22. R. M. Sundrum, *A Comparison of Occupational Data in 1921 and 1931 Censuses* (University of Rangoon, 1957), table x.

23. On the economy in the period of the Burmese kings, see L. J. Walinsky, *Economic Development in Burma, 1951-60* (New York: The Twentieth Century Fund, 1962), ch. 2; and F. N. Trager, *Burma from Kingdom to Republic* (New York: Praeger, 1966), pp. 140-143.

24. Walinsky, *Economic Development,* appendix xiii, pp. 660-661.

25. Mya Maung, "Cultural Values and Economic Changes," *Asian Survey,* IV, no. 3 (March 1964), p. 761.

26. Summarizing the reasons for the failure to develop and modernize agriculture, Walinsky states: "First, the agricultural program aid did not appraise and clearly define priorities in program objectives and implementation." Second, "implementation of the program was adversely affected by political pressures exerted by local AFPFL and all Burma Peasants Organization authorities." Third, "the lack of civil orders in the countryside constituted a persistent and omnipresent limitation on program implementation, not only because it hampered agricultural production programs but also because it was possible for ineffective officers to use insecurity as an excuse for failure in performance"; Walinsky, *Economic Development,* p. 297. See also ch. 16 for details on public capital expenditures for agriculture, crop expansion, irrigation, mechanization, agricultural credit, and land nationalization. For similar and other details, see also Trager, *Building a Welfare State in Burma: 1948-56* (New York: Institute of Pacific Relations), pp. 35-51; Pfanner and Ingersoll, "Theravada Buddhism," p. 343; Wichman, "Burma," p. 73. For the rice economy

analyzed as indicator of the success or failure of the Revolutionary Council's economic policy, see L. D. Stifel, "Burmese Socialism: Economic Problems of the First Decade," *Pacific Affairs*, XLV, no. 1 (Spring 1972), pp. 64-71.

27. Mehta, "Labor Force " table 31.

28. In cottage industry, the average number of workers per unit was 3; 1.5 were hired laborers. In industry, the average number was 4.5. See ibid., pp. 180, 222.

29. Everett E. Hagen, *On the Theory of Social Change* (Homewood, Ill.: Dorsey Press, 1962), pp. 469-470.

30. Walinsky, *Economic Development*, p. 349. This assessment has been rejected by other scholars. See, for example, Mya Maung, "Socialism and Economic Development of Burma," *Asian Survey*, IV, no. 12 (December 1964), p. 1185.

31. Walinsky, *Economic Development*, p. 566.

32. The declared economic policy, accepted in August 1952 by the Pydawtha Conference, included (1) making Burma self-sufficient in commodities for nutrition and clothing, increasing agricultural production and crops for export, and reaching a national income of K. 700 crores (K. 7 billion or $1.48 billion) by 1959, an increase of 78% over 1951. This required an investment program of approximately K. 750 crores (about $1.59 billion) between 1952 and 1960 designed to restore to the 1966 population the prewar per capita standard of consumption; (2) nationalizing land and developing the underdeveloped areas; (3) providing Burma with free public education from primary through professional levels; also mass adult, technical, artisan, and vocational education; and (4) supplying medical and public health facilities. For details see Trager, *Building a Welfare State*, pp. 20-21; Walinsky, *Economic Development*, pp. 153, 158-162, 371-375, 378-379.

33. For a detailed discussion of the problems of public and business administration in Burma, see Walinsky, *Economic Development*, chs. 27-29; Trager, *Build in a Welfare State*, pp. 97-100.

34. Walinsky, *Economic Development*, p. 404; see also the discussion of foreign aid, chs. 31-32.

35. Ibid., p. 566.

36. T. V. Tai, "The Role of the Military in the Developing Nations of South and Southeast Asia with Special Reference to Pakistan, Burma and Thailand" (Ph.D. diss., University of Virginia, 1965), pp. 396-397. See also J. F. Guyot, "Political Involution in Burma," *Journal of Comparative Administration* II, no. 3 (November 1970), pp. 309-311.

37. L. J. Walinsky, "The Role of the Military in Development Planning," in *Man, State and Society in Contemporary Southeast Asia*, ed. R. O. Tilman (New York: Praeger, 1969), p. 348. See also Stifel, "Burmese Socialism," pp. 62-63.

38. Tai reports that "the allotment for economic development in this sector was raised by Kyats 1,100 million to Kyats 2,181 million, or by 109% during 1962-63. The projected investment for 1963-64 was raised by Kyats 2,023 million or by 93%" ("Role of Military," p. 399).

39. R. Butwell, "Burmese Political Development: Impact of a National Heritage," in *Nationalism and Revolution in Southeast Asia*, ed. M. Leifer (Zug: Hull Monographs on Southeast Asia, no. 2, 1968), p. 137.

40. J. Silverstein, "Problems in Burma: Economic, Political and Diplomatic," *Asian Survey*, VII, no. 2 (February 1967), pp. 117-126. For the economic situation in 1968, see J. Silverstein, "Burma: Political Dialogue in Burma: A New Turn on the Road to Socialism?," *Asian Survey*, X, no. 2 (February 1970), pp. 134-136. Nationalization was more effective in trade, marketing, and big business. However, in the late 1960s "the private sector still owns 94% of the industrial plants (25% of factories with over 50 workers) and most of the buses

and river and coastal vessels" (Stifel, "Burmese Socialism," p. 71). About two-thirds of the Indian and most of the Chinese communities remained (ibid.).

41. *Far Eastern Economic Review,* 16 January 1964, pp. 105-107.

42. J. Badgley, "The Union of Burma: Age Twenty-Two " *Asian Survey,* XI, no. 2 (February 1971), p. 153.

43. For changes in the economic situation in the 1970s, see J. Badgley, "Burma: The Army Vows Legitimacy," *Asian Survey,* XII, no. 2 (February 1972), p. 179; Stifel, "Burma Socialism," p. 73.

44. This may be seen in productivity and export. For a comparison of agriculture in various countries in southeast Asia, see G. Myrdal, *Asian Drama: An Inquiry into the Poverty of Nations* (New York: Pantheon, 1968), p. 494. For natural resources, see ibid., pp. 512-513.

45. G. L. Harris et al., *Area Handbook for Thailand* (Washington, D.C.: The American University, 1963), p. 44.

46. Harris, *Area Handbook for Thailand,* p. 45.

47. J. C. Caldwell, "The Demographic Structure," in Silcock, *Thailand,* p. 29; Myrdal, *Asian Drama,* p. 396.

48. T. H. Silcock, "Summary and Assessment," in Silcock *Thailand,* p. 290; Caldwell, "Demographic Structure," pp. 53-64.

49. Thailand, National Economic Development Board, Office of the Prime Minister, *Performance Evaluation of Development in Thailand for 1969,* p. 14.

50. Thailand, National Statistical Office, Office of the Prime Minister, *Preliminary Report of the Labor Force Survey, July-September 1969* (Bangkok, Government of Thailand, n.d.), p. 31, table 6B.

51. Ibid.

52. Thailand, Central Statistical Office, *Economic and Demographic Survey, 1954* (Bangkok: Government of Thailand, 1955), tables 15-1, 15-2, 15-3.

53. Caldwell, "Demographic Structure," p. 44. Russett, *World Handbook,* p. 49.

54. See above, chapter 6.

55. Important evidence of the large-scale immigration to Bangkok is the fact that in 1965, 300,000 inhabitants (out of 2 million) had lived there fewer than eight years. See *Economic and Demographic Survey,* table 7-11.

56. The accelerated monetization actually started after World War II. See E. Ayal, "Private Enterprise and Economic Progress in Thailand," *Journal of Asian Studies,* XXVI, no. 1 (November 1966), p. 8.

57. J. C. Ingram, *Economic Change in Thailand since 1850* (Stanford: Stanford University Press, 1955), p. 44. See also E. Ayal, "Value Systems," pp. 37-38.

58. K. Tominaga et al., "The Modernization and Industrialization of Thai Society," *East Asian Cultural Studies,* VIII (1969), pp. 10-11.

59. T. H. Silcock, "Outline of Economic Development, 1945-65," in Silcock, *Thailand,* pp. 16-17.

60. Ibid., p. 7.

61. For economic development in the first years after Phibun's 1947 coup, see ibid., pp. 8-13.

62. Ibid., p. 14.

63. Ibid., p. 17.

64. For details, see E. Ayal, "Thailand's Six-Year National Economic Development Plan," *Asian Survey,* I, no. 11 (January 1962), pp. 34-35; K. Somvichian, "The Thai Military in Politics: An Analytical Study" (Ph.D. diss., University of London, 1969), pp. 259-260.

65. Silcock, "Outline of Economic Development," pp. 23-25.

66. Somvichian reports "within five years of the 1958 coup the gross national produce increased by 50 percent while export rose approximately 55 percent. National income went up steadily from 41,000 million baht in 1950 to 46,000 million baht, 50,000 million baht and 53,000 million baht in 1960, 1961, and 1962 respectively" ("Thai Military," p. 266). For more details on economic growth during Sarit's and Thanom's rules, see F. von der Mehden, "The Military and Development in Thailand," *Journal of Comparative Administration*, II (1970), pp. 329-335.

67. Silcock, "Summary and Assessment," p. 296.

68. D. Wit, *Thailand: Another Vietnam?* (New York: Scribner's, 1968), p. 77.

69. Myrdal, *Asian Drama*, pp. 479-484.

70. Ibid., p. 488.

71. Ibid., p. 488.

72. Ibid., p. 417.

73. Russett, *World Handbook of Political and Social Indications* (New Haven: Yale University Press, 1964), p. 157.

74. I. Adelman and C. T. Morris, *Society, Politics and Economic Development: A Quantitative Approach* (Baltimore, Md.: Johns Hopkins, 1967), pp. 84-128.

Chapter 8

A COMPARATIVE ANALYSIS AND

SOME GENERAL CONCLUSIONS

A. THE MICROFACTORS AND MILITARY INTERVENTION

This chapter is devoted to a systematic comparative analysis of the civil-military relations in Burma and Thailand, with reference to the typologies and paradigms mentioned in the two introductory chapters. Their validity can thus be at least partially examined. The role expansion of the military with regard to the political, economic, administrative, and social spheres was the focus of both the analytical presentation and the historical description of Thailand and Burma. A military coup d'etat per se should be perceived as only one dimension of the possible variations of military role expansion. Some evidence of the existence of such variations is contained in the studies of Burma and Thailand. Any case studies of neighboring countries, for example Indonesia and Pakistan, would show further varieties of patterns or profiles of role expansion.[1]

The main differences between Thailand and Burma will be considered later. Now, let us mention that the differences—either in terms of the intensity of the role expansion in different spheres stemming from a different range of priorities, or in terms of the scope of penetration and expansion—are the product of very different historical conditions.

We have distinguished between two groups of factors which were intended to explain (1) the specific conditions for the execution of a coup, and (2) the difference in the direction and the intensity of role expansion. We have referred to the internal factors exclusive to the military social system and to external factors. They may perhaps be defined as micro- and macrofactors. What was the weight of the microfactors in the circumstances brought about by the military coups in Thailand and Burma? And to what extent were they responsible for the different patterns of military regimes which subsequently emerged?

The two military establishments were similar in the instrumental dimension, i.e., the quantity and the quality of material and other resources necessary for implementing military rule. They were also similar in the logistic dimension, i.e., the dimension which can be measured by knowledge of the extent of mechanization, number of units, and degree of coordination between the different services.

Military experts can probably point out more specific differences with regard to logistic capacity in the light of the Burmese army's experience in warfare against various guerrilla movements. Nevertheless, one may reasonably say that those differences between the Burmese and the Thai armies had little if any impact on the patterns of the coups, much less on the types of the military regimes. However, the differential, internal cohesiveness and the different types of self-identity undoubtedly had a great effect on the number of the coups, on the scope and intensity of internal purges, and, of course, on the social and political features of the military regimes. In social cohesiveness, the Burmese army had a great advantage compared to the Thai army. Nevertheless, this did not prevent the Thai army from carrying out coups and from being, in its own way, consistent in economic and social policies. It was precisely the internal, personal conflicts within the Thai military elite in the 1950s and 1960s that strengthened the predisposition to solve conflicts by coups and countercoups. On the other hand, the stability of the military regime in Burma, and the fact that there was no countercoup up until 1973, can be explained by the relatively strong internal social cohesiveness of the Burmese military elite. This social cohesiveness must be described cautiously, since some internal purges occurred. However, they were limited in scope, and the measures taken against the deposed officers were very mild. This particular type of purge within the Burmese army can be attributed less to the social cohesiveness than to the ideological controversy which began in the 1950s and became more heated after the 1962 coup. The Burmese army's internal social cohesiveness actually involves only those armed forces which were under the direct control of the general staff—not all the armed forces at the disposal, in one way or another, of the Burmese political elite. These include the various paramilitary units in the periphery and even the Union Military Police, under the control of the Ministry of Interior. For these units, internal rifts and conflicts were no less significant than in the Thai military. The strengthening of these paramilitary units and the danger of confrontation between them and the regular army was a major cause for the establishment of the caretaker government in 1958 and for the coup in 1962. The Thai military was spared such an unpleasant experience.

The more ruthless and resourceful officers of the Thai military expected to gain from the weak internal social cohesiveness. When there is relatively easy access to social and economic benefits and an absence of normative restrictions,

Comparative Analysis and Conclusions [229]

there is a very high probability of personal conflicts and institutionalized corruption. It would be misleading to argue that personal corruption was a rare phenomenon in Burma during either civilian or military rule. However, although the Burmese military became almost the exclusive channel of mobility, the exploitation of power positions at the disposal of the officers for personal gain was very different in scope and intensity from that of Thailand. It would, perhaps, be naive to assume that the ideological approach of the Burmese military elite to public issues and social programs was what kept it from this sort of moral deterioration. In any case, this ideological approach is a salient feature of the Burmese army; while in Thailand, the ideological approach is marginal and, in the opinion of some observers, even entirely absent.

Any explanation of the differences between the Thai and Burmese military officers in terms of personal histories would probably point out the socio-economic backgrounds of the senior officers and their families, and the circumstances of political socialization, especially during the crucial adolescent period. The political education of the upper echelons of the Burmese military occurred in a particular political framework, i.e., the national independence movement or in the militant student organizations which eventually became the spearhead of the national movement.

Although the data concerned with the social origins of the military in Burma and in Thailand are very limited, the agrarian background which, in many cases, may explain the distinctiveness of the military vis-à-vis other elites plays a smaller role in these countries.[2] In spite of the fact that Thailand did not experience colonial occupation, in both countries the background of the military elites did not greatly differ from the geographical origin of the other elites. It is, however, plausible that Janowitz's observation[3] about the social origin of the military may be true for the junior officers. They are continually being recruited from the rural sector, while the other elites come from a more heterogeneous background, especially from urban areas. Nevertheless, the proportion of officers coming from urban middle-class backgrounds will increase, especially in Thailand where opportunities for enrichment and economic progress are much greater.

In any case, the general observation about the social origins of the officers in developing nations may not be applicable to Burma and particularly to Thailand.

There is a great deal of selectivity in recruiting the officer corps. But in Burma, the selection is first and foremost on the basis of ideological commitment and through a political organization, i.e., the *Lanzin* Party; in Thailand, the selection is assured by informal mechanisms, for example, the encouragement of officers' sons to choose the military career. One may even say that in Thailand there is a consolidation of a military oligarchy in which the ascriptive criterion plays a very prominent role. However, in spite of this difference in selective criteria, class interest cannot be considered the dominant factor explaining the role expansion of the military establishments or their general attitudes toward social change and modernization. The distinction made by Finer between class interest and corporate interest is applicable here. The corporate interest, i.e., the demand for large budgets and other material privileges, does not play a smaller role than class interests and its presence, especially in Thailand, cannot be ignored.[4]

B. THE MILITARY PROFESSION IN THAILAND AND BURMA

Since World War II, the Burmese and Thai armies substantially improved professional standards. The question is, however, whether one can confidently assert that these two military elites became full-fledged professionals. Any judgment in this respect is contingent on the definition of the concept of professionalism and especially on how the relationship between the different components of professionalism is perceived. From this point of view one can find many new clues to the professional character of the two countries. In Huntington's terminology, in the Thai army the corporate loyalty of the military professionals is more important than expertise or public responsibility. On the other hand, the Burmese military have made a great effort, with relative success, to reach an integrated and balanced conceptual relationship of the components. Is it possible that these nuances may explain the differences in the political militancy of the two military elites? At face value, it would seem that a more integrated approach to professionalism would restrain the inclination toward political activism. The qualifications mentioned earlier with regard to this thesis are reinforced by the Burmese case. These qualifications stem from the fact that in many cases, and especially in societies undergoing rapid social and economic modernization, the professionalization of the army intensifies rather than reduces the feeling of mutual alienation between the civilian and the military sectors. Burma between 1958 and 1962 provides an excellent example. An accelerated process of professionalization of the military in developing countries like Burma, where political, economic, and cultural backwardness is prevalent, makes the officer corps stand out much more sharply as an elite group. The capacity to manipulate manpower and other resources goes hand in hand with the power and prestige of this group. The combination of prestige and the ability to manipulate administrative tools and material resources provides an ideal incubator for the growth of ideas about shaping the civilian society according to particular ideological doctrines. On the other hand, the slow rate of development of administrative and social systems sometimes creates the proper conditions for megalomaniac postures. The feeling of "historical mission" was used by the Burmese military elite as a justification for its political activism and role expansion.

Comparative Analysis and Conclusions

In Thailand, as well, the pretensions of the military in the economic and political spheres are discernible—they stem from the sense of being a professional elite with a greater organizational capacity than any other social or political organization in Thailand. The gap between the rate of professionalization of the military and that of the civilian sector in Thailand brought with it a great deal of alienation and resistance by the military elite to any significant civilian control of the processes of decision making. Nevertheless, the Thai military regime is entirely different from its Burmese counterpart. The ideal of the Thai military regime is an apolitical society, namely, a society which allegedly releases the executive from harassing pressures by interest groups and permits a maximum avoidance of "compromise politics." The granting of optimal priority by the officer corps both to private interest and to corporate interest, at the expense of social responsibility and even specific professional qualities, may well explain the Thai military's inclination to depoliticize the society.

Thailand and Burma raise some additional questions about the circumstances which decrease the alienation and conflict between the military and civilian elites. These circumstances include, first and foremost, the necessity of a greater similarity between civilian and military practices. This similarity is due to the processes of bureaucratization, professionalization, and occupational differentiation in both sectors that increase mutual dependence and interaction. We have defined these processes as those of *militarization* of the civilian sector and *civilianization* of the military sector. However, this concept of civilianization does not apply to the specific civilianization patterns which characterize the Burmese and Thai military establishments. The civilianization processes in both are only partially a result of technological changes and innovations within the military system. In Burma, the dominant factor is the desire to impose a specific doctrine of social change and to assume an exclusive monopoly of the techniques of modernization. In Thailand, the dominant factor is the desire to impose the corporate interest of the military on the civilian society as a whole. These specific patterns of civilianization, especially in the Thai case, differ to a great extent from that described by Janowitz in the Western societies. This is reflected also in the possibility of interchangeability between civilian and military roles. The absence of such interchangeability is one of the unique features of the military profession compared with other professions in developed societies. Another proof of civilianization based on intensive role expansion in either the Thai or Burmese style is the fact that, simultaneously with the inclination to role expansion, in many cases the military has an inclination for autarky or autonomy in the socialization of manpower as well as in judicial processes. In other words, the crystallization of *permeable* boundaries between the two sectors does not contradict the establishment of more or less invisible barriers which prevent effective political, economic, and judicial control by the civilian elites over the military. On the contrary, the accumulation of resources within the internal barriers of the military establishment guarantees a more effective manipulation of the civilian social resources which are, for all practical purposes, available to the military elite as a result of role expansion.

C. THE POLITICAL AND SOCIAL STRUCTURE AND MILITARY INTERVENTION

The structural dissimilarities of the two military establishments, as well as their style of government, are, at least in part, a result of the original political characteristics of the Thai and Burmese societies which the military elites inherited and did not change to any great extent. Nevertheless, the two political cultures became vulnerable to military coups. In Finer's terminology, both belong to an immature political culture characterized by a low consensus about the procedures for transferring power and by the absence of a widespread political public mobilized into associations. The latter characteristic is more typical of Thailand than of Burma. However, even in Burma there is an imbalance between the consensus about the rules of the game and the capacity of the central political party to mobilize politically.

The mere existence of several parties in Burma and not in Thailand—which for many political scientists is an important indicator of the potential vulnerability of Burma's political system—is not a significant variable in comparing the two countries. The emphasis on the importance of consensus about the rules of the political game does not contradict the fact that the absence of consensus is not confined to this sphere. It may spread to other spheres, for example, to ad hoc issues or to the ultimate and sacred values of the society. In Burma, and to a lesser extent in Thailand, examples can be found of a lack of consensus about specific ad hoc policies of the civilian elite.

All researchers who abide by the thesis which correlates the absence of an indigenous middle class to the frequencies of coups will find additional examples in Thailand and Burma. The importance of the middle class, according to these researchers, is primarily due to the fact that its existence allows a real alternative for social mobility and for another access to prestige and political and economic power. In the absence of a middle class, the civilian and, especially, the military bureaucracies are for all practical purposes the exclusive substitute for what the classical and modern middle class could offer. The conclusion applies to both Burma and Thailand. Moreover, in both the civilian and the military bureaucracies were forced to compete with an alien middle class which had accumulated extensive economic power. True, in Burma another option was open, namely, the political sphere. But the low level of institutionalization of

Comparative Analysis and Conclusions

this sphere, the large extent of oligarchization, nonconsistency, and corruption damaged the image of political activities as a suitable mobility channel.

The fact that the middle class had limited scope because it was mainly composed of aliens and the dubious character of the political channels for social mobility contributed to the imbalance between the rates of upward and of downward social mobility. Reliable quantitative data are absent, but this gap is reflected in the relatively great amount of upward social mobility compared with the low rates of downward mobility. This state of affairs is likely to produce frustration which can influence the predisposition of the officer corps to become an active partner, if not the sole participant, in policy making, especially with regard to the criteria which permit access to the political center, in order to reshape the patterns of mobility. Is it possible to say that reshaping these patterns by the officer corps means modernization of the system of stratification? If this is the case, the officer corps fulfills a very similar function, at least in this respect, as the middle class in Europe fulfilled in struggling for a redefinition of the criteria of social stratification and especially for access to the center.[5]

One crucial indicator of modernization of stratification is the emergence of specific status groups within a socially and culturally pluralistic society which, owing to their particular entrepreneurial qualities, function as meeting points among various strata. They thus facilitate the upward and downward flow of persons who become released from various ascriptive and particularistic frameworks. Analysis of social stratification in Thailand and Burma indicates the development of a limited number of objective conditions which enable their officer corps to serve as intermediaries or brokers among the various sectors and elites. However, the differences between the two countries is reflected in the officers' willingness to exploit these conditions and to cooperate with other elites or status groups in fulfilling such functions. The Burmese officer corps expressed the desire to fulfill them, although it advocated total monopolization of the interactions with the various associational groups via an exclusive political organization. The Thai military elite, however, expressed indifference to this issue. It was ready, by and large, to cooperate with the royal court, the civilian bureaucracy, the intelligentsia, and even with other political organizations—as long as this cooperation did not endanger its own corporate interest. These differences between the two countries explains, from another point of view, the differences in the scope of role expansion, its intensity, and the list of priorities of their military elites.

D. THAILAND AND BURMA AS PROTOTYPES OF CIVIL-MILITARY RELATIONS

Intermediation between the different sectors in a pluralistic society is in a sense only a particular case of a broader issue: that is, intermediation between the political and cultural center, which is basically urban and Westernized, and the periphery, which is basically, although not exclusively, rural and traditional. The function of intermediation among the various sectors of the elites is not confined to intermediation per se. It is also related to the mobilization capacity of the elite of both traditional and modernized status groups. The greater the differentiation and political activism of the periphery, the greater is the challenge confronting the ruling elites. Often the demands of the different groups conflict with each other. Thus it is much more difficult for the political elite to respond to these demands, either because of the absence of various facilities and social services or because of basic political principles.

We have made two assumptions about the various prototypes of action between the center and periphery. The first is that the extent of stimulation and temptation the military has for extending its conventional roles differs according to a specific prototype. The second is that the military's ability to make a new, enlarged definition of its role varies from one prototype to another according to the military's character, magnitude, and power. Thailand may be classified as prototype C, where the strengths of the center are relatively unchallenged because of the periphery's apathy and the lack of mobilization. Such a situation is not static. There were certainly periods when the center reflected weakness, for example, in the late 1940s, the middle 1950s, and the beginning of the 1970s. Some changes occurred in the periphery as well. However, except in the northeast and the southeast, the major part of the Buddhist periphery was distinguished by its extreme passivity, at least until the late 1960s, in comparison not only to Burma but to all other countries of southeast Asia. Hindley states that Thailand lacked the conditions which elsewhere allowed for the politicization of the society as a whole and particularly the periphery, or, as he says, the non-elite groups.[6]

1. Thailand was never a colony. A colonial regime generally serves as a catalyst for political and social development. Colonialization effects the crystallization of militant political elites which are the products of the colonial regime's educational system and demand social and political reforms. The more radical frequently advanced their cause by mobilizing the urban and rural periphery. The degree to which Thailand was exposed to colonial influence only strengthened the ruling elite, compared to the periphery, by improving the military's warfare capacity and introducing administrative reforms, etc.

2. Thailand was not involved in large-scale wars with its neighbors or the big

Comparative Analysis and Conclusions [235]

powers. This saved her from the humiliation of defeat which, in other countries, usually causes social and political ferment among the counterelites.

3. The governing was uninterrupted, whereas in ex-colonies there was the transfer from colonial rule to political sovereignty. Thailand was thus ensured a relatively high level of physical and economic security and a minimum level of social services both in the center and at the periphery.

4. Thailand had no key groups (excluding the Chinese minority and recently the intelligentsia) which suffered from severe frustrations[7] and made excessive demands that the political center was unwilling to fulfill.

In addition, the specific cultural characteristics of the Thai Buddhist society also had a great impact on political behavior—the deference to authority, the unquestioning acceptance of existing rules of conduct, and the belief that an individual's position in life is the result of good deeds and good luck.[8] These factors made it much easier for the royal court, until 1932, and for the various military cliques, after 1932, to handle the relatively moderate demands from the margins of the center or from the periphery itself. The channels connecting the periphery to the center were largely one way, used for the transmission of instructions and demands from the elites to the periphery. The best examples of these channels are the bureaucracy, the parliamentary framework, and the Buddhist church. Other frameworks, for example, the trade unions, student organizations, and the intelligentsia, were organizationally and economically too weak to be institutionalized, enduring channels for transmitting demands.

In sum, the Thai elite was not compelled to develop political frameworks which could be used as "institutional means of bridging the rural urban gap."[9] In the period concerned in this study, the passivity of the periphery enabled roughly the same pattern of military bureaucratic regime that had emerged in 1932 to continue. Nevertheless, in those cases where frustrated groups, especially among the officers, emerged, "the looseness of allegiance and the flexibility of standards of status have permitted the groups which circulated around the center of power to absorb new elements without difficulty."[10]

Burma belongs to a very different kind of prototype, namely, prototype B—a society where the power of the center is inferior. In other words, it is a center which cannot cope with the demands and pressures from the accelerating process of differentiation, formation, and consolidation of new groups within the periphery.[11] Historically, conditions in Burma were conducive for the political activization of the periphery and of various groups within the center—a phenomenon relatively absent in Thailand. The long-lived colonial government completely destroyed the monarchy and, more important, prevented the emergence of any alternative power, either local or national. This was accomplished by the system of direct rule, which was an exceptional principle with regard to the general imperial policy and was applied mainly in Burma.

British economic policy brought about the disintegration of the periphery as well, by not taking any measures to prevent peasants from being evicted from their land and becoming rural and urban proletariat. The side effects of this disintegration were extremely high rates of physical and economic insecurity, increased by the destruction of the Burmese economy during World War II. The large number of minorities and the military power of the various underground groups added to the general administrative and economic chaos and encouraged the more militant political socialization of peasants, students, and monks. Thus the leaders of the national movement were confronted, immediately after independence, with a full spectrum of political groups. However, in Burma this broad basis for political recruitment—in other words, this political and social "catching area" of the various political parties—was actually responsible for the almost total collapse of the political system in the early 1950s.

We have seen the differences between the Burmese and the Thai officer corps in terms of the stimulus and impetus to intervene. But, as suggested ealier, it would be worthwhile to refer to two more variables, although only the first is really relevant to our discussion—namely, the propensity and the predisposition to intervene, and the real and effective power of the military. We have suggested, in regard to the former, the willingness or unwillingness of the officer corps to maintain a balance between group cohesiveness or ideological exclusiveness, and promotion of professional standards, especially in technology, logistics, and warfare strategy. A distinction between the two officer corps from this point of view is more difficult to make than from the point of view of the stimulus to intervene. However, the Burmese officer corps can be classified as one which is typical of prototype C, namely, a military system in which integrative and pattern maintenance are overemphasized at the expense of logistic and technical performance. This general characterization of the Burmese officer corps describes the situation which began in the middle of the 1950s, on the eve of the establishment of the first Ne Win government. The senior officer corps then started to devote more and more attention to more general policy issues, followed by their exclusive and different political stand toward the civilian political elites. This process reached a climax in the first years after the 1962 coup, when a great part of the officer corps' activities were devoted to indoctrination and political resocialization of officers and rank and file,[12]

This trend in the Burmese officer corps indicates very clearly the propensity to intervene in the decision-making processes within political and other important spheres. The Thai military officer corps was, at least until the middle 1960s, very close to prototype D, namely, to an officer corps characterized by relatively low achievement in the logistic, technical, and cohesive ideological spheres. This sort of "negative" balance does not necessarily decrease the basic propensity for intervention. Sometimes it does the opposite. However, the

Comparative Analysis and Conclusions [237]

general trends of intervention after the seizure of power and the general quality of the political regime will be very different from the case where the officer corps belongs to the opposite prototype, as in the Burmese example.

Some of the most important differences between the two armies, in the essence if not the magnitude of military propensity to intervene, are reflected in the entrepreneurial qualities and the ideological articulation accompanying role expansion. It would be very easy to perceive the Burmese army as an almost classic illustration of prototype A, which distinguishes itself both by a high level of entrepreneurial activities and by ideological articulation. Typical are the far-reaching economic reforms, on the one hand, and the great extent of "productivity" in the ideological sphere, manifested by the publication and the declaration of a series of political, economic, and social programs, on the other. Thailand may also be classified, without much hesitation, in the fourth prototype, namely, as a military in which the principle motive of the army or its powerful cliques is the consumption of economic and political benefits and rewards. There is hardly any incentive to create new economic and social institutions and to toy with abstract ideologies. The distribution of private and collective, legal and nonlegal, corruption, the extent of symbiosis between the senior officers and the economic elite—these fit very well into this schematic description.

There is still another dimension for distinguishing between the two armies: their relative power vis-à-vis the underground or subversive groups. Undoubtedly the relative power of the Burmese army is less than that of the Thai army, because Burma's enemy forces are bigger and better trained. However, the relative power of the Thai army is decreasing as the underground organizations grow stronger. But it seems unlikely that the Thai army will come close to the kind of military standoff as occurred in Burma.

E. COUPS, REBELLIONS, AND REVOLUTIONS IN THAILAND AND BURMA

In the period involved in our study, the Burmese military executed one and a "half" coups, while the Thai military executed about half a dozen successful or nonsuccessful coups. Were all these coups of the same order or quality? The answer is obviously negative. It is possible to say that Ne Win's coup d'etat was basically, in Johnson's terminology, a *simple revolution*—i.e., a case where the revolutionary ideology was restricted to more or less fundamental changes of only a *few* values. In Burma, there were changes in the political rules of the game from a multiparty, parliamentary system to a one-party system. There was also an almost total nationalization of the means of production. We can include in this category the 1932 coup in Thailand, since it eliminated the principle of absolute monarchy. It would be more questionable to include the 1947 coup against Pridi, although it removed the short-lived parliamentary regime. Nevertheless, all other coups that occurred in Thailand may be defined without any hesitation as *simple rebellions*—violent action or the threat of using violence against the ruling elite that was not motivated by new, ideological motives or by a desire for the rehabilitation of ancient norms. Instead, they were motivated first and foremost by the urge to use the existing rules of the game to become a more active partner in the decision-making process and to be able to distribute the rewards.

The difference between the two types of coups is also reflected in the patterns of role expansion before and, especially, after the coup. This may be examined from three aspects: (1) from the order of priorities of the aims of role expansion; (2) from the point of view of the intensity of role expansion; and (3) from the point of view of the simultaneity of role expansion. The Burmese military is distinguished in its desire to monopolize control both of the political and of the economic spheres. Previous to the 1962 coup, clear priority was given to economic development. After 1962, equal weight was apparently given to both, although the activities in education and indoctrination lagged behind slightly. The intensity of activity was very high, as measured by the willingness and actual use of power. Between 1962 and 1972, the Burmese army engaged not only in intensive role expansion but also in attempting to achieve simultaneously a variety of economic and social aims. All of this was done without neglecting routine military activities against insurgents.

The order of priorities of the various Thai military cliques between 1932 and 1972 was rather different. Excluding the seizure of power per se, role expansion was largely in the economic sphere. But this was accomplished mainly through competition between military cliques and not through collective endeavor by the military as a whole. The penetration of the Thai army into the civilian economy was less than that in Burma. The training of manpower within autonomous frameworks was very high on the Thai list of priorities. In the political sphere, however, there were only bursts of activities—for example, the party political activity in 1955 to 1957 and on the eve of the election in 1969.[13] The intensity of the role expansion was fairly moderate, as the military elite did not show de facto a clear intention to monopolize resources and services in the sphere of their action. This moderation may also stem from the fact that the military was not inclined to act simultaneously in many spheres and did not try to set unrealistic goals that could not be achieved with a reasonable investment of resources and within a reasonable period of time. The differences between the two military establishments are summarized in Table 8.1.[14]

Toward the end of the 1960s, Burma and Thailand were ruled by officers

Comparative Analysis and Conclusions

TABLE 8.1

| | High Intensity ||| Low Intensity |||
| | Multidimensional Simultaneity ||| The Absence of Multidimensional Simultaneity |||
	The Economic Sphere	The Political Sphere	The Educational Sphere	The Economic Sphere	The Political Sphere	The Educational Sphere
Burma until 1962	1	2	3			
Burma after 1962	1	1	(1)			
Thailand until 1955				1	3	2
Thailand after 1955				1	2	3

who served simultaneously as cabinet ministers, commanders in the armed forces, and leaders of political parties. Nevertheless, the similarity between the two officer corps, at least in participation in executive positions of political parties, is only formal. There is almost no common denominator between the United Thai People's Party in Thailand and the *Lanzin* Party in Burma. This is particularly true of their basic aims. Although the *Lanzin* is essentially an elitist party, its objective is optimal mobilization of the Burmese population and resources, working either within the party framework itself or within the various affiliated organizations. This mobilization is aimed at achieving total control and regulation of the economy and society. The *Seri Manangkhasila* Party during Phibun's rule and the UTPP in the late 1960s were, in a sense, elitist political organizations as well. However, for all practical purposes, they were not more than popular cliques aimed at participation in the political parliamentary game according to the rules established by the military elite.

These and other characteristics previously discussed may also help explain some of the different alternatives of civilianization of the military regimes in the two countries. The Burmese military elite, which evolved as an entrepreneurial and ideologically articulated elite, preferred to civilianize itself at least partly and to find a proper ideological justification for doing so.[15] The military elite's main argument was that there was no place for any alternative social doctrine or for any other competing social and economic organization. On the other hand, the Thai military elite, which is basically nonentrepreneurial and not ideologically oriented, did not show an inclination to civilianize. However, it was ready to make some gestures in order to become involved in party politics during election campaigns. Moreover, when it faced the danger of a fullscale showdown with important social and political forces, the Thai military elite preferred, at least temporarily, to withdraw—as it actually did in October 1973.

In his interesting comparison of the different styles of the two military regimes, Badgley states that

> Political development reproduces infinite variations. Although Burma and Thailand have more in common with one another than with any of their neighbors they continue to pursue sharply different public policies by most standards. Thailand and the Thai government have conducted their development with greater skill and reached a higher technical level than the Burmese. But that success is still irrelevant to the Burmese, just as Burma's problems in minority integration and economic development are irrelevant to the Thai. Both peoples are caught by an understandable compulsion to create political forms that will enable their prospective states to survive.[16]

This evaluation could serve as an adequate summary of the comparative analysis suggested in this chapter.

F. THAILAND AND BURMA: TWO PATHS TO MODERNIZATION

In previous discussion about the concept of modernization (see chapter 2), four central dimensions have been suggested as a departure point for the definition and analysis of various phenomena of modernization: (a) structural changes involving institutional differentiation, functional specialization, and increasing complexity of the stratification system; (b) social economic changes stemming from different patterns of social mobilization; (c) changes in the value system; and (d) the capacity for sustained growth. Our assumption is that the process of modernization, like any other kind of social change, is linked in some way to the fluidity or the ongoing thawing and refreezing process of the society's social, political, and economic resources. However, the intensity and the quality of these social processes are not identical in all institutional spheres. The main reason (to borrow a concept from physics) is that the power of resistance or conductability of the stream of reforms is different from case to case. This assumption is relevant to the discussion because one departure point of the theoretical presentation has been that the multidimensionality of modernization creates serious problems as a result of the difficulties of ensuring (if it is indeed desirable at all by the elite) internal compatibility of synchronization of changes in different institutional spheres. The capability to handle the almost unavoidable effect of a lack of synchronization dictates the degree to which development will become lopsided. It also dictates the chances for breakdown of the political system as a result of this lopsided development.

Comparative Analysis and Conclusions [241]

Our earlier emphasis on the risks and the danger of breakdown does not at all exclude the potential development of positive effects from unbalanced modernization. However, these are rather rare, because unbalanced development makes the institutional interchangeability of means and resources very difficult. As a result, severe obstacles to social mobilization may arise and the channels of change may become clogged. The danger of this increases in those circumstances where there is either objective or subjective necessity for the simultaneous solution of a range of problems, for example, law and order, economic problems, or problems of national identity. Very few political centers are able to withstand such pressure without adequate economic and political resources, which are usually very scarce in developing societies. It seems that there is not only a statistical but also a logical relationship between the processes of modernization and the frequencies and patterns of military coups. Our hypothesis is that certain profiles of modernization, or, more specifically, certain profiles of unsuccessful processes of modernization, may result in certain profiles of coups and military regimes. The specific pattern of the coup or the revolution will have an impact on as well as be influenced by the treatment given to the bottlenecks which emerge from the absence of synchronization in the processes of modernization.

All the evidence we have brought indicates the great differences between the military regimes of Burma and of Thailand. Is it thus possible to say that the two countries are marching down different roads and are therefore at different stages of modernization, all of which explains their different characteristics? The answer is at least partially positive, as can be seen from an analysis of the processes of modernization and the implication for the interchangeability among various institutional spheres.

We have indicated that a distinction should be made between political development and political modernization. We may now say that, generally speaking, in both countries there are more significant indicators of the former than of the latter. In both, on the eve of the first military coup, there were some changes in the distribution of power and in the amount of power within the political system. This was manifested, for example, in the administrative, economic, and military reforms initiated by the two great reformers of Thailand, King Rama IV and King Rama V.[17] In Burma this was also certainly true after independence. But while Thailand reached a large degree of unification and centralization of the political system, Burma greatly lagged behind in this respect. However, Burma was more advanced in its continuous development of free-floating political power. In both countries, these floating political powers were very attached to particularistic frameworks. Moreover both countries failed to create sustained frameworks and new mechanisms for enlarging the absorption capacity of the system. This is true even in Burma, where both the civilian and the military regimes made a more sincere and courageous effort than in Thailand. For example, during U Nu's rule, there were sincere—although unsuccessful—experiments to encourage the participation of the population in the selection of the rulers and in decision making. In this respect, indicators for political modernization in Burma were, at least in U Nu's time, more numerous than those in Thailand.[18] There were differences between the two countries with regard to the lack of synchronization between the development of the executive bodies and the development of mechanisms of articulation and aggregation of interests. In Burma, a complicated system of political organizations which indicated a great involvement in politics emerged. In Thailand, there was no kind of a party system on the eve of the 1932 coup. Even later—actually, until the end of the 1960s—Thailand did not experience the sort of parliamentary and extraparliamentary activities so typical of Burma between 1948 and 1962. Although one should not exaggerate the modernity of the Burmese political system, modernization was certainly more apparent there than in Thailand.

With some reservations, one could say that the opposite situation existed in Thailand concerning the development of executive bodies. Since the nineteenth century, many reforms were introduced which resulted in strengthening the control of the political center over large parts of the periphery. However, in the absence of the legacy of a colonial regime, Thailand never experienced a breakdown of the central executive machine. The colonial power in Burma not only adopted the system of direct rule (at least in Burma proper), it also totally destroyed the central executive mechanisms, although leaving some remnants in the villages. The direct result was a retardation in the institutionalization of new executive frameworks in comparison to development in the political party sphere.

The differences in the profiles of modernization are also manifested to some extent in the economic sphere. So far, neither country has suffered acutely from the disparity between population growth and agricultural productivity. When some symptoms of this sort of disparity emerged, both governments succeeded in preventing the destructive outcomes which occurred frequently in other countries, for example, India and China. Nevertheless, in Burma the rate of economic growth was greatly hindered by wars and radical changes in the structure of marketing and in the import and export systems. After Burma's independence, there were sharp fluctuations in economic growth and frequent changes of the focus of economic development. In Thailand, however, economic growth was very gradual, balanced, and continual after the development of agriculture and industrial products connected with agriculture, as for example rice mills, was emphasized. Only a very small part of the available resources was allocated to heavy industry.

Comparative Analysis and Conclusions   [243]

The variations in the process of change and modernization in the two societies showed in the cultural and normative spheres as well. A thorough analysis by experts of Buddhism in Thailand and Burma would reveal many variations, especially with regard to the inclination, willingness, and internal transformative ability of the Buddhist establishment, in the two countries. For example, in Burma the sangha basically "rejected Western culture and knowledge in the course of their revivalism and their demand for the restoration of an idealized past." Thailand, on the other hand, "is in many ways today more open to Western influence. This is clearly reflected in the orientations and aspirations of the monks: Theirs is not a rejection but an active adaptation to the West—at least in regard to their thirst for Western secular knowledge and their borrowing of certain organizational techniques."[19] The general impression is that the transformative ability is not so low. It is possible that this stems from the fact that the two societies are more "traditional" than "traditionalist"—they are the kind of societies where many cultural attitudes are more instrumental and pragmatic, and the range of permissiveness available for personal and collective interpretation is rather broad.[20] This is especially true for the elites of these countries. However, while the bureaucratic and military elites of Thailand demonstrate great willingness to absorb, in a diffused, eclectic, and selective way, ideas and values from Western culture,[21] in Burma the absorption was initially compulsory, because of the colonial regime and was restricted to very specific aspects of British culture. After independence, when the absorption of foreign values became voluntary, it nevertheless continued to be selective and specific. The range of variation was mainly within the framework of socialist ideology. Later, when the military regime was established, the selective process of absorption became more defined and rigid. It was accompanied by a clear-cut policy of isolation toward the external world—to the extent that symptoms of xenophobia developed.

However, a great deal of similarity exists between the two countries with regard to certain dimensions of social stratification. This is especially true of occupational differentiation of the composition of the labor force and the standard of living. The similarity also extends to the pehnomenon of the two ethnic minorities within the two societies that have attained economic power positions and have thus become the backbone of the small middle class. Nevertheless, in the interrelationships among the different strata of the society, there is a large difference between Burma and Thailand. We refer here to the character of the groups intervening between the elite and the lower classes of the society. In Thailand, these groups are composed of patrons who are civilian bureaucrats, officers, or monks who also are actually part of a bureaucratic machine which is much more developed than the clergy in Burma.[22] In Burma during the civilian regime, these intervening groups were composed first and foremost of members of the party machine and to a certain extent of businessmen, officials, and officers. The relatively low status of the civilian bureaucracy and the unstable security situation prevented this category of people from functioning effectively as brokers between the elite and the rural society.[23] After the coup, the officers replaced the politicians as brokers between the political center and the farmers or the urban proletariat. However, the officer-politician with the ambition of indoctrinating his clients differs very much from the partisan of the AFPFL.

The meeting points between the patrons and clients thus differ in Thailand and Burma, although the function they fulfill is similar. In Burma the meeting point is mainly in the political sphere—local party branches, party seminars, village committees, peasants' and workers' organizations, etc. In Thailand, the meeting points are mainly within the bureaucratic sphere. This undoubtedly has a great impact on the channels of mobility and the criteria of social stratification. The evidence is that the Burmese officer corps adopted the image of the reform oriented officer with a positive attitude toward change oriented ideology. The Thai officer corps still adheres to the image of the conservative officer, loyal to the corporate interests of the military and especially to certain cliques within it.

The challenge confronting the intervening groups in Burma is much greater, because of the heterogeneous character of the Burmese society and the pluralistic attributes of its culture. The lack of consensus among the minorities about their sheer belonging to Burma as a sovereign state testifies that Burma is indeed very far from having a crisscross of converging points which make communication between the different ethnic, linguistic, and cultural groups easier. In this respect, the system of economic partnerships between the Thai military elite and the Chinese elite to a certain extent aided the crystallization of such vital meeting points. Nevertheless, even in Thailand, these frameworks lack one of the most important characteristics of a modern stratification system, namely, the abolition of the total monopoly by the senior partner (the officer corps) in such social interactions of political power. Because of this monopoly, these relations actually lack a genuine voluntaristic basis which can guarantee exchange relationships based on universalistic principles. The absence of such a basis is also reflected in the very slow and unsatisfactory growth of voluntary associations which would be able to provide formal and informal social relations between newer and older status groups.

The differences between the military regimes of the two societies are not confined to the differences of the process of modernization within the various institutional spheres; they also involve the extent of synchronization between spheres. For example, the lack of balance between the low rate of economic development in Burma in comparison to the relatively high intensity of political

Comparative Analysis and Conclusions [245]

participation is relevant. The Thai profile in this context is much more balanced. U Nu, in particular, felt that it was possible to achieve radical economic changes without introducing far-reaching changes in the traditional value system.[24] In Thailand, conservatism in economic development seems more compatible with the Thai traditional value system. Another example is the intense antagonism between the Burmese political elite and its bureaucratic counterpart. This antagonism had the character of a multidimensional conflict over political, cultural, and social superiority. Such sharp antagonism never developed in Thailand—and, to the extent that such an antagonism did emerge during the short periods of civilian rule, the balances of power were reversed. The civilian political elite was subordinated to the administration and the military. This reflects the fact that the institutionalization of the competitive political system in Thailand lagged behind the institutionalization of the administrative system.[25]

It is impossible to sum up the differences between Thailand and Burma with regard to the internal balance of the process of modernization without mentioning again the differences between the power relationships of the center and of the periphery. As emphasized earlier, the main vulnerable point of the Burmese political regime was first and foremost the inability of the civilian elite to mold and crystallize organizational instruments and the social and political frameworks necessary to permit the consolidation of its own power basis. Burma was also unable to respond satisfactorily to the demands of various groups—for example, the elite's inability to solve the problem of the minorities and to crush Communist insurrectionists. Several times, Burma found itself on the brink of disintegration. Even now that this danger has been averted, the question of territorial sovereignty is still theoretically unresolved for certain important minority groups. Burma is still today what Nash calls a multiple society: "a segmented social order welding a territory and its population together by a single set of political and economic bonds."[26] This definition may be extended to the government itself (until 1962), a shaky coalition of political factions. The government's success in holding out for more than a decade can be attributed mainly to the similar disunity of the opposition. Moreover, any real opposition was located outside of the parliamentary system: underground Communists, students, the sangha, and the army exerted pressure in other noncompetitive public or semipublic channels.

The failure in the economic area is even more dramatic, considering the country's richness in natural resources and land, and the absence of overpopulated areas. The failure is generally attributed to the fact that Western organizational norms were absorbed only in a haphazard, partial way. Along with the absence of requisite knowledge and know-how, this prevented modern forms of economic organization from being adopted and then adapted to local needs.

The fragmented adaptation of Western economic norms was apparently linked to Buddhist counterinfluences, which to some extent neutralized efforts to implement large-scale economic reforms. However, the destructive effect of Buddhism on economic development should not be exaggerated either on the local level or on the national level where the influence of the sangha was actually negligible.[27]

U Nu's interesting attempt to found a democratic regime on cultural retraditionalization failed despite the absence of intensive contradictions between Buddhism and democracy[28] and in spite of the fact that Buddhism showed a promising capacity to adapt itself to modernization processes.[29]

The weakness of the center was first revealed by the malfunctioning of the main mechanism of government, which had grave difficulty in establishing and then maintaining the means and the institutions for articulating the interests of different groups of citizens. Other shortcomings were a lack of consensus and the existence of hostile attitudes toward many ad hoc aims, significantly toward parliamentary government itself. Continuous searching for an acceptable basis of legitimacy was yet another weak point. In many respects, both the strong and weak traits of the center reflected the composition and dynamics of the periphery. Differentiation in the Burmese periphery is very intensive, and there is substantial overlapping among economic, political, and ethnic (particularistic) divisions. Only because this overlapping was not total and because of important ethnic and religious cleavages was the polarization of Burmese society prevented. When only Burmese Buddhists are taken as the frame of reference, differentiation has another face. Here polarization was between the small Western elite and the rural population and was manifested in the standards of living and sources of income. The result was a shortage of sectors to mediate between the elite and the rank and file.

The political center of Thailand was perhaps not so strong in absolute terms in comparison with Burma. But in light of the passivity of the major part of the periphery in the period concerned, the political elite could allow the internal struggle between the various cliques to continue without endangering the corporate interests of the military bureaucratic establishment at large. Corruption fulfills an important function in promoting the corporate interest of Thai elite in spite of the internal strain accompanied by the competition for rewards and privileges.[30] Nevertheless, one cannot avoid mentioning the vulnerable points of the Thai political system. The most salient are the continuing subversive actions in the northeast and the southeast, the decreasing ability to absorb economic and social mobile groups (for example, educated youth), the recent increasing antagonism between the bureaucratic military elite and the progressively more militant political groups, the problem of integrating the Chinese beyond business partnerships, and finally, the increasing signs of inability to cope with the problem of the high demographic growth. All this raises doubts about whether Thailand will be able to continue to develop and institutionalize mechanisms of sustained growth. It is also doubtful whether the internal transformative capacity which the Thai rulers have exhibited so far can ensure Thailand against severe crises in the more distant future, when the balance of profit and loss of the different sectors of the society will become much clearer as a result of this policy.

G. THE MILITARY AS A PSUEDO-MODERNIZER

In the first chapter, we tried to question some of the beliefs about the advantages and disadvantages of the military framework in general and of the officer corps in particular. The armed forces have been considered modern social systems possessing the institutional and personal qualifications for leading and directing social change and modernization in developing countries. Some of the most popular arguments in this respect are based on a belief in military superiority in technology and administration over civilian managerial units, and the military's application in, for example, maritime and land transport or engineering services. Although this issue was never examined in a comparative, systematic way, it seems that, at least in Burma, where one can compare the situations before and after 1958, the argument for the superiority of the military was corroborated, especially with regard to brief and short-range operations—for example, cleaning the streets of Rangoon, taking measures against black marketeers and money changers, and assisting victims of natural disasters. On the other hand, when more administrative, routine work extending over a long period of time was involved—like the problem of food marketing, etc.—the efficiency of the military administration decreased over time. The accusations against it were not different from those raised against the civilian regime.[31]

Such a comparison for Thailand is much more difficult, because there has been no true civilian government since 1932. It is thus possible only to compare different periods of the history of modern administration in Thailand and to evaluate the degree of improvement. In this respect, it would be difficult to say that the initiative and ideas for greater rationalization and improvement of the civil bureaucracy came particularly from the military elite. The various administrative reforms in the nineteenth and early twentieth centuries were initiated by the royal court through foreign experts. After World War II, foreign experts played a very important role in planning reforms in the bureaucracy. Although the military supported these reforms, officers as individuals or as a collective did not serve directly as agents of change and modernization.

Another type of evidence about the military establishment as an agent of modernization has been that the military more than any other organization combines traditional structural features with a division of labor based on universalistic principles. Thus the military establishment may be considered as one of the most adequate frameworks for absorbing new and innovative concepts by people raised in and accustomed to a traditional background. This argument has validity theoretically and empirically. However, until a comparative study has been made of the processes of socialization and its consequences for the military system, on the one hand, and for the various civilian sectors, on the other, it would be premature to generalize about the two case studies concerned here, let alone formulate a generalized rule.

With regard to the alleged advantage of the military as an organization capable of assuring law and order to the population, the evidence is quite conclusive. The success of the two military establishments, especially the Burmese one, in imposing law and order has been partial and limited. The military power and managerial qualities could not serve as a substitute for adequate political leadership able to solve the problem of subversion and guerrilla warfare.

It seems that, of all the alleged positive qualities attributed to the army, one is undebatable: More than any other social organization, except the royal court in Thailand, the army served in the period involved as a focus of solidarity and an embodiment of the respected and sacred symbols of society. However, this status does not necessarily go along with the political capabilities of negotiation, bargaining, brokerage, and appeasement between ethnic minorities and the dominant segments of the population. In Burma, the officers succeeded from time to time in destroying the social networks vital to a two-way political interaction. We may refer here to the contacts with legal oppositional groups, such as students and the different national minorities. In Thailand, one can also discern failures in interaction with minorities and opposition groups, but it seems that while in Burma the failure stems mainly from *overpoliticization* of the society at large, in Thailand it is related to the officer corps' adherence to a specific model, namely, a *nonpolitical* model of power relationships. This model is based more on imposed cohesion than on comprehensive social consensus.

The optimistic observers' disappointments about the qualities of officers as agents of modernization strengthen the felt need for demystification of the advantages of the military sphere. In any case, it would be advisable to construct a more balanced picture. The fact that some military establishments have succeeded in opening up bottlenecks within frozen and rusty social frameworks does not mean that the same officers would necessarily exhibit aptitude or willingness to provide new infrastructures in order to prevent further bottlenecks from developing.

NOTES

1. M. Lissak, "Modernization and Role Expansion of the Military in Developing Countries: A Comparative Analysis," *Comparative Studies in Society and History*, XIV, no. 3 (April 1967), pp. 223-255.
2. This does not take into consideration the unquestionable urban character of the Chinese elite.
3. See above, ch. 1, n. 9.
4. See above, ch. 4.
5. S. N. Eisenstadt, "Continuities and Changes in the Systems of Stratification," *Megamot*, XIX, no. 1 (November 1972), pp. 13-14. (in Hebrew)
6. D. Hindley, "Thailand: The Politics of Passivity," *Pacific Affairs*, XLI, no. 3 (Fall 1968), pp. 359-363. See also J. C. Scott, *Comparative Political Corruption* (Englewood Cliffs, N.J.: Prentice-Hall, 1972), p. 58.
7. Hindley, "Thailand," pp. 364-367; N. J. Mosel, "Thai Administrative Behavior," in *Toward Comparative Study of Public Administration*, ed. W. J. Siffin (Bloomington: Indiana University Press, 1957), pp. 24-26.
8. Hindley, "Thailand," p. 363.
9. S. P. Huntington, *Political Order in Changing Societies* (New Haven: Yale University Press, 1968), p. 433.
10. D. A. Wilson, "Thailand and Marxism," in *Marxism in Southeast Asia*, ed. F. N. Trager (Stanford: Stanford University Press, 1959), p. 80.
11. See above, ch. 1.
12. See above, ch. 3. One may also define the propensity of the Burmese military in terms of Janowitz's concept.
13. See above, ch. 3.
14. For another version of this scheme, see Lissak, "Modernization."
15. J. A. Wiant, "Burma: Loosening up on the Tiger's Tail," *Asian Survey*, XIII, no. 2 (February 1973), pp. 180-181.
16. J. H. Badgley, "Two Styles of Military Rule: Thailand and Burma," *Government and Opposition*, IV, no. 1 (Winter 1969), p. 117.
17. For a summary of the reforms executed by these Thai kings, see F. W. Riggs, *Thailand: The Modernization of a Bureaucratic Policy* (Honolulu: East-West Center Press, 1966), pp. 108-109.
18. For a pessimistic view of the development of a national political process in Burma, see J. Badgley, *Politics among Burmans: A Study of Intermediary Leaders* (Athens, Ohio: Ohio University, Center for International Studies Southeast Asia Program, 1970), no. 15, p. 82.
19. S. J. Tambiah, "The Persistence and Transformation of Tradition in Southeast Asia, With Special Reference to Thailand," *Daedalus* (Winter 1973), p. 77. In recent years new directions in the interpretation of canonical texts have developed. See the discussion of Buddhadasa Bhikkhu, the most renowned religious thinker in Thailand, in ibid., pp. 67-70. Modern forms of Buddhism are found in Ceylon as well. See H. Bechert, "Sangha, State, Society, 'Nation': Persistence of Traditions in 'Post-Traditional' Buddhist Societies," *Daedalus* (Winter 1973), pp. 91-93. Nevertheless, with regard to the basic system of

relationships between the Buddhist establishment and the ruling elite, Thailand still preserves a more traditional pattern than Burma and Ceylon. See E. Leach, "Buddhism in the Post-Colonial Order in Burma and Ceylon," *Daedalus* (Winter 1973), p. 37.

20. See above, ch. 2.

21. N. Jacobs, *Modernization without Development: Thailand as a Case Study* (New York: Praeger, 1971), ch. 12; T. Pronsiri, *Thailand's Transition* (Bangkok: Prae Pittayer, 1965), pp. 12-13.

22. One can find interesting examples concerning the function of monks as a channel of communication between the rural population and the central authorities in the analysis of the *Dhammathad* program. See Tambiah, "Persistence," pp. 70-71.

23. The most comprehensive study on intermediary leaders in Burma which deals with their socioeconomic characteristics and their capacity to fulfill the functions of intermediation between the center and the periphery is Badgley, *Politics*, pp. 2, 70, 83, 86-87.

24. M. Maung, "Cultural Values and Economic Changes," *Asian Survey*, IV, no. 3 (March 1964), p. 757; M. Nash, "Southeast Asian Society: Dual or Multiple," *Journal of Asian Studies*, XXIII, no. 3 (May 1964), p. 421.

25. D. Wit, *Thailand: Another Vietnam?* (New York: Scribner's, 1968), pp. 124-126.

26. Nash, "Southeast Asian Society," p. 420.

27. M. Nash, *The Golden Road to Modernity* (New York: Wiley, 1965), p. 157.

28. D. E. Smith, *Religion and Politics in Burma* (Princeton: Princeton University Press, 1965), pp. 311-312.

29. S. N. Eisenstadt, "The Protestant Ethic Thesis in Analytical Comparative Framework," in *The Protestant Ethic and Modernization*, ed. S. N. Eisenstadt (New York: Basic Books, 1968), p. 76.

30. Scott, *Comparative Political Corruption*, ch. 4; J. C. Scott, "An Essay on the Political Functions of Corruption," *Asian Studies*, V, no. 3, pp. 501-523.

31. See the discussion of the psychological-administrative profile of the Burmese military in J. F. Guyot, "The 'Clerk Mentality' in Burmese Education," in *Man, State and Society in Contemporary Asia*, ed. R. O. Tilman (New York: Praeger, 1969), pp. 219-220.

INDEX

Abrahamson, B., 39-42, 44, 46
Abrams, P., 42
Adelman, Irma, 68, 109, 141, 204, 219, 225
All Opposition Alliance (AOA), 176
All Shan States Organization, 176-177
Almond, Gabriel A., 51, 53, 67-71, 222
Ananda Mahidol (Rama VIII, King), 74, 77
Anderson, B., 140
Anderson, C. Arnold, 70
Ansuchote, C., 110
Anti-Fascists People's Freedom League (AFPEL, in Burmese, PASABALA), 146-149, 160, 163, 173, 176, 178, 214, 222, 244
Apter, David E., 22, 66-69
Arakan National United Organization, 148
Arendt, Hannah, 28
Aung Gyi (Brigadier), 161, 180-181, 215
Aung San (General), 146, 155, 163
Ayal, Eliezer, B., 138, 221-222, 224
Aye Hlaing, 175
Azmon, Y, 67, 175

Badgley, J. H., 176, 179, 182-184, 204-205, 224, 240, 249-250
Ba Maw, 178
Banerji, S. C., 180
Banks, Arthur S., 42, 67, 70-71
Bauman, Mary Jean, 70
Bavaradej (Prince), 77
Bechert, H., 183, 249
Bell, F., 113-114
Bellah, Robert N., 69
Ben-David, Joseph, 41
Bendix, Reinhard, 66-67
Bennet, Alan, 108, 113
Berger, J., 70, 140
Bernstein, Frieda, 69
Bernstein, Henry, 67
Bhumipon (King), 77
Bienen, H., 39, 42, 45, 68-69
Binder, Leonard, 69
Blackmer, Donald L.M., 70
Blanchard, Wendell, 108, 110-115, 137, 139-142, 221

Bobrow, Davis B., 39, 45-46
Bodhisattva (King), 76
Braibanti, R., 178
Breese, G., 203
Buddhadasa Bhikkhu, 249
Burma Democratic Party (BDP), 148
Burma Nationalist Bloc (BNB), 176
Burma's Way to Socialism (BWS), 169-171
Burma Workers and Peasants Party (BWPP), 147, 176-177
Burmese Community Party, 148
Butwell, Richard, 176, 178-181, 223

Cady, John F., 181, 183
Caldwell, J. C., 139, 224
Calvert, Peter, 44
Campbell, Alex, 112, 114
Chinese Communist Party of Malaya (CCPM), 111
Chinese Communist Party of Thailand (CPT), 85, 111
Chong-Do-Hah, 66-67
Chulalong Korn (Rama V, King), 77, 84, 112, 119
Coast, John, 108
Cole, 179
Coleman, James S., 67, 70-71, 222
Communist Party (Burma), 146, 148, 165-167, 169, 171-172, 176, 245
Communist Party of Vietnam (CPVN), 111
Constitutional Front Party *(Naew Rathathammanum)*, 110
Cooperative Party *(Sahachip)*, 110
Coughlin, Richard J., 111, 139-140, 142
Cutright, Phillips, 140

Daalder, A., 45
Darling, F. C., 110-114
Davies, D., 183
Depuy, Traver N., 178
Desai, A. R., 66-68
Deutsch, Karl, 66-68, 70-71, 205
Djilas, 179
Dobratz, Betty A., 40
Dowse, R. E., 9, 40, 43
Dudley, B. J., 42

[251]

Eckstein, 44
Economist Party, 110
Einstein, Albert, 179
Eisenstadt, S. N., 11, 48, 53, 66, 68-69, 70-71, 175, 249-250
Embree, John F., 138-139
Engels, F., 179
Erickson, J., 42
Etzioni, Amitai, 66-67
Evers, H. D., 108, 112, 114. 118 131 138-142, 221

Fairbairn, G., 176
Fast, Howard, 179
Feierabend, Ivor K., 70
Feierabend, Rosalind L., 70
Feld, Maury D., 41-42, 44
Feldberg, Roslyn C., 39, 43
Finer, S. E., 17, 21-22, 40-42, 44-46, 115, 232
Fischer, Joseph, 111 141-142, 205
Fogg, E. L., 111, 142
Fossum, Egil, 42-44
Free Democratic Party *(Prachatipat)*, 82-83, 98-100, 110
Free Thai Movement, 110
Freyn, Hubert, 113-114
Furnivall, J. S., 175-176, 179

Galtung, Johan, 70, 140
Geertz, Clifford, 9, 70, 184
Germani, Gino, 43, 68, 71
Girling, J.L.S., 110, 114
Glick, Edward B., 39, 115
Goffman, Irving W., 40, 140
Gordon, M., 69
Gould Julius, 40
Gregg, Phillip M., 70-71
Grossman, 179
Gutmann, E., 71
Guttridge, William, 44
Guyot, J. F., 178-184, 203-205, 223, 250

Hagen, Everett E., 69, 181, 222
Hanks, L. M., 117, 138, 141-142
Hanning, Hugh, 115
Harris, George L., 112-113, 115, 138-139, 141-142, 224
Hass, Mary R., 139
Hindley, Donald, 108-112-113, 249
Hla Han (Colonel), 182
Hofstader, R., 9

Holmes, R. A., 183, 204
Hopkins, Keith, 22, 39, 42-43, 45
Horowitz, D., 71
Horowitz, Irving L., 43-45
Hsueh, S. S., 109
Huntington, Samuel P., 22-23, 35, 39, 41-46, 53, 66-70, 230, 249
Huvanandana, Malai, 109
Huxley, Aldous, 179
Hyde Park Movement Party, 98

Independent Party, 110
Indian Communist Party, 148
Ingersoll, J., 204-205, 221-222
Ingram, J. C., 224
Insor, D., 111, 114

Jacobs, N., 109, 111-112, 138 210, 221, 250
Janowitz, Morris, 11, 15-16, 31, 39-41, 43, 45-46, 229, 231, 249
Johnson, Chalmers, 28-29, 40 44, 184
Johnson, John, 43-44, 115, 181
Jordan, A. A., 113
Justice Party (Burma), 148
Justice Party *(Tharmathipat)*, 82

Kahin, M. G., 175
Karen National Defense Organization (KNDO), 148, 177
Kaufman, H. K., 112, 142, 221
Khuang Kowit Aphaiwong (Prime Minister), 74-75, 82, 108
Kirsch, A. Thomas, 141
Koestler, 179
Kornhauser, William, 44
Kourvetaris, George A., 40
Kukrit, Pramot, 110
Kuper, Leo, 69
Kyaw Soe (Colonel), 182
Kyaw Zaw (Brigadier), 181

Labor Party (Thailand), 98
Lanzin Party (Burma Socialist Programme Party–BSPP), 165-166, 168-169, 181-183, 229, 239
Leach, E., 176-177, 183, 222
Lehman, E. W., 111
Lenin, 145, 166, 179
Lenski, Gerhard E., 40, 140
Lerner, Daniel, 67, 69
Levy, Marion J., 44, 66
Leys, Colin, 9, 40

Index

Lipset, S. M., 9, 45, 67, 70-71
Lissak, M., 39, 45, 67, 69-71, 249
Little, Roger W., 44
Lovel, J. P., 114, 178
Luckham, A. R., 39, 41, 45-46

Manoprakorn, 97
Marx, Karl, 145, 166, 179
Maung Lwin (Colonel), 182
Maung Maung (Colonel), 157, 176, 178-179, 181, 183, 250
Maung Shwe (Colonel), 182
McClelland, David, 69
McKinlay, R. D., 41-42, 45
McKinney, J. C., 66
Mehta, Surider K., 188, 198, 203, 205, 222-223
Mendelsohn, Michael I., 178
Midlarsky, Manus, 44
Might is Right Party, 98
Miller, S. M., 43
Millikan, Max F., 70
Moerman, M., 142, 221
Montgomery (Viscount), 179
Morell, D., 110, 113, 115
Morris, Cynthia T., 68, 109, 141, 203-204, 219, 225
Mosel, N. J., 108-109, 115, 127, 138, 140-142
Moskos, Charles C., Jr., 41
Mulder, J. A. Niels, 141
Muscat, Robert J., 115
Mya Maung, 176, 183, 203, 222
Myrdal, G., 145, 176, 203, 205, 219-220, 224-225

Nai Pridi, 73-75, 77, 81, 86, 108 110, 114, 238
Narayan, 179
Nash, Manning, 142, 175, 177, 196, 203-205, 209, 221-222, 245, 250
National Democratic Party (The Unionists), 98
National Socialist Party, 83, 99, 110, 114
National United Front (NUF), 176
Nationalist parties, 99
Neher, Clark D., 108, 110, 113-114
Nettl, J. P., 67
Ne Win (General), 157, 160-161, 163-165 169, 176, 178-181, 183-184, 215
Nisbet, R. A., 66
Nordlinger, Eric A., 16, 40, 45 68

Nuechterlein, Donald E., 108
Nyi Nyi, 205

Parsons, Talcott, 70
Patriotic Front (Thailand), 94
Pawngyaung National Democratic Front, 176
People's Voluntary Organization (PVO), 146, 155, 176
Perlmutter, Amos, 11, 42-43, 45
Pfanner, David E., 204-205, 221-222
Phahon Phonpha Yuha, 74
Phao Sniyanonda (General), 75, 85-86, 98-100, 110, 114
Phibun Songkhram (Field Marshal), 74-75, 77, 81, 85-86, 88, 91, 97-100, 103-104, 108, 110, 130, 218, 224, 239
Phillips, H. P., 111, 142
Pickerell, Albert G., 111
Piker, Steven, 142
Polanyi, Karl, 67
Prachatipok (King), 74
Pramot, Seni, 83
Praphas Charusathien (General), 75, 83, 95, 104, 107
Progressive Party *(Kau-na)*, 82, 110
Promoters (The People's Party), 73-74, 76-78, 80-81, 98, 108, 110
Pronisiri, T., 250
Punyodyana Boonsanong, 141-142
Putnam, Robert D., 43
Pye, Lucian W., 44-45, 51, 53, 68-69 175, 180-181, 204-205, 222

Rama IV (King), 241
Rama V (King), 241
Rapport, David C., 46
Red Flag Communists, 148, 155, 171, 177
Redick, Richard W., 212
Revolutionary Council (of Burma) (RC), 168-172, 175, 181-183, 215-216, 223
Riggs, Fred W., 66, 97 108-111, 113-115 139-140, 142, 249
Rosenberg, Carl G., Jr., 71
Rostow, W. W., 48, 66-67, 179
Rudner, Martin, 175-176
Russell, Bertrand, 179
Russett, Bruce M., 70, 112, 123, 139, 204, 219, 225
Rustow, Dankwart A., 42

Sakai, R. K., 179
Sanya Thammasah, 87
Sanye (Brigadier, vice chief of staff), 167
San Yu (Brigadier), 181
Sarit Yuthasin (General), 75, 77, 83-86, 88, 95, 97-100, 103, 105, 108, 110, 114, 218, 225
Sarkisyanz, E., 175-177
Sathyamurthy, T. V., 177
Sayadaw U Nanda Thami, 177
Scalapino, R. A., 176
Schneider, Y., 66-67
Schnore, Leo F., 67
Scott, J. C., 109, 140, 250
Sein Win, 176, 182
Seri Manangkhasila Party, 83, 98-99, 110, 239
Shils, Edward A., 8-9, 43, 45, 69
Shor, Edgar C., 109, 138-139
Siffin, William J., 109, 111-113, 131, 138 140-141
Silcock, T. H., 108, 114-115, 139-142, 221, 224-225
Silverstein, Josepf, 175-178, 181-183, 204-205, 223
Silvert, Kalman, 43
Simpson, Dick, 68
Simpson, John, 44
Sjoberg, Gideon, 204
Skinner, G. W., 111, 122, 128-130, 138-142
Smelser, Neil J., 70-71
Smith, Donald E., 151, 175, 177-178, 180, 183, 222, 250
Smith, Michael G., 69
Social Democratic Party (Burma), 165-166
Socialist Party (Burma), 146-147, 149, 176, 181
Soedjatmoko, 69
Solari, A., 46
Somvichian, Kamol, 108, 110-115, 224-225
Southall, Aiden, 71
Soviet Communist Party, 148
Srinivas, M. N., 71
Stalin, J., 179
Stifel, L. D., 223-224
Stinchcombe, Arthur, L., 66
Stone, Lawrence, 44
Strachey, 179
Suhrke, Astri, 107
Sundrum, R. M., 191, 193, 203-205 213, 222

Sun Yat-sen, 110
Sutton, J. L., 109, 138
Swe-Nyein, 163

Tai, T. V., 223
Tambiah, S. J., 141, 177, 222, 249-250
Tanter, Raymond, 43-44, 70
Textor, Robert E., 42, 67, 70-71
Thakin Kudaw Hmine, 176
Thakins, 145, 152, 155, 175
Thakin Soe, 148
Thakin Than Tun, 148
Thamrong Navasawat (Prime Minister), 74
Thanat Khoman, 115
Thanom Kitikachorn (Field Marshal), 75, 77, 87-88, 95, 99, 105, 107, 110 225
Than Sein (Colonel), 181
Thaung Kyi (Colonel), 182
Tilman, R. O., 178, 205, 223, 250
Tinker, Hugh, 175, 177-179, 203-204
Tin Pe (Brigadier), 181
Tin U (Colonel), 179
Tiryakian, E. A., 66
Tominaga, K., 138-139, 141-142, 217, 224
Trager, F. N., 111, 175-176, 181, 183, 204, 222-223

U Nu, 145-146, 148, 150, 152, 155, 160-165, 169-171, 176-177, 179-183, 214, 242, 245-246
Union Party (U Nu's), 163, 177
Unionist Party (National Socialist Party), 83, 99, 110
United Thai People's Party (UTPP), 83, 99, 110, 239

van der Mehden, Fred R., 70, 151, 177 179, 181, 225
van Doorn, Jacques, 41-42
Van Gils, M. R., 41
Vella, Walter F., 108, 110, 113
Verba, Sidney, 51, 53, 67-69
Vibhatakarasa, Jin, 108, 112-115
Viksnins, George J., 113

Walinsky, Louis J., 175, 178-180, 183, 194, 204, 212, 222-223
Ward, R. E., 42
Weatley, Charles W., 39-40, 44-45, 108, 112, 114
Weber, Max, 69, 222
Weinberg, Ian, 68
Weintraub, Dov, 67-69, 71

Index

Whitaker, Jr., 67
White Flag Communists, 148, 155, 171, 177
Wiant, Jon A., 179, 249
Wichman, A. A., 222
Wijeyewardene, G., 142
Williams, Robin M., Jr., 57, 70
Willner, A. R., 33, 40, 45, 66, 69
Wilson, David A., 109-111, 113-115, 118, 138, 140-142, 249

Wit, Daniel, 109, 113, 218, 225 250
Wohl, J., 177, 205
Wolfe, J. N., 42
Wolfstone, D., 179-180

Yoneo Ishii, 111

Zelditch, M., 70, 140